First Reader for
Antique Collectors

BOOKS
by Carl W. Drepperd

FIRST READER FOR ANTIQUE COLLECTORS

THE PRIMER OF AMERICAN ANTIQUES

First Reader for Antique Collectors

by

CARL W. DREPPERD

Garden City Books

GARDEN CITY, NEW YORK

GARDEN CITY BOOKS REPRINT EDITION 1954, by special arrangement with
Doubleday & Company, Inc.

This book is dedicated to four career women—

E.R., K.K., V.W., *and* C.D.,

because they have researched without seeming end, have checked and rechecked, and have spared neither eyesight nor patience in their efforts to correct errors of omission and commission and, finally, when the last proofs were corrected, said, "When do we start on the next one?"

Acknowledgments

For permission to use certain pictures of types and styles of furniture, glassware, silver, pewter, and other objects in this *First Reader for Antique Collectors*, the author desires to thank Thomas H. Ormsbee for pictures in his collection and used also in his book, *The Story of American Furniture*, published by The Macmillan Company; the Parke-Bernet Galleries; Stephen G. C. Ensko; Southern Comfort Corporation; *House and Garden*; George S. and Helen McKearin, and the Crown Publishing Company, publishers of *American Glass*; the New York Historical Society; William Helburn, Inc., publishers of *Scale Drawings of Colonial Furniture*; and the Smithsonian Institution, Washington, D.C. Many line drawings illustrating this work are taken directly from objects on sale somewhere in an antiques shop during the year 1945. Innumerable illustrations derive from early periodicals and from illustrated catalogues of manufacturers of furniture, stoves, tinware, and elegancies, issued between 1840 and 1900.

Preface

More American men and women, and boys and girls, than at any time in our national history are now collecting objects which, rightly or wrongly, are called antiques. Yet not all Americans today concerned with antiques are concerned as collectors or dealers. Some, like the old New Englander who had a houseful, don't collect them; they just have them by inheritance. Any descendants of families living in America since, say, 1860, are now apt to own relics of past decades that have been handed down to them. This is not to say these relics are, actually, antiques. But plenty of other people regard them in that light, want to buy them, and seem willing to pay fair to good prices for them.

Therefore, without pointing a single page of this *First Reader* at the fortunate inheritors of hand-me-downs of other days, it is hoped this book will be of service to you in at least one dimension: if you have anything pictured or mentioned in these pages, you can know your stuff is not junk but near, or perhaps even real, antiques of some value.

Between 1844 and 1876—or even later, if you please—a staggering amount of so-called Victorian-style furniture was made and sold generally throughout this country. When this furniture was outmoded by the very worst furniture ever produced, either in style or quality, the "Victorian" was either disposed of or retired to storage in garret, outhouse, or barn. Newly marrieds during the Gay Nineties often became the recipients of a gift set of Victorian that Aunt Eliza or Grandmother felt would be very nice because it had once graced a bedroom or parlor when they were young. By 1910 nobody seemed to want Victorian stuff. A lot of it, carefully and even meticulously fashioned from rosewood and walnut, was just too good to chop up for firewood. So it was either again stored, sold, or given to the very poor. The Little Italy, the gas works section, and the Jim Crow part of every town sported the furniture that had once graced the homes and the mansions of the middle classes and the well to do.

By 1942 Victorian furniture was back in vogue with a bang. It was bringing higher prices secondhand, or as the "next antique," than it had commanded when new. Now, really good Victorian furniture, more properly "nineteenth-century 'Chippendale,' " as a writer in *American Collector*, May 1945, suggested, is commanding prices that would make Hepplewhite envious and cause the eighteenth-century Chippendale to blush.

The reason for Victorian popularity is to be found somewhere between the psycho-complexities of human emotions and the good old law of supply and demand. For many years Victorian was hidden behind the curtain of the future as the next thing to come of antiques age. Its predecessor in point of time, Empire furniture, had been launched and, not without some misgivings, accepted as antique between 1920 and 1935. Certain museums, notably in the Middle West, put Empire to the forefront when they exhibited it as the first furniture of the region. Then acceptance spread. More pieces were dragged from obscurity. Some really engaging chairs, sofas, and bureaus of Empire status were brought to light. Duncan Phyfe was discovered to have made furniture in the Empire style. That, in some quarters, did not detract from Phyfe and also put a sort of halo over Empire. It moved out of antiques shops into homes and from other homes into antiques shops, clearing the decks for the next in line—Victorian.

Now Victorian is going through a grand period of brisk trading. It is received with an altogether different attitude than that which marked and sparked Empire acceptance. Victorian has more qualities of the sort that create verve, nostalgia, enthusiasm, and sweet emotions. It has more "points," as they say; it is "gracious" (which Empire isn't), and it is "lovely." All these attributes and qualities are, I think, due to the not always apparent parentage of Victorian at its best. There is Chippendale revival in it, out of the Chippendale book of Old French and antique styles issued in 1834. And there is also considerable of the styling of Louis XV and of Robert Manwaring who, in 1765, advocated the making of some chairs that could almost pass as Victorian of 1865.

These echoes, reverberating out of the eighteenth and nineteenth centuries, give to Victorian a certain something that, to many people of quite good taste, is ageless charm. They may be right. They may be as right as the people who first saw charm, rather than mere antiquity, in a William and Mary six-legged highboy, or a three-legged turned chair of 1630. It is now apparent that Victorian is here to stay. Just yesterday I had all the proof I need of its permanence. Outside my office window there was a traffic jam. A huge truck stood there, loaded to its tailboard with newly made Victorian sofa frames—at least fifty of them. New Victorian sofas! I, for one, am convinced that when a furniture is reproduced it has truly arrived as an antique. And that is why so much is said here, and will be said later on, about Victorian furniture in this *First Reader for Antique Collectors*.

All of the decorative appurtenances of the Victorian era (I wish we had another name for it!) seem to have achieved antiques status whether they are antique or not. Lamps, glassware, pottery, china, Parian, iron, brass, Britannia, silver, rugs, draperies—all of the Victorian period—are now to be found in the shops. When, in 1918, the late Abner Haberbush of Lancaster, Pennsylvania, showed me a blue Stiegel saltcellar and said, "You should buy this for twenty-five dollars, my lad," I thought the man balmy. Now, twice twenty-five dollars is paid for a piece of Victorian glass which sold, originally, for just about as much as William Stiegel got for his blue saltcellars in 1770—a shilling then, a quarter for the Victorian in 1850.

Some of the things—the "appurtenances"—sold as Victorian today were in common use after Victorian furniture was passé. Oil-burning parlor and bedroom lamps, made as late as 1900, are so much sought after that antiques dealers must scour the back country to supply (or attempt to supply) the demand. This, too, is a story that needs telling.

That is why, it is hoped, this book will be of some real value to the upstanding, run-of-the-mill, and salt-of-the-earth Americans now indulging in what they call antiques collecting. It is doubtful whether anything in the book will be helpful to the experts. All the types of objects mentioned or pictured in this little reader, with but few stated exceptions, stood somewhere in an antiques shop or auction room during the year September 1944 to August 1945. Many of the pictures are taken directly from original woodcuts or engravings used to portray or to advertise the antiques when they were "modern" furniture and new goods. Others have been included because they most effectively illustrate certain so-called "antique" objects. We have butchered scores of merchandise catalogues, posters, billheads, and books, issued between 1815 and 1895, to reproduce many pictures for your enjoyment. Some of them derive from newspaper advertisements appearing as early as 1768.

Approximately two thirds of the items pictured are of things first made by mass-production methods in America. There is glassware representative of mass-production pressing and blowing. There is furniture made in steam-powered factories. There are chairs made by the mass-production plant of Lambert Hitchcock, and furniture from factories in Boston, Providence, Bridgeport, New York, Baltimore, Philadelphia, Pittsburgh, Cincinnati, and St. Louis. There is pottery mass produced at Bennington; by Remmey of Philadelphia; and by Farrar, of Geddes, New York. There are things mass produced in woolen mills, ironworks, tin mills, and foundries. These various factories turned out an enormous production of one-time luxuries and, in so doing, made them staples at fair prices for all people. Time has turned these things back into luxuries. They are now verging upon being antiques, or are antiques. They are collected by some, and still owned as family possessions by others. And in this, from first to last, resides that present-day business and pleasure, profit and fun, collecting antiques.

Carl W. Drepperd

January 10, 1946

Contents

	Preface	vii
I	Introduction	1
II	Chairs	21
III	Settles, Settees, Sofas, and Seats	50
IV	Tables, Stands, Sideboards, and Dining-room Cabinets	62
V	Highboys and Lowboys	79
VI	Desks, Bureaus, and Chests of Drawers	86
VII	Bedroom and Boudoir Furniture	93
VIII	Clocks	101
IX	Mirrors	107
X	Elegancies, Conceits, Fancies, and Fads	112
XI	Silver and Sheffield Plate	138
XII	Pewter and Britannia	151
XIII	Lamps and Candlesticks	157
XIV	Pottery and China	167
XV	Blown Glass, Bottles, and Flasks	182
XVI	Pressed Glass	194
XVII	Paintings, Engravings, and Lithographs	216
XVIII	Children's Toys	232
	Glossary and Index	243

*First Reader for
Antique Collectors*

CHAPTER I

Introduction

Since it is the purpose of a First Reader to "tell a series of stories," that is the pattern which, for better or worse, you, the reader, will have to contend with; a series of short, short stories about—and a lot of pictures of—Antiques You Can Collect.

Some few years ago a nationwide dairy organization retained a publicist to write the history of ice cream. In that history the publicist said, "Dolly Madison, first lady of the land during gay Colonial days, served ice cream for the first time at a function of state in this country." Read it again. Laugh to your heart's content. First lady of the land during gay Colonial days! But don't laugh too loudly. Thousands of people who shouldn't and tens of thousands of others unthinkingly tack the term "Colonial" to many things made for the American home in our Federal period, and in the administrations from Jackson through Buchanan to Lincoln, and even to Grant. It is all very well to know that Italian pastry cooks and French sugar bakers offered ice cream to the colonists in Colonial days prior to 1776. It is nice to know that in early Federal days Dolly Madison served the delicacy at the White House. But we should never mix Federal with Colonial. It is too much like saying "Hiya, toots," to a nice old grandmother in a wheel chair.

Prior to the Revolution what we call antiques were made by hand. During the Revolution a certain amount of furniture was made in the same way. But after the Revolution came another revolution. American artisans began to think in terms of factories. Alexander Hamilton, in 1791, reported to Congress on manufactures. He spoke in favor of a division of labor because a workman doing one thing repetitively would achieve great dexterity in that one operation, thus saving time and making production easy. Mr. Hamilton also said that this constant application will provoke thought in respect of better and quicker ways to perform the operation, and the application of machinery to the operation. By 1800 many American artisans had factories in which this philosophy of production had become a fact.

The *Philadelphia Cabinet and Chair Maker's Book of Prices*, 1795, and the *New York Cabinet Maker's and Chair Maker's Book of Prices*, 1796, deal with the costs to be applied to making each item of furniture. In other words, the operation is broken down in order that a division of labor in cabinet shops could be set up and the costs charted.

The late Edgar G. Miller, Jr., of Baltimore, whose monumental two-volume work *American Antique Furniture* was written for amateurs, but not published in a format amateurs in general could enjoy or afford, credits John Hall of Baltimore (1840) with issuing the first illustrated cabinetmaker's assistant published in the United States. Mr. Miller was careful (as he was in all things) to state that this is the opinion of librarians. As it happens, the librarians were wrong; at least in part. Illustrated books were issued by and for American cabinetmakers and chairmakers before Hall's little volume appeared. The New York (1817) and some Philadelphia price books of issue prior to 1840 were illustrated. So also was that now excessively rare little volume the *Pittsburgh Cabinet Makers' Book of Prices*, printed by John Snowden at Pittsburgh in 1830, and that almost as rare volume, *Book of Prices of the United Society of Journeymen Cabinet Makers of Cincinnati, for the* Manufacture *of Cabinet Ware*, at Cincinnati in 1836.

Both of these latter books, as well as the Philadelphia and New York illustrated price books, predate Hall's *Cabinet Maker's Assistant*. Hall's book depicts furniture of the very worst Empire style in which little of the genesis of the style remained; little of the original designing of the Directoire, of Robert Adam and Hope; of Sheraton-inspired Regency. Yet Hall's little book was almost unobtainable as a relic, or research aid, for many years. Now you may procure a facsimile reprint for two dollars. Hall's furniture designs—if one may call them designs and not abortions—were reproduced in tens of thousand of pieces and sold all over America.

But to blame Hall for all this production is to err. Joseph Meeks's huge furniture factory at New York was producing

THE CABINET MAKERS ASSISTANT

DESIGNED, DRAWN AND PUBLISHED, BY JOHN HALL,
ARCHITECT.
BALTIMORE

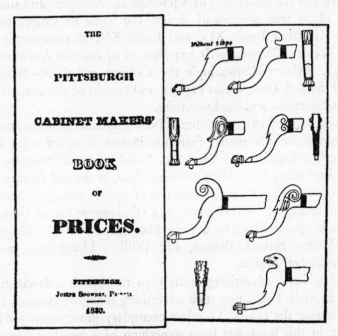

THE

PITTSBURGH

CABINET MAKERS'

BOOK

OF

PRICES.

PITTSBURGH.
JOSEPH SNOWDEN, PRINTER.
1830.

Top: Hall's *Cabinet Maker's Assistant,* 1840.
Bottom: *Pittsburgh Cabinet Maker's Book of Prices,* 1830, and One of Its Plates

in 1832, furniture of the sort that Hall pictured, although Hall drew his with a slightly heavier pencil. In 1833 the Meeks firm retained an advertising agency to promote the sale of their goods. If this sounds like Grand Rapids and the year 1933, you'll know why a revision of our thinking about American antiques furniture production is in order. The promotion for Meeks was a huge poster, picturing forty-four items including three of window draperies. This was lithographed by Endicott & Swett of New York. Prices ranged from seven dollars for a mahogany chair to six hundred dollars for a canopy bedstead with curtains and top!

In 1842 R. Conner, designer, of New York, issued the *Cabinet Maker's Assistant*, published by Faxon & Read. This is a far more important book than Hall's because, while Hall pictured the awful end of Empire fashions and styles, Conner pictured the birth of the so-called Victorian fashion. It is in this book that we can see something of Victorian as "Antique" and something of its true sources of design—the work of Chippendale borrowed from Louis XIV and Louis XV, as resurrected in John Weale's *Chippendale's 133 Designs of Interior Decoration* (1834), Robert Manwaring's the *Cabinet and Chair-Maker's Real Friend & Companion* (1765), and certain of the designs of Adam, Sheraton, and the Directoire.

In 1828–29 and 1830 a number of New England furniture manufacturers were advertising furniture in something of what has been called Empire and Victorian. Notable in this category of advertisers were Isaac Miles of Greenfield, at the old factory of Bancroft & Miles; Roger Portington of 656 Washington Street, Boston; George & Philip Graves, 554 Washington Street, Boston; Sherlock Spooner's Chair & Sofa Manufactory of Washington and Warren Streets, Boston; and William Handcock, 37–53 Market Street, Boston.

Chairmakers' advertising from 1770 to 1870 is a fascinating study in itself. Collecting such advertising is almost as much fun as collecting the chairs. To select exemplary illustrations for inclusion in this book has been something of a problem because no one section of the country had a corner on chairmakers' advertising. As the frontiers moved westward, so did the chairmakers. Wherever they located, they advertised. Not infre-

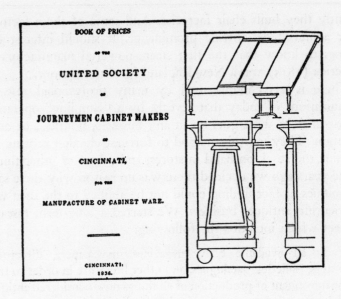

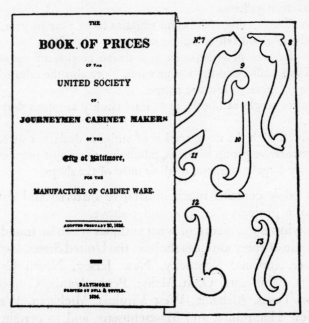

Top: Cincinnati *Cabinet Maker's Book of Prices,* 1836, and One of Its Plates.
Bottom: Baltimore *Cabinet Maker's Book of Prices,* 1836, and One of Its Plates.

quently they built chair factories. And some of those factories later achieved nationwide prominence. It should interest collectors to know that the first steam-powered manufactory in America (1815) was a New England furniture factory.

There is a technique used by many professional research organizations of today that reveals, by a "sampling" operation, approximately what goes on in any business, political, or other situation. They use this method to forecast election returns, determine the stock on hand in stores, and a host of other things. Some years ago we decided there was no reason why these same techniques of fact finding could not be applied to the then very unscientific antiques business. We started a long-term research project which included the following:

1. Study all available early magazines, newspapers, directories, posters, bulletins, catalogues, and other literature in order to trace the movement of production of all things now considered antiques.
2. Make a continuous study of what kind of antiques pass through the auction galleries.
3. Note all collecting trends and vagaries from year to year, charting the rise and fall of public interest.
4. Note the uses of Americana as a theme in current national advertising, radio, and motion pictures. Note also the sales of books on any American historic theme.
5. Tabulate stocks at booths in at least twenty antiques shows each year.
6. Conduct, with the co-operation of antiques dealers, a survey of a representative group of shops, tabulating the major portion of inventory largely common to all or most of the shops.

This book contains much illustrative material and data discovered in projects 1, 2, 3, 4, and 5 above.

Following is the record of what antiques are to be found today in a sample of forty antiques shops in the United States, located in Delaware, Indiana, Kentucky, New Jersey, North Carolina, Montana, Minnesota, Ohio, Maine, Pennsylvania, Connecticut, Oregon, Texas, Alabama, West Virginia, Michigan, Washington, New Hampshire, and Massachusetts, and in certain shops in the cities of Philadelphia, New York, Baltimore, and York, Pennsylvania.

This sample of shops includes, perhaps, seven that may be

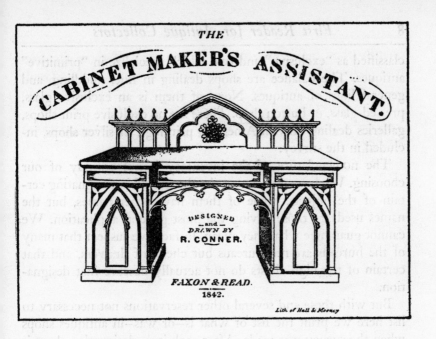

THE CABINET MAKER'S ASSISTANT.

DESIGNED
—and—
DRAWN BY
R. CONNER.

FAXON & READ.
1842.

Lith. of Hall & Mooney

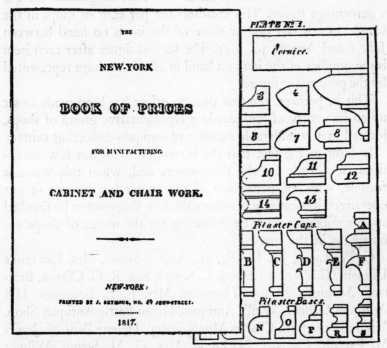

THE

NEW-YORK

BOOK OF PRICES

FOR MANUFACTURING

CABINET AND CHAIR WORK.

NEW-YORK:
PRINTED BY J. SEYMOUR, NO. 49 JOHN-STREET.

1817.

PLATE Nº. 1.

Cornice.

3   4
5   7   8
10 11 12
14 15

Pilaster Caps.

A
B   C   D   E   F

Pilaster Bases.

N   O   P   R   S

Top: R. Conner's *Cabinet Maker's Assistant*, New York, 1842.
Bottom: *New York Cabinet Maker's Book of Prices*, 1817, and One of Its Plates.

classified as "exclusive" and two which specialize in "primitive" antiques. The balance are shops dealing in fine, middling, and general lines of antiques. None of them is an exclusive glass, pressed-glass, or button shop. There are no exclusive print shops, galleries dealing only in American paintings, or silver shops, included in the survey.

The nomenclature of the inventory is not entirely of our choosing. We have used names the shops used in designating certain of the objects. Some of them have other names, but the names used are those having the most general application. We cannot guarantee what they mean. In fact, we suspect that many of the bureaus are not bureaus but chests of drawers, and that certain of the high chests do not actually deserve that designation.

But with these and several other reservations not necessary to list here we print the list of what is—or was—in antiques shops when the survey was made. After each item designation there is a percentage figure. This indicates the per cent of shops in the sample which had one or more of the items on hand between July 1 and August 30, 1945. The second figure after each item is the number of the item on hand in *all* of the shops represented by the percentage figure.

This is, perhaps, the first time an effort has been made to set up an inventory of antiques in a representative group of shops, located in a considerable number of antiques-collecting centers.

In light of the fact that the inventory, with but few exceptions, was made by the shopowners and, when this was not feasible, with the permission of the owner but by one of our operatives, it is entirely in order that these shopowners be thanked and mentioned here. The following are the names of shops cooperating in the survey:

C. W. Lyon, Joe Kindig, Jr., Arthur Sussel, Mrs. Lawrence Ullman, Ginsburg & Levy, J. C. Seng & Son, R. G. Clifton, Bretman Antiques, Nancy Thornton, Mrs. F. E. Brammer, Hill Antiques Gallery, Weil's Antiques, Green Battle Antiques Shop, Mildred Simmons, Charles Montgomery, Helena Penrose, James M. Parrish, Clarence N. Flood, Mrs. G. M. Strom, Wilmer Moore, Tryphose-Barrett House, Carroll Simmons, Hobbyana' Shop, Ox Shoe Shop, Seven Hearths Shop, Don Maxwell, Marie

CHIPPENDALE'S
One Hundred and Thirty-three
Designs
OF INTERIOR DECORATIONS
in the Old French & Antique Styles,
for Carvers, Cabinet Makers,
Ornamental Painters,
Brass Workers,
Modellers, Chasers,
Silversmiths,
General
Designers,
and
ARCHITECTS.

LONDON
Published by
JOHN WEALE.
Nº 59, High Holborn.
1834.

Chippendale's One Hundred and Thirty-three *Designs in the Old French and Antique Styles*, London, 1834.

Irvine, The Bristol Company, Mrs. W. O. Crawford, John Schwarz, Florian Papp, Inc., The Macberns, Lockard's Antiques, George Richardson, Mrs. W. W. Husband, and Esther Rockey. Certain shops did not sign the inventory questionnaires and hence cannot be mentioned by name.

Item	Per Cent of Shops Having Item	Total Number of Items on Hand
Windsor Loop-back Side Chairs	40	260
Windsor Hoop-back Armchairs	15	80
Windsor Comb-back Side Chairs	5	15
Windsor Comb-back Armchairs	5	12
Windsor Settees	2½	2
Windsor Brace-back Chairs, Side or Arm	5	20
Early Slat-back Chairs, Rush or Rope Seats	15	75
Banister-back Side Chairs	15	50
Panel-back (Fiddle) Side Chairs	20	100
Panel-back Armchairs	20	26
Hepplewhite Chairs (Any Kind)	20	125
Queen Anne Side Chairs	30	60
Queen Anne Armchairs	25	30
Hitchcock Type Side Chairs	50	250
Hitchcock Type Armchairs	15	25
Other Fancy Chairs	50	150
Empire Side Chairs	40	100
Empire Armchairs	20	25
Corner Chairs (Fine)	35	40
Corner Chairs (Pioneer Type)	15	20
Ladder-back Side Chairs, Four or More Shaped Crosspieces, Rush or Rope Seats	35	55
Ladder-back Armchairs, Four or More Shaped Crosspieces, Rush or Rope Seats	35	40
Sheraton Style Chairs	40	70
Duncan Phyfe Style Chairs	20	75
Early Rocking Chairs	40	60
Boston Rockers	55	125
Pioneer or Primitive Chairs	45	70
Victorian Side Chairs	60	200
Victorian Armchairs	40	60
Upholstered Wing Chairs (Eighteenth Century)	40	43
Upholstered Armchairs (Eighteenth Century)	30	33

Item	Per Cent of Shops Having Item	Total Number of Items on Hand
Gate-leg Tables	15	45
Butterfly Tables	15	16
Queen Anne Drop-leaf Tables	25	33
Chippendale Drop-leaf Tables	35	50
Chippendale Tilt-top Tables	30	70
Queen Anne Tea Tables (Without leaves)	25	30
Sawbuck or Trestle Tables	30	36
Hepplewhite Drop-leaf Tables	35	44
Hepplewhite Fold-over Leaf Tables	25	30
Hepplewhite Tea Tables	20	33
Sheraton Drop-leaf Tables	25	36
Sheraton Dining Tables	25	35
Hepplewhite Dining Tables	15	18
Sheraton Side Tables	15	27
Hepplewhite Side Tables	20	30
Duncan Phyfe "Lyre" Side Tables	10	35
Other Duncan Phyfe Type Tables	20	36
Empire Side Tables	25	39
Empire Folding-top Tables	30	39
Empire Drop-leaf Tables	35	40
Victorian Side Tables, Marble Top	45	90
Victorian Dining Tables	25	30
William and Mary Lowboys	10	21
William and Mary Highboys	10	15
Queen Anne Lowboys	20	33
Queen Anne Highboys	30	33
Queen Anne Chests-on-frame	10	11
Chippendale Lowboys	10	15
Chippendale Highboys	10	20
Hepplewhite High Chests of Drawers	20	27
Hepplewhite Bureaus	35	44
Federal Period High Chests of Drawers	10	24
Federal Style Bureaus	10	27
Empire High Chests of Drawers	30	30
Empire Bureaus	60	100
Victorian Bureaus	30	42
Hepplewhite Sideboards	25	30
Sheraton Sideboards	20	24
Duncan Phyfe Style Sideboards	15	12

Item	Per Cent of Shops Having Item	Total Number of Items on Hand
Empire Style Sideboards	30	31
Victorian Style Sideboards	15	19
Grandfather Clocks	50	62
Banjo Clocks	40	44
Terry Style Clocks	30	39
Mantel Clocks, Other Kinds	75	135
Queen Anne Sofas	10	9
Queen Anne Love Seats	5	3
Chippendale Sofas	15	14
Chippendale Window Seats	5	5
Hepplewhite Sofas	5	12
Hepplewhite Window Seats	10	15
Sheraton Sofas	20	21
Sheraton Window Seats	10	12
Duncan Phyfe Style Sofas	15	18
Duncan Phyfe Style Window Seats	5	3
Empire Sofas	45	123
Victorian Large Sofas	35	72
Victorian Settees	35	66
Early Settles	25	30
Table Settles	20	30
Hitchcock Type Settees	10	12
Settees, Other Types	20	42
Directoire Settees	10	12
Directoire Sofas	10	5
Four-poster Beds, Queen Anne	15	5
" " " Chippendale	15	21
" " " Hepplewhite	10	15
" " " Federal	15	42
" " " Phyfe	10	12
French or Sleigh Beds	15	18
Spool Beds	40	240
Empire Beds	25	60
Victorian Beds	35	65
Slope-fall Secretary Desks	45	92
Desks-on-frame	20	48
Fire-screen Desks	10	11
Desk-bookcases	40	63
Brass Andirons	70	300

Item	Per Cent of Shops Having Item	Total Number of Items on Hand
Wrought Andirons	65	210
Brass Fire Tools	60	180
Wrought Fire Tools	36	200
Hooked Rugs	50	375
Lamps, Early	60	260
Lamps, Victorian	60	700
Historic Bottles and Flasks	50	280
Historic Blue Staffordshire	45	390
Historic Liverpool	20	75
Pattern-woven Coverlets (Dated and Signed)	25	68
Lowestoft China	45	300
Pottery or China Figures and Figurines	60	600
Victorian Glass Objects	60	600
Victorian Pottery and China Ornaments	35	420
Early American Silver Spoons	30	300
Nineteenth-century Silver Spoons	35	1500
Early American Silver Creamers, Sugars, Teapots, or Mugs	20	270
Nineteenth-century Silver Creamers, Sugars, Teapots, or Mugs	30	300
Pewter Plates	60	1200
Pewter Teapots, Sugars, Creamers	50	300
Britannia Wares, General	20	300
Paperweights	35	240
Dolls	40	225
Children's Wood Toys	20	36
Children's Mechanical Toys	20	150
Mechanical Banks	20	30
Decanters	70	400
American Rifles	30	210
American Pistols	15	180
Children's Furniture	45	240
Japanned Tinware	50	270
Currier & Ives Prints	70	690
Other American Lithographs	45	300
Early American Prints, Engravings	40	180
Silhouettes	45	80
Hobbyhorses	20	20
Carousel Horses	5	20

Item	Per Cent of Shops Having Item	Total Number of Items on Hand
Spice Cabinets	30	50
Blanket Chests	50	180
Student Lamps	30	69
Fractur Paintings	15	27
Primitive Paintings	35	102
Small Portraits	25	71
Miniatures	45	60
Buttons	30	25,000
Candlesticks, Brass	75	390
Sandwich Glass	75	900
Pressed Glass	60	16,500
Early Blown Glass	50	900
Gaudy China	30	210
Patch Quilts	35	90
Pattern-woven Coverlets (Undated and Unsigned)	45	90
Early American Pottery (Jugs, Pots, et cetera)	60	600

Now that we have seen something of how American furniture production was fostered, promoted, and sold as our nation was expanding, and something of what there is of it in antiques shops today, it is entirely in order to consider the pattern of presenting the story in reader style.

Chairs, because they were made by more chairmakers and more chair factories—and because they have always been used in greater numbers than any other kind of furniture—come first. Then benches, settees, sofas, and such. Then tables and sideboards, highboys and lowboys, desks and bureaus, bedroom and boudoir furniture, clocks, mirrors, elegancies and conceits, silver and Sheffield plate, pewter and Britannia, lamps and candlesticks, pottery, china and glass, paintings and engravings, and toys.

All these are antiques you can collect; antiques you can find in antiques shops or buy in auction rooms. Much of it is nineteenth-century made. Some, however, is eighteenth century, and some even dates from the seventeenth century. The paintings or lithographs mentioned are mostly nineteenth century. The mirrors and clocks are almost wholly in that same period. But if you collect, and have a pocketbook well filled, any of these things you can buy and, barring prior sale, can buy right now.

Conversely, if you have any of what is pictured, you may know you have something of value. But don't ask, or expect, this book to tell you what those values are. Prices current, as this is written, are one thing. Tomorrow they may change up or down. Even auction prices have far from the stability of the stock market. At some auctions certain types of antiques go for a song. A month later the same type of things (and sometimes, it

Grand French *Settee Chair*

Settee Design by Robert Manwaring, London, 1765.

must be said, the *same* things) sell at amazingly high prices. At almost every auction some things are sold at rare bargains while others hit new highs in price.

To those of you sufficiently interested to want to follow auction price records, I can offer no better advice than to subscribe to price catalogues of well-known auctions[1]. Then you will have factual records of what was sold and of what, at that particular moment, somebody was willing to pay. The price will tell nothing about whether the buyer was excited, whether he was buying for a client who said "go the limit, I want that," or whether the buyer didn't like the bidder-up and decided to show the so-and-so he couldn't have the thing.

[1]It is possible to procure priced catalogues of the sales at the Parke-Bernet Galleries of New York at the nominal price of the catalogue plus a fee of one dollar per session for insertion of the price brought by each item.

At auctions of famed collections often prices are high because of the prestige, real or fancied, that goes with owning a piece from a great collection. It has been said with some truth that if, for example, the duPont collection was ever placed on the market, it would bring the absolute record in prices. When, in 1929, the Reifsnyder collection was sold at auction, a highboy sold for $44,000, a wing chair for $33,000, and a side chair for $15,000. But that was 1929, and the pieces were superb examples. Had that sale occurred in 1932 the prices would perhaps have been half, or less. In January 1930, with the financial market beginning to rock on its foundations, a tambour secretary in the Flayderman sale brought $30,000 and a tea table brought $29,000. Such figures sound astronomical even today. They most certainly would sound astronomical to the collector who first rescued the items from oblivion. And it may well be that the price paid for a superfine Victorian sofa, with maker's label dated 1853, will be considered astronomical by the bidders at a sale of antiques sometime during the year 2046.

Meanwhile, here we are, down to earth and dealing with things we can buy in the antiques line today—things that are, or were, in antiques shops as this book is written.

American antiques do get around. Not long ago I met a man in an antiques shop at Bronxville, New York. He was looking for pressed glass and milk-white animal-headed glass wares. Upon asking him from whence he came, he said, "Nebraska." It developed that he had carried some early twentieth-century lamps from Nebraska to New York, sold them at a good price, and was buying stuff that he wanted with the money he got for the lamps. The Bronxville man bought one of the lamps. The following day he sold it to a woman from South Carolina!

They won't stay put, these antiques we collect. They won't even stay put after we collect them. But within the movement of our antiques—and especially the movement of antiques we can collect—there is fun in big doses. So here's to you who want to have fun! Your chairs are waiting for you in Chapter II!

CABINET WARE
OF EVERY DESCRIPTION·

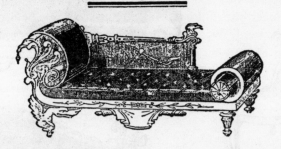

THE SUBSCRIBER would tender his thanks to the public, for the liberal share of patronage bestowed on him thus far, and would inform those not acquainted with his Warehouse, that he has on hand, and is constantly manufacturing at the old stand of Bancroft & Miles,

Cabinet-Ware of every description---such as---

Secretaries, Sideboards, French, Toilet and Common Bureaus, Sofas of various patterns and prices, Mahogany and Cherry Card, Center, Dining, Tea and Breakfast Tables, Work and Dress Tables, Wash & Light Stands, High Post, Field, French, Press and Common Bedsteads, Music Stools, Curled Hair Matresses, &c &c.

All of which will be sold cheap for cash, produce, most kinds of Lumber er approvod credit.

Greenfield, Dec. 2, 1834.   ISAAC MILES.

Cabinet and Chair Manufactory.

ROGER PORTINGTON,
NO. 656,
Washington-Street,

HAS on hand, and is constantly manufacturing, of the best materials, and of the most fashionable patterns, a variety of *CABINET FURNITURE.*
He also manufactures *Mahogany CHAIRS, SOFAS,* and *COUCHES,* and the spring seat *ROCKING CHAIRS,* which have been so universally admired.

GEORGE & PHILIP GRAVES,

RESPECTFULLY wishes to inform the Ladies and Gentlemen of Boston, and its vicinity, that they have commenced a Factory, No. 554, *Washington-Street,* where they intend to manufacture all kinds of *MAHOGANY CHAIRS, SOFAS,* and *COUCHES,* to any pattern or design whatever—and all kinds of *CHURCH FURNITURE,* with neatness and despatch.

UPHOLSTERY

GOODS, of every description, for CHURCHES, HOUSES, and SHIPS, constantly on hand, and the business, as usual, attended to in all its branches, by

WILLIAM HANCOCK,
Upholsterer,
NO'S 37, 39, 41, 45, 49, & 53,
MARKET-STREET,
BOSTON.
Where may be had every article of *CABINET FURNITURE*—and
A great variety of *CHAIRS, &c. &c.*

Isaac Miles of Greenfield, Massachusetts, 1834; Roger Portington, Boston, 1829; George & Philip Graves, Boston, 1829; and William Hancock, Boston, 1829, illustrate the newest furniture styles in their newspaper advertising.

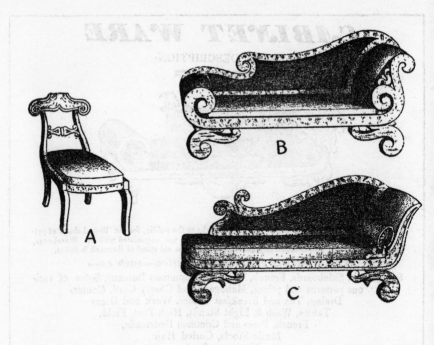

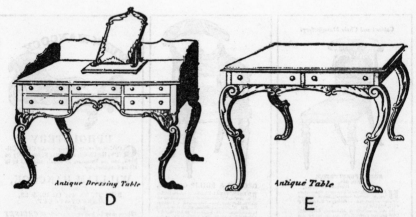

A, B, and **C:** Sofas and a Chair Designed by John Hall, 1840.
D and **E:** "Antique" Furniture Designs, Now Called Victorian, by R. Conner, New York, 1842.

FANCY CHAIR STORE.

WILLIAM BROWN, Jun.

No. 50 Beckman-street, New York, has constantly for sale, a large assortment of elegant, well-made and highly finished Fancy Chairs, Settees, Conversation, Ehair, Rocking, Sewing, Windsor and Children's Chairs, of every description, on the most moderate terms.

Orders from any part of the continent will be attended to with punctuality and dispatch. A liberal allowance made to shippers, &c.

N.B Old chairs repaired, varnished and re-gilt.

JAMES R. HEATON,
FANCY & WINDSOR CHAIR MAKER,
No. 240 GREENWICH STREET,
between Robinson & Murray streets,
NEWYORK.

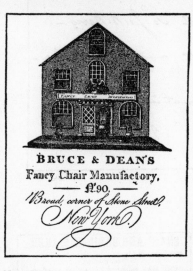

BRUCE & DEAN'S
Fancy Chair Manufactory,
No. 90,
Broad, corner of Stone Street,
New York.

Allegheny Chair Manufactory.

WHITE & HAMILTON,

keep constantly on hand a large and general assortment of

Chairs and Settees,

of every description, of the latest and most approved patterns, which they will warrant, and sell at the most reduced prices, at their old stand, corner of Ohio street and the Diamond, Allegheny Borough. The citizens of Pittsburgh and Allegheny are respectfully invited to call and examine for themselves.

N. B. Steam Boats and Hotels furnished at the shortest notice.

New York, 1810–18, and Pittsburgh, 1837. Chairmakers' Advertisements Showing, in One Instance, That Considerable Stocks Were Carried in Anticipation of Quick Orders.

Isaac Washburn of Taunton, Massachusetts, in 1828, Sold Ten Dining Chairs and Two Small Chairs for $10.58.
Joseph Barry, Philadelphia, 1797, Billed an Easy Chair at $25. Fancy Chair Advertising by Cowperthwaite of New York, 1830, and John May of Lancaster, Pennsylvania, 1849.

CHAPTER II

Chairs

The American Windsor chair, first appearing at Philadelphia about 1725, and the American slat-back chair, dating from around 1700, made simultaneously in New England, New York, and Pennsylvania, were the first chairs to go into what might be called repetitive manufacture. The makers could produce the chairs by spending time on the making of a number of legs, which were turned on a lathe, then in shaping slats or spindles, then in making rails, seats, and stretchers, and finally in assembling the chair for sale. The Philadelphia or Windsor chairmakers seem to have been among the first artisans generally to advertise their wares. Windsor chairs are among the first illustrated items advertised in early newspapers. In the Carolinas, Maryland, and Delaware, in Pennsylvania, New Jersey, and all over New England, he who scans the early newspapers from 1735 down to 1840 will find Windsor chairmakers advertising their wares.

These chairs were made for everybody. They were cheap but handsome; common but good. The rich bought them, the poor bought them. They were everywhere. A great deal has been written about the different kinds of Windsors, the significance of the turnings, the quality of the saddle seats, fashioned from a solid plank of wood, and even the original colors of paint used on them. One expert has said: "Windsors were painted red, brown, and green, in various shades, but never white." It is a pity he has passed on to his reward because he would be amazed to see the manuscript bill of John Letchworth, Windsor chairmaker of Philadelphia, dated "1st day, 5th month, 1796," itemized as follows: "To William Meredith, 18 Oval back Windsor chairs painted green at 13/9 each, and 18 ditto painted *white* at 15/ each; 2 ditto Arm Chairs painted *white* at 22/6 each and 2 ditto painted green, 21/6 each!" Thus we know that Windsors were originally painted white, and that they cost a bit more than Windsor chairs painted green. Another bill, by Francis Trumble, dated 1758, itemizes a "Mahogany Tea Table £4,5/0 and six Windsor chairs at 14/ each." Enoch Storey, of Philadelphia, made this purchase and, according to certain experts who have examined the bill, it marks an early mention of "mahogany" as a cabinet wood.

In 1818, at the village of Barkhamsted, Connecticut, Lambert Hitchcock established a factory for the production of fancy chair parts. These he shipped to Charleston, South Carolina, and other Southern ports, where they were assembled by fancy chairmakers. By 1821 he was so busy making chair parts that a little village of workmen's homes had grown up around his factory. This settlement was named Hitchcocksville. The mass production of chair parts had by 1823 become so lucrative an undertaking that Hitchcock decided to cash in on the chair business in a big way. He used his own parts to make Hitchcock chairs and sold them in tremendous quantities.

Two well-turned front legs, with a nicely turned stretcher; seats wide in front and narrowing to the rear; bent and shaped back posts and legs in one piece, with shaped back rails; rush seats and stenciled decoration—these were the earmarks of the first Hitchcock chairs. His stenciled designs included the "horn of plenty," grapes, and other fruits, birds drinking at fountains, eagles, et cetera. He stencil marked his chairs, "L. Hitchcock, Hitchcocksville, Connecticut, Warranted." By 1826 he had erected a large three-story factory with a cupola, and in it had production lines that included children painting the chairs and women applying the stenciled decoration. In 1829 Hitchcock went bankrupt, owing more than $20,000. His assets included fifteen hundred chairs at the factory, fifteen hundred on consignment in Hartford, five hundred at New Haven, and many other thousands on consignment—unsalable in the general depression of the times. His assignees worked the business out of bankruptcy. By 1832 it was again in full production, with Hitchcock serving as sales agent and a former employee, Arba Alford, as production manager. The stenciled label was changed to read, "Hitchcock, Alford & Co., Warranted," and business again boomed. But not only for the Hitchcock works. Other

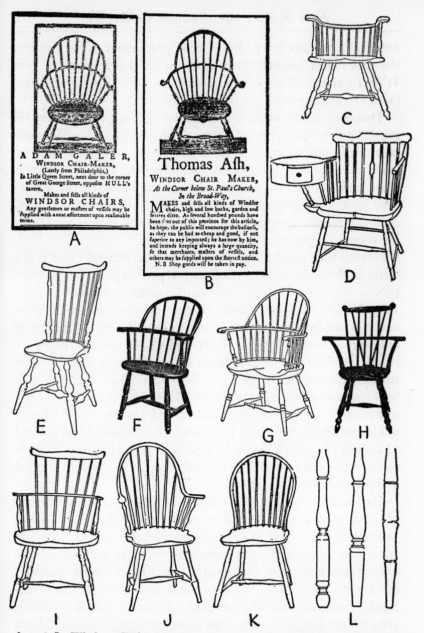

A and **B**: Windsor Chair Advertisements, 1774. **C**: Low-Back or Horseshoe Windsor Armchair. **D**: Late Windsor Writing Armchair, 1840. **E**: Fanback Windsor Side Chair. **F**: Factory-Made Hoop-Back Windsor, 1875-95. **G**: Hoop-Back Windsor Armchair. **H**: Early Type Brace-Back Windsor. **I**: Comb-Back Windsor Armchair. **J**: Loop-Back Armchair. Loop and Arm in One Piece. **K**: Loop-Back Windsor Side Chair. **L**: Pennsylvania, New England, and Bamboo Type Leg Turning

fancy chairmakers were also in mass production, some rivaling the Hitchcock output. Steamboats were multiplying on our Western rivers. Most of the steamboats were furnished, from saloon to stateroom, with fancy chairs.

Thus the fancy chair was duplicating the phenomenon of general production enjoyed by the slat-back and by the Windsor chair. It could be repetitively manufactured by a division of labor and the parts brought to assembly. The people loved the chair and bought (conservatively) about 6,000,000 in a ten-year period. Many homes used sets of six, with one an armchair, in dining rooms. They were used in bedrooms, parlors, and sewing rooms, on piazzas, and on front "stoops."

Having thus fixed the three most popular general chair types made in America, we can look at the periods of great production as beginning at both ends of the century of years, 1735–1835. Within that century all other types of antique chairs generally available to collectors of today were also made, excepting only seventeenth-century chairs and these specific types of chairs: William and Mary, Queen Anne, Victorian, some Boston rockers, Shaker chairs, and late slat-backs. With just so much background and the tail end of the Hitchcock story (Hitchcock left his first factory in 1841 and started another chair factory at Unionville, Connecticut, from which he shipped chairs marked "Lambert Hitchcock" until he died in 1852), we can begin a review of the chairs available generally today in the shops called antique and in the auction rooms.

Slat-back or Ladder-back Chairs. This form of simple turned chair, or assembly of turned members into a chair form, dates from at least 1700. It is generally agreed that the type having front legs and back posts turned in what is now called the sausage-and-ball form, and chairs turned from square members but having short vase-and-ball turnings between the square sections (somewhat like the turnings of certain gate-leg tables), are of New England make, and those having plain turned back legs and posts, but with some turning on the finials of back posts, and turned front legs, are the Pennsylvania type. The slats, or rungs, in the backs of these chairs range, in the earlier examples, from four to seven down to two and three in late examples. Also, these slats are known in several varieties: (1) curved laterally to

Top bill:

1st of 5th mo 1796

William Meredith
　　　Bought of Jno. Litchworths
18 Oval back Windsor Chairs, painted green a 13/9 — £12..7..6
18 Ditto _____ do — do white a 15/ — 13..10..—
2 Ditto Arm Chairs — do — do a 22/6 — 2..5..—
2 Ditto ___ do ___ do green a 21/6 — 2..3..—
　　　Doll.s 80.73　　　　£30..5..6

Middle bill:

Philada June 1791
Frend Meradeth
12 Green Chairs　Bot of William Cox
　　　a 6/3 — £3..15..0

Bottom bill:

Edward Shippen Esqr
　　　　Bot of Frans. Trumble —
July 24 — To 2 Windsor Chairs with Mahy. Arms £ 2..0..0
　　　Received the Contents 29. Augt 1769
　　　　　　James Leet

Top: Bill for Windsors Painted White, 1796. **Middle:** Bill for Twelve Green (Windsor) Chairs. **Bottom:** Bill for Windsors with Mahogany Arms, 1769.

fit the back of the sitter and shaped in a bow or wave-like form; (2) laterally curved and also shaped (a) in the form of dolphins head to head, (b) in cyma curves, and (c) in double waves; (3) curved laterally but cut straight across the bottom and with tops curved in a bow or wave shape.

Two turned front stretchers grace the chairs of this type made in New England. The Pennsylvania chairs usually have one finely turned stretcher of the bulb-and-wheel type. Two plain side stretchers and one back stretcher are common to both the New England and Pennsylvania slat-back chairs.

This is the quick-fact story about slat-back chairs. Within it is buried material for a book, or at least the monograph that Mr. Thomas Ormsbee is now writing. What is pertinent further to say here is that New England, New York, and Pennsylvania slat-back chairs were made for at least one hundred years; that various communities of Shakers in the nineteenth century made slat-back chairs for sale through shops; and, finally, that scores of furniture factories made them as common chairs for kitchen, garden, porch, and as general chairs for cottages, down to 1890. The early slat-back chairs had flag, or rush, seats, or what is known as a rope seat—a seat woven very much as a rush seat but using good stout cord or rope. The latter lasted longer, especially when the cord was of flax or the rope of hemp.

Rarely hemp rope seats may have been called hangman's seats. There is a tradition that a sheriff once had the slat-back chairs of his office seated with ropes used to hang malefactors. When we realize that certain booklovers once had such atrocious taste as to have books bound in the tanned skins of executed malefactors, the vagary of the sheriff isn't hard to believe.

Our pictures of slat-back chairs do not include all types and styles, and display some early and late nineteenth-century examples. But the pictures do represent the types and styles of slat-backs you can expect to find now, in either antiques shops or auction rooms. If you want slat-back chairs, these are the ones available. When you find them, they're yours at the prices current.

Fancy Caned Chairs. These are early and mid-seventeenth-century luxury chairs made for top-drawer people. They are carved and turned, and they have caned seats and panels of caning

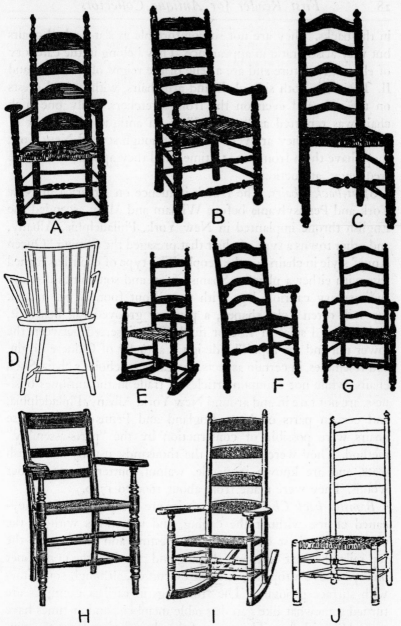

A: Slat-Back Armchair, New England Type, Maple. **B:** Slat-Back New England Armchair. **C:** Pennsylvania Slat-Back Side Chair, 1750–90. **D:** Square-Back Windsor Armchair, about 1840. **E:** Slat-Back Rocking Chair, New England Type, Maple. **F:** Pennsylvania Slat-Back Armchair, Early Type. **G:** Pennsylvania Slat-Back Armchair, 1750–70. **H, I,** and **J:** Late Slat-Back Chairs, 1870–90.

in the backs. They are not so comfortable as slat-backed chairs but very aristocratic in appearance. They belong in the category of elegant furniture and are a relic of the reigns of Charles I and II. There are both side chair and armchairs, with carved crests on the rails and even on the front stretchers. Only one such chair was reported as "on hand" in an antiques shop west of Philadelphia. They are very scarce, although several New York shops have them from time to time. And they appear, with some frequency, at auctions.

Splat-back Chairs. The Dutch influence on America in New York and Pennsylvania before William and Mary ascended the English throne implanted in New York, Philadelphia, Albany, and other towns a type of chair that presaged the coming "Queen Anne" style in chairs for the people. This type of chair has turned legs with either a plain or Spanish foot, and sometimes displays rudimentary cabriole legs with turned-out foot. It has a back top rail, often yoke shaped, a plain or grooved rail below it, and a shaped splat in vase or fiddle form inserted between the lower rail and the top. The design is actually of Chinese origin, and resembles, in certain aspects, the Chinese scholar's chair. Such chairs, while not common articles of trade in the antiques business, are not rare in and around New York, Albany, Philadelphia, and certain parts of New England and Pennsylvania. These chairs were possible of construction by the "parts-assembly" method. They were made by the thousands, usually with rush seats, and are known in maple, walnut, butternut, and other woods. They were made from about 1690 to 1750.

Banister-back Chairs. These chairs are the poor man's fancy-caned chairs, without the caning, and sometimes without the carving. The best examples have cresting and carving on the top rails, the next best have shaping and piercing, the commoner ones just have a top rail, straight or curved, although sometimes with surface grooving. The front legs in earliest examples are turned somewhat like gate-leg table members, and at times have carved Spanish feet. The name of the chair derives from the construction of the back, a series of split, vase-turned banisters set between top rail and seat rail. Splitting a turned banister reveals its turned form in flat silhouette and gives such chair backs a delightful quality. The flat side of the banister is toward the

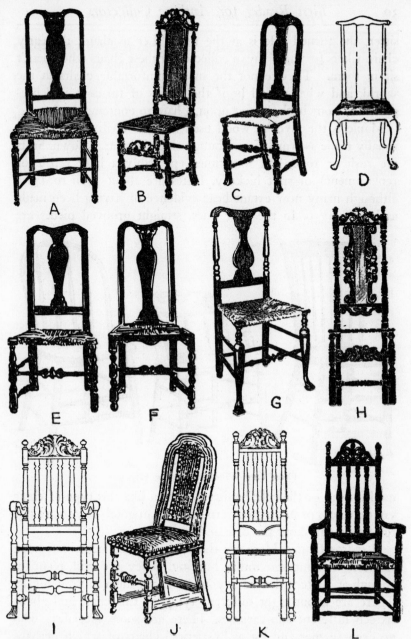

A: Splat-Back, Similar to Chinese Scholar's Chair. **B** and **H:** Fancy Caned Chairs with Carved Crests and Stretchers. **C:** Splat-Back Chair with Spanish Feet. **D** and **G:** Splat-Back with Yoke Top and Cabriole Legs. **E** and **F:** Splat-Back Chairs with Turned Legs. **I:** Banister-Back Armchair, Carved Top Rail and Spanish Feet. **J:** Splat-Back with Leather Covering, 1710. **K:** Banister-Back Side Chair. **L:** Banister-Back Armchair, Pierced Top Rail and Plain Turned Legs.

sitter, the turned side is at the rear. "Let us thank the early chairmakers for that," says a collector of these chairs who doesn't sit in them. "They're not the most comfortable chairs in the world, and what they'd be if that series of turnings was presented to your back, to rest upon, I hate to contemplate."

Maple is the favorite wood used in these chairs. They were usually made as armchairs, although side chairs are known. Seats are rush or rope, and sometimes (probably a later repair or replacement) of split hickory. Dates are about 1680 to 1720, although many now extant bear evidence of having been made as late as 1750. In the later ones, straight grooved pieces are

Three Late Windsors, Dating 1870–90.

used instead of the split banisters. If you like this type of chair your chances of finding one are better than good—if you are not too particular about the date and style.

Windsor Chairs. Here are the chairs any collector can hope to own without too much hunting. They are still plentiful enough at Eastern dealers if you can't find them in your locale. There are about eight different types of this chair and about sixteen different sub-varieties. There are some specialists who go even further and list as "varieties" chairs of which perhaps only one example was made.

Simplification, however, is easy in our case, for we are dealing only with chairs you can buy and not with chairs in private collections or in museums. The oval-back Windsor side chair,

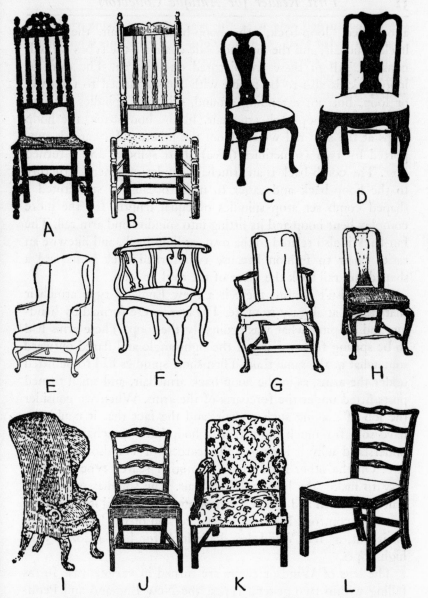

A and **B**: Banister-Back Side Chairs. **C**: Queen Anne Dining or Side Chair. **D**: Georgian Period Chair in Queen Anne Style. **E**: Queen Anne Upholstered Armchair. **F**: Queen Anne Corner Chair. **G**: Queen Anne Armchair. **H**: Queen Anne Side Chair. **I**: Chippendale Upholstered Armchair from Cabinetmaker's Advertisement, 1769. **J**: Chippendale Ladder-Back Side Chair. **K**: Chippendale Upholstered Armchair, Square Legs. **L**: Chippendale Ladder-Back Side Chair.

also called "loop-back," the hoop-back armchair, the comb-back armchair, and the fan-back side chair are the types we will consider. All of these are pictured on page 23. The oval, or loop-back, is also to be found with arms attached to the oval, or loop, but not extending around, with the spindles through it, as in the hoop-back armchair. In the hoop-back, the hoop stops at the arm rail which, from the juncture forward, is supported by two (sometimes three) short spindles and a turned post. The comb-back is an armchair, similar in general structure to the hoop-back and easier to make because it substituted a shaped comb set atop spindles of equal length, for the more complex bent hoop and its fitting into spindles and arm rail. The fan-back is also related to the oval, or loop-back, and likewise an easier chair to fashion because two turned back posts and a shaped top rail took the place of the oval or loop.

Simple, isn't it? But there is a New England type armchair that wasn't at all easy to make. The arms were formed by bending and shaping what was ordinarily the loop. These arms had to be sprung forward at just the right angle and flared outward somewhat at the same time. Then short spindles had to be fitted under the arms, as in the hoop-back armchair, and small turned posts fitted under the foreparts of the arms. When we consider the job of making such a chair, and the fact that it could not have sold for much more than a hoop-back armchair, we can understand why it is among the scarcest of Windsor chairs today. On the other hand, there is another scarce type that was easy to make—the low-back armchair. The spindles end at the arm rail, which had a heavy section nicely rounded into a pillow form for comfort. It is a high-class version of the later barroom chair but, as real Windsors, don't look for half a dozen with high hopes.

The legs of Windsor chairs are turned in various vase forms falling within two general types: the New England and Pennsylvania. There is also a bamboo type of turning. Simple line drawings among our pictures show these three turnings. The seats of Windsor chairs are solid, worked from a slab of poplar or similar soft wood into a saddle shape which one wit has called "a perfect sitting-down place." Windsors were originally sold painted green, red, brown, and white. Occasionally they were

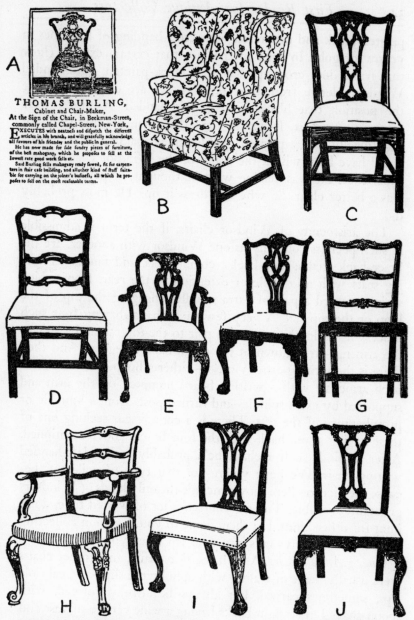

A: Chippendale Chair in Cabinetmaker's Advertisement, 1770. B: Chippendale Style Wing-Back. C: Gothic-Back Chippendale Chair, Square Legs. D and G: Chippendale Ladder-Back Side Chairs with Carved and Pierced Slats. E and F: Chippendale Armchair and Side Chair. H: Chippendale Armchair with True Chippendale Turned-up Scroll Feet. I and J: Two Fine Chippendale Style Chairs of Philadelphia Make.

painted black and decorated with cross-banding of fine lines in yellow or gold. In spite of the fact that certain experts (how that name does crop up) say that black-painted, gold-banded Windsors derive from later repaints, we are disposed to take the position that black-painted, gold-banded Windsors were among the earliest. It was in 1725 that memory—and sight—of traditionally black-painted, gold-banded banister-back chairs could have been within the realm of the Windsor chairmaker's experience. He was making what he thought, or perhaps knew, was a better chair. So why not dress it up? He most probably did.

The aristocrats of Windsor chairs, if the term is admissible in such peerless company as one Windsor with another, are the brace-back chairs; loop-backs, comb-backs, and fan-backs having seats with a knuckle or extension to the rear, from which spring upward a pair of extra spindles engaging the top of the loop or the top rail. A very few such chairs—having four such braces, or "flying buttresses," a pair to the top rail and a pair to the arm rail—are known in the comb-back category. And then there is the writing-arm Windsor—either a hoop-back or comb-back armchair with a writing board mounted on the arm and supported by extra spindles and turned posts from a knuckle or protuberance of the seat. There is a connoisseur seeking one of these having also a back with the four braces above mentioned. After he finds such a chair, he'll probably seek a left-handed writing chair. We hope you're not that type of collector, because the pictures here shown include the only kinds of Windsors generally available. To save yourself a lot of wasted time, don't hunt for other kinds. Let them come to you. Keep on collecting —the unusual always falls into your lap when you do.

Queen Anne Chairs. Armchairs, side chairs, and corner chairs were usually made of walnut with upholstered slip seats, cabriole legs, sometimes carved, but always beautifully formed, with spoon-shaped or straight backs having a wide variety of vase and fiddle-form splats. They are very fine chairs. They are aristocratic chairs and, believe it or not, they are not so scarce as their place in time (1702–60) would have you think. Which is not to say they are cheap. And also not to say that all of these chairs now in America, or even in America for two centuries, were

A: Chair Designed by Manwaring. **B** and **C:** Hepplewhite Armchairs. **D** and **F:** Hepplewhite Dining or Side Chairs. **E** and **I:** Very Fine Hepplewhite Type Side Chairs with Over-upholstered Seats. **G:** Typical Adam Style Chair. **H:** Fancy Chair Factory Advertising, 1818. **J:** Badge of the Fancy Chairmakers in Erie Canal Celebration.

made here. One may suspect considerable importation as part of the goods of early gentlemen and merchant settlers, and representatives of proprietors and the Crown. It doesn't matter how they got here, if imported. What does matter is that cabinet-makers in town and country made these chairs for fifty years or more and in that time made them for a great many people. The chairs were so unquestionably good they were never ruthlessly junked, at least in the eighteenth century. If, in the nineteenth century, they fell into less moneyed hands, there was apparently no lack of appreciation for them. That's why you can today collect them one by one, and even splurge and purchase a half-dozen matched ones with an armchair. Pictured are examples of the kind you can collect today. You may, conceivably, find their counterparts in some museums, but the kinds here shown you can find in dealers' shops.

Chippendale Chairs. There aren't many of this type of chair in most dealers' shops for the simple reason that dealers usually have to compete with private buyers in order to procure them, be it in the auction rooms or in private homes. But some Chippendale chairs, and fortunately the less ornate and hence more satisfying ones, are to be found in both dealers' shops and at auctions. It would be very nice to go into rhapsodies over this style of chair and tell all about it in words. But we can picture only the types of chairs that antiques dealers now have on hand and chairs which, to our knowledge, have been offered at auction within the year of this book's preparation. Hence no rhapsodies. At any rate, Thomas Chippendale has been greeted by thousands and said "good-by" to by but one, so the man and his style need no comment here. The captions under each Chippendale chair tell all of the story that needs telling. After you own a Chippendale chair, you'll want to know more about the style, its genesis, and its variants.

In this day and age it's easier to find a little Chippendale in a Victorian chair than it is to find a lot of Chippendale—plus a lot of American styling—in an American-made Chippendale chair of the Chippendale period. Let it suffice here to say that the Chippendale style is adapted from Queen Anne, the Georgian, the French, and the Chinese. It is characterized by carving, without inlay of any kind, and the favored woods are mahog-

A

D   E   F   G

A: Tweed Chair Factory Advertising, 1857. B and C: Boston Rockers with Painted and Stenciled Decoration. D and E: Late Fancy Chairs by the Heywood Company of New England. F: Stencil Decorated Fancy Chair, Caned Seat, 1840. G: Baltimore Style, Stenciled, All-Wood Fancy Chair, 1850–80.

any and walnut with an occasional piece of maple, cherry, and even pine. Also, some bilsted, or gumwood, was used. This is very much like mahogany although it is a native north American wood. A few American cabinetmakers made country Chippendale chairs with crudely shaped legs and rush and rope seats. Herewith are pictures representative of the Chippendale chairs waiting somewhere for collectors to purchase them.

Adam, Hepplewhite, and Manwaring Style Chairs. These three styles, all having something in common, are attempts to escape from the Georgian and Chippendale influence. Adam and Manwaring made their respective bids for recognition in 1760 and 1765. Adam achieved great popularity in England, but not in America. Hepplewhite made his bid in 1780 and in his posthumously published book of designs issued in 1788. Both Adam and Hepplewhite designs are based upon a classic revival. Manwaring, on the other hand, just tried to go Chippendale one better—something that was accomplished more successfully in the nineteenth-century Chippendale we now call Victorian. There are no Adam and Manwaring style chairs of the period to be found in any but the most exclusive antiques shops. They are probably importations. Any American-made Adam and Manwaring style furniture of the period was captured long ago, and is now either in private or museum collections. But American-made Hepplewhite is another story. Hepplewhite chairs, particularly dining chairs and easy chairs, were made here in considerable numbers. Pictured are the types you can hope to find in antiques shops or at auctions. During the past six months, as this is written, several sets of Hepplewhite dining chairs have sold for less money than parlor sets of Victorian. Hepplewhite furniture is characterized by square tapered legs, inlaid or plain. Chair backs are generally shield shaped and heart shaped in many varieties—sometimes inlaid, sometimes carved, sometimes pierced and fretted. Mahogany was the favorite wood, but the furniture is known also in walnut, cherry, and other woods.

Directoire, Sheraton, and so-called "Phyfe" Style Chairs. When in 1791–93 Thomas Sheraton published his *Cabinet-Maker's and Upholsterer's Drawing Book*, he gave to cabinet-makers and chairmakers a lot of new chair patterns. His chief departure from the styles of Adam and Hepplewhite is found in

A: Eagle-Back Fancy Chair, 1830. **B, C,** and **D:** Three Late Fancy Chairs, Two All Wood, Stencil Decorated, One Cane Seated and Gold Outlined. **E:** Fancy Folding Chair, 1856. **F:** Fancy Chair as Pictured by Its Maker, 1840. **G** and **H:** Two Chairs of So-Called Duncan Phyfe Style. **I:** Wing Chair, 1810, with Empire "Bedpost" Front Legs, Sheraton Back Legs, and Hepplewhite Body. **J:** Sheraton Style Armchair. **K:** Sheraton Influence Fancy Chair.

the backs of his chairs, which are rectangular or square in general shape no matter what other patterns were imposed upon them for decoration or what other elements were introduced. Many chairmakers in America used Sheraton designs but did not copy exactly the models he drew. Certain other of our chairmakers appear to have arrived at designs comparable to Sheraton, but without benefit of his book. The style we call Sheraton includes simple as well as ornate chairs, some of which have carved and reeded banister-like elements, others carved slats, and still others modified heart, vase, oval, and lyre forms. Legs are turned, reeded, square, tapering; some joined by stretchers but mostly without. Chair seats are leather, fabric, and rush. Some of the seats are "over-upholstered"; that is, the covering is carried down over the seat rails and fastened with tacks over tape or with fancy nails; and some are slip-seated. Many Sheraton chairs were made in America between 1795 and 1815.

The French Directoire which, in France, lasted from 1793 to 1804, gave us another new furniture style characterized by delightful curves and simple classicism. The style was received here with enthusiasm, and perhaps as many chairs were made in the Directoire as were made in the Sheraton style. Certainly they were made for a greater number of years and, as our population was increasing each year, we can assume an ever-increasing annual production of this popular chair style.

The French began to drop the Directoire and developed the Empire style in 1804. In parts of our country, at least, we stayed with the Directoire until 1830. Most of the designs in the *Pittsburgh Cabinet Makers' Book of Prices* of 1830 are Directoire in influence. Our Duncan Phyfe was making Directoire influence furniture up to at least 1825. The pictures here displayed by no means cover the gamut of Sheraton, Directoire, and Phyfe type chairs, but they do represent the chairs of these styles to be found in antiques shops and sold in auction rooms today. Many Directoire style chairs, made in America by perhaps hundreds of cabinetmakers, have been called "Duncan Phyfe style" because they, and Phyfe, made chairs in the same styles—a blending of Sheraton and Directoire, or chairs in which the Sheraton or Directoire style is dominant. Pittsburgh, Ohio, and Mississippi Valley chairmakers produced such chairs long after Phyfe

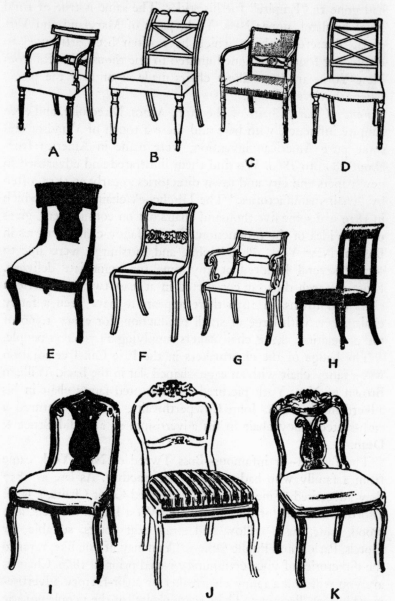

A, B, C, and **D:** Two Armchairs and Two Side Chairs of Sheraton Influence.
E, F, G, and **H:** Directoire Influence Chairs, Fancy and Plain. **I, J,** and **K:** Late
Directoire Influence Chairs, 1830–50.

had gone to "Empire" for his styles. The same is true of rural New England, upper New York, parts of Maryland and Virginia. Therefore, chairs which have often been attributed to Phyfe, yet found from one hundred to one thousand miles from New York, are most likely chairs made at or near the places where they were found.

Fancy Chairs. Chairs of Sheraton, Adam, Directoire, and even Empire influence, with here and there a touch of Windsor and some pure American invention, were made in America from about 1800 to 1860. We find them illustrated and advertised in newspapers and city and town directories as early as 1815, often by "chair manufactories." The Hitchcock chair factory, which in 1829 had some five thousand chairs out on consignment, gives us some idea of the production. Certain fancy-chair factories in Boston, New York, Philadelphia, and Pittsburgh were able to supply several hundred at any time for immediate delivery. From research thus far conducted in at least twenty American cities and towns, in 1830 there appears to have been a fancy chairmaker, with large or small production, for every 1,560 of the population: 8,128 chairmakers supplying 12,700,000 people.

The badge of the chairmakers in the Erie Canal celebration was a fancy chair with an eagle-shaped slat in the back. William Brown of New York pictured a cane-seated fancy chair in his advertising in 1818. John Cowperthwaite, in 1818, pictured a rush-seated fancy chair in his advertising; so also did Bruce & Dean.

The famous—or infamous—Boss Tweed of New York came from a family who had a fancy-chair factory. As late as 1857 they advertised "Fine Gilt and Variegated Color Chairs, a large assortment boxed for the Spanish and West Indian markets, also wood, cane, rush, willow and straw seat chairs, suitable for Hotels, Parlors and Public Offices." You may, if you like, refer to the directories of your community issued prior to 1860. Chances are you will find a fancy chairmaker or chair-factory advertisement in that directory. These were chairs for the people—of the people—by the people. Every family had them, many families still have them, and almost every antiques shop has them on sale now.

Our pictures include some fancy-chair factory advertising

A and **B**: Pair of Empire Style Chairs. **C**: Empire Chair Showing Directoire Influence. **D**: Chair in High Empire Style with Roman Elements for Arm Supports. **E**: Empire Armchair, Grecian Influence. **F**: Empire Stool, 1850–60. **G, H, I,** and **J**: Four Side Chairs, Empire Style, Greek Revival Influence, 1830–40.

and a group of fancy chairs of the kind you can buy now. These embrace a variety such as Tweed advertised, but dating from about 1820 down to the all-wood fancy chairs made as late as 1860 or even 1875. These latter chairs in Pennsylvania have been called "Pennsylvania Dutch," which, of course, they aren't. They are chairs which appealed to the Swiss Amish and Mennonites because they were both colorful and sturdy. They still appeal to these people who, never collectors of antiques, will bid up to a pretty penny at country auctions to get solid-wood fancy chairs.

Do you need to be told these chairs are lovely, or nice, or engaging? That they were painted, carved, gilded, stenciled, and decorated freehand? That examples bearing the mark of the maker cost more as antiques than unmarked ones? Then you must read many books about antiques to satisfy your hunger. If you like the chairs and are a collector who wants them, you'll go out on a hunt, in person, or by mail. If you have a few by inheritance, you'll know they're worth money as antiques, and, better still, worth keeping as antiques.

Empire Chairs. The French "Empire" style of furniture was developed in France when Napoleon took over the leadership of that nation. The Directoire, one of the finest furniture styles ever created, was gently suppressed in the France of 1804 by the simple process of coarsening its graceful curves, doubling and trippling its weight, and then grafting improved classic patterns from Egypt, Greece, and Rome—not to mention a salting of rococo and a peppering of sixteenth-century Swiss. Thus the way was paved for France's Empire furniture. This furniture adapted the bad from many sources and made it worse, and appropriated the best from other sources and made it not so good. Yet, as has been said over and over again, a superlatively good workman cannot produce a completely bad piece of furniture even from a hodgepodge of designs. Many superlatively good cabinetmakers turned to making Empire mainly because it was new and reflected the age—the Empire—that was making newspaper headlines all over the civilized world.

America did not, apparently, get around to the Empire style until long after Napoleon's Empire had crumbled to dust. But when we did get to it, with Duncan Phyfe in New York and

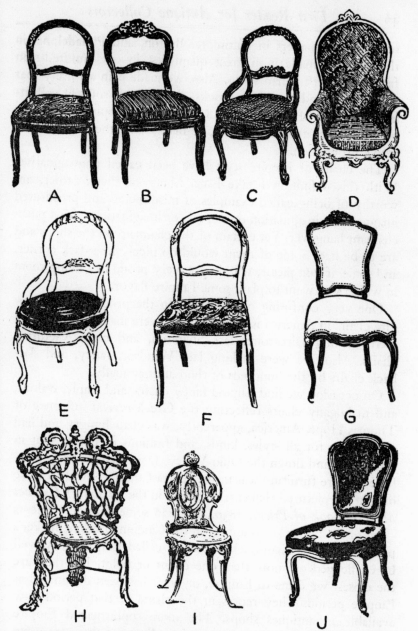

A, B, and C: Three Victorian Chairs of Rosewood. D: Early Victorian Armchair.
E: Victorian Chair, 1855. F: Victorian Chair, 1855–60. G: Victorian Chair of
French Make. H and I: Victorian Garden Chairs of Cast Iron, 1856–80. J:
Victorian Chair, Advertised in 1857.

other cabinetmakers in Baltimore, Boston, and Philadelphia in the van, we made it in great quantities, in one-hundred-man factories and two-man shops. Also, we made it in a variety that still amazes—and sometimes shocks—the aesthetic souls of collecting. The end of the period, 1840, displays Empire in its very worst aspects and, conversely, it marks also the era of most active production.

The chairs of Empire style have been called unimaginative. With this definition I take issue. Many of them, rather, are worthy of being called examples of misdirected and prostituted imagination: imagination on a spree, or imagination with a pink-elephant hangover. Yet certain of the chairs are in the shops and are to be had. Some of them would do nicely in a dark corner, and some, if you please, will do you very proud in a living room in which you want to plant some Empire flavor.

One very confusing circumstance in the production of Empire chairs in America is that while we were making Empire we were making Directoire, late Sheraton, and early Victorian chairs. Also, we were making late Windsor, fancy, and slat-back chairs by the hundreds of thousands annually.

On occasion we find painted fancy chairs, and maple, walnut, and mahogany chairs reflecting the Greek-revival influence of Thomas Hope. America, apparently, was chair hungry and had an appetite for all styles, kinds, and fashions of chairs. Out in Pittsburgh and down the Ohio Valley, from 1810 to 1835, very little Empire furniture was made. At least there is hardly a trace of it in the pictured elements of design in the *Pittsburgh Cabinet Makers' Book of Prices*, 1830. By 1836 some Empire elements —but of the better kind—appear in the Cincinnati cabinetmaker's price book. The chairs here pictured, called Empire, may well be challenged on more than one count or point. But they are the closest we came to Empire, or what has been designated as Empire period. They represent the chairs of that period now available in antiques shops. The more sophisticated Empire chairs occasionally turn up at auctions. Some of them are quite good examples of a style and period that has little otherwise to recommend it.

Victorian Chairs. It would be delightful to say, "Here is a near-antique chair you can go right out and buy in any quantity

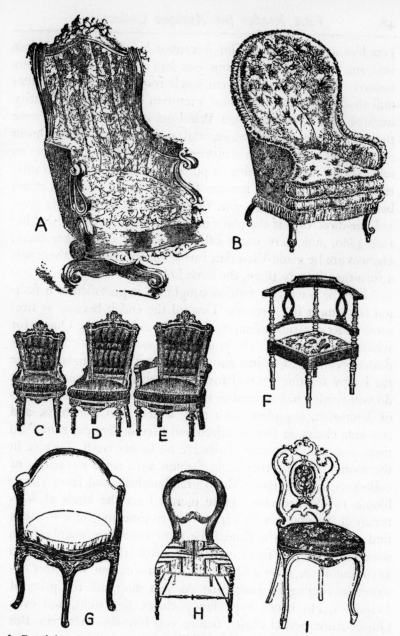

A: Revolving Armchair, Victorian, 1856. **B:** Victorian Upholstered Easy Chair, 1856. **C, D,** and **E:** Late Victorian Chairs, 1875. **F:** Victorian Corner Chair, 1894. **G:** It looks like Victorian but it isn't. It was made in Paris, 1750–60, in the style Chippendale copied and which, revived in the nineteenth century, is now called Victorian. **H:** Top-Heavy Victorian Chair, Advertised, 1856. **I:** American Chair, 1852, in the French Style.

you like at low prices." But it cannot be said because it just isn't so. In sophisticated shops you can't buy Victorian chairs because they won't give them stock room. In the run-of-the-mill shops you can't find good Victorian chairs in any quantity because they're scarcer than Windsors or Hitchcocks; scarcer than slat-backs, Hepplewhite, and even country-made Queen Anne. That is, Victorian chairs are harder to find—and easier to sell. Also, it would be nice to put down here a lot of information about who made Victorian furniture in these United States between 1842 and 1872. But that would mean writing a five-volume directory. If the place in which you live was settled before 1860, and there was a cabinetmaker or chairmaker there, chances are he made Victorian furniture and chairs. If there was a furniture factory there, the same holds true.

After the Victorian fashion caught on it prevailed as a fashion for almost five decades. Toward the end it became as tiresome to its one-time admirers as did the reign of the Queen for whom it was named. "Do you know," said a seasoned antiques dealer recently, "I've just come back from New England, once the happy hunting ground for Early American antiques. What do you think I had offered to me in Boston? Three parlor suites of Victorian, complete with sofa, settee, two armchairs, and two side chairs, at four hundred and fifty dollars per suite." So there you are. Victorian chairs are no longer trash. They're in the money because they're in fashion with some thousands of collectors, from career girls to grandmothers, and from young bloods to old bachelors. Here pictured are the kinds of Victorian chairs you can find from time to time and some you can find almost all of the time. The illustrations are mainly from advertisements by factories which made the chairs between 1850 and 1870. If you like them, buy them, but with this admonition ringing in your ears: As you shop, ask the price of Windsors, Hitchcock type fancy chairs, slat-backs, and even Queen Anne period chairs, before you buy the Victorian. But will you buy them? You'll buy Victorian or nothing, for nothing else will do. And that's what I'd do too—if I wanted Victorian chairs.

Post-Victorian Chairs. Eastlake? B-r-r-r-r! Horrible! Its cousins; brothers, and contemporaries? Another shudder. The end of Victorian, like the end of Empire, was—and is—awful. Here are pictured some of the chairs. They, too, are edging into antiques shops. But since this *First Reader* may, conceivably, fall into the hands of the very young, the words in order now must

Gothic, or Eastlake Chairs, as Advertised, 1877.

remain unsaid. And that leaves nothing more to be said. The curtain of the chapter is drawn over this anticlimactic scene featuring a few of the next chairs destined to be called antique. Perhaps if we are lucky that will not happen until 1960. But more likely it will be not later than 1950.

Eastlake Corner Chair, 1883.

CHAPTER III

Settles, Settees, Sofas, and Seats

Seventeenth-century Settles. The high-backed, shallow-seated settle with curved and sometimes "eared" end pieces, usually fashioned of pine or tulipwood, dates from about 1640. Settles were designed primarily to stand by the fireside and even inside cavernous fireplaces. The high backs and sides, or "arms," kept off drafts. That was the chief element of comfort. Seats were often quite shallow and never upholstered. They were sometimes fitted with a long cushion, a strip of drugget or carpet, or a folded bedcovering. Sometimes these settles had narrow hoods to stop downdrafts and perhaps protect the sitters from soot-laden raindrops falling down the chimney. Often a folding wooden candlestand was fitted in the back of the settle. Such settles, in a variety of sizes and with certain variations in styling, were made until about 1850. Strangely enough, these relics of America's first great century of colonization are still to be found in antiques shops. And they are not priced nearly so high as the chests, tables, and other furniture of the period. No less than thirty early settles were recorded as "for sale" in the shops co-operating in the research project conducted preparatory to the writing of this book.

Settle Tables. A dual-purpose piece of furniture, dating from perhaps 1650 and made right up to 1900! That's the record of the settle table which, on occasion, was a dining table and then, by the simple process of removing two wooden pins, the top was tilted, the table base became a settle seat and the tilted top a settle back. We do not know who made these settle tables in the seventeenth century. Perhaps they were the cheapest article offered by joinery-turnery shops. But we do know who made them in the nineteenth century—at least who made a lot of them. The J. W. Mason Company of New York, established in 1844, made and sold these tables, fashioned of unpainted pine, up to

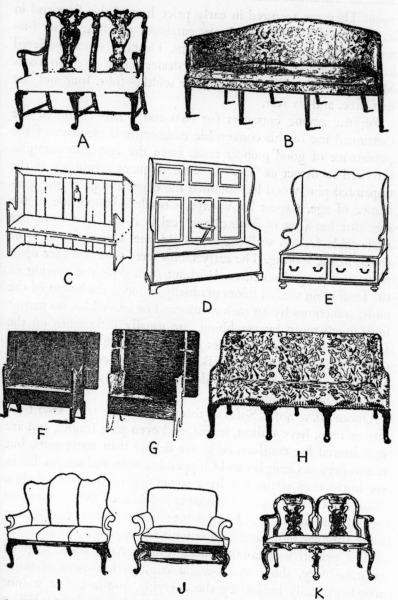

A: Chippendale Chair-Backed Settee. B: Hepplewhite Sofa. C and D: Hooded Settle and Paneled Settle of 1680. E: Cottage Settle, 1835. F: Pine Settle Table, 1850–90. G: Pine Settle Table, Seventeenth Century. H: Queen Anne Sofa. I and J: Queen Anne Sofa and Settee. K: Georgian Chair-Backed Settee.

1900. They are featured in early price lists of this firm and in its illustrated fiftieth-anniversary catalogue of 1894. Other furniture catalogues carry the same items. The table was also offered in the catalogues of woodenware dealers from 1850 to 1900. Mason made the table-settle in four widths—four, four and one half, five, and six feet.

Popular among cottagers for two and a half centuries, the continued use of this convertible table-settle is evidence of the persistence of good pioneer taste. Even the very late examples are hard to detect as "late" because frequent scrubbing of the unpainted pine wood has rounded the edges and given the semblance of age. Expert knowledge is needed—knowledge of the sort that has a lot of instinct and feel in it—to tell a worn late settle table from a well-preserved old one. One guide is to be found in the footing. The early tables were sometimes set upon skids, and pegged on them. Without such skids the moving of the footing on sanded floors gradually reduced the height of the table, sometimes by an inch or more. The late tables, no matter how much worn by scrubbing, are usually little worn on the footing. Also, the early tables have wider pine boards, thinner tops, and are hand wrought. Both kinds, and settle tables of all ages between two hundred and ninety and forty-five years, can be found in the shops.

Queen Anne Sofas. Sofas of this period, made from 1702 to as late as 1760, have walnut, maple, and even pine frames, and are upholstered for comfort. Seats are deeper than settle seats, but not so deep as Georgian and Chippendale sofas and settees. Backs are lower than settles but have something of the settle design. Also, these sofas usually have ends redolent of the curvate and "eared" ends of settles. Queen Anne style sofas are to be found in some antiques shops and appear with fair regularity at auctions. A few primitive or country-made Queen Anne sofas, stripped of upholstery, show an all-wood construction—pine or tulipwood originally hidden by the covering, and maple or walnut where the wood was exposed. Some, though, are all pine. When thus stripped they look like low settles with open bottoms and cabriole legs. Today these frames or forms are sometimes covered with coverlets of the pattern-woven variety, dating about 1820–50. It is a moot question as to whether, as some aver, this

A: Chippendale Sofa. **B:** Chippendale Upholstered Settee. **C:** Directoire Window Seat. **D:** Hepplewhite Sofa. **E:** Hepplewhite Settee, or Double Chair. **F:** Empire Cottage Sofa, 1850. **G:** Sheraton Sofa. **H:** Sheraton Sofa Attributed to McIntire of Salem. **I:** Directoire Influence Sofa, 1820–25. **J:** Fancy Settee, 1825–35. **K:** Empire Sofa. **L:** Directoire Sofa. **M:** Fancy Settee, 1820–30. **N and O:** Early Pictures of a Directoire Sofa, 1825, and Empire Sofa, 1840.

is in bad taste. It is an arbitrable point, but the point is missed if we make the decision in light of this day's standards. The question should be, "Would an American of 1835 have re-covered a country-made Queen Anne style sofa with coverlet material?" And the answer most logically is, "Yes, if no other appropriate material was readily at hand."

Chippendale Sofas. These appear at auctions with fair frequency, some of those offered being of English origin—imported antiques. Others, of course, are American made and may date from before Chippendale's book of designs first appeared in 1754 (and which depicted only a very few sofas) to 1780. Also, the same sofas are to be found in many antiques shops of the so-called fine or sophisticated type. Just why we have come to regard shops which feature only eighteenth-century and early Federal furniture as "sophisticated" is a mystery. One of the largest and finest stocks of antiques of this kind in America is housed in two old dwellings and a big barn. There is no effort to put on "front" and certainly no sophistication about it. But there is profound knowledge of antiques, and a stock to make the mouth, or the eye, of a museum director water. Chippendale sofas with carved cabriole legs are now quite rare. Hence you only see one in a blue moon. But the square-legged type, with gracefully curving back and roll-over arms, can be found without too much trouble. Also, Chippendale chair-backed settees (which Chippendale seems to have favored above the upholstered sofa) are occasionally to be found at auctions and in the better shops. The prices, of course, are in the higher brackets. What is important to the collector with a desire for a Chippendale sofa is the news, authentic and of fact, that the sofas can be found, obtained, and enjoyed today.

Hepplewhite, Sheraton, and Directoire Sofas and Settees. From 1785 to 1800 American cabinetmakers made Hepplewhite style sofas. From 1795 to 1830 they made Sheraton and Directoire style sofas, often blending Sheraton and Directoire. From about 1800 the Sheraton and Directoire inspired sofas and settees enjoyed what might well be called a monopoly in public taste. Hepplewhite sofas and settees are quite scarce, and even rare. The Sheraton-Directoire sofas (at least according to the prices asked) are anything from excessively rare to plentiful.

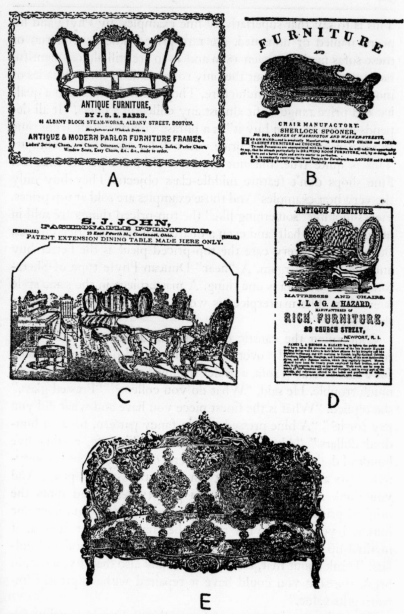

A: "Antique" Was Its Name, 1852; Now It's "Victorian." **B:** Whoops! Sofas as Advertised, 1829. **C:** Cincinnati Victorian Furniture, 1856. **D:** "Antique" Instead of "Victorian" at Newport, Rhode Island, 1856. **E:** "Antique" or Victorian Sofa by Roux, New York, 1852.

This is to say that superlatively fine examples, by Phyfe and his peers, named or unnamed, are rare prizes. The general run of these sofas made between 1800 and 1830 are still almost plentiful because they were about the only sofas made in three decades of mounting quantity manufacture. They are to be found in a quality and price range to fit almost any collector's purse. "It all depends on where you buy it" is a phrase you may hear from time to time in respect of the price you will be asked for an antique. This is quite true, but not in the sense most people imagine. Fine shops don't feature middle-class objects. They buy only the very best examples. And those examples are sold at top prices. Pieces looking "something like" the top-priced things are sold in other shops for half, and even a quarter, of the top-priced pieces. But in almost every case the top-priced piece is the better buy and the better bargain. A "near" Duncan Phyfe type of Sheraton-Directoire sofa is one thing. A masterpiece in the same style is another. The masterpiece is worth a lot of money. The near thing isn't.

Concerning the caustic comments of a lady collector ("It's robbery!" she said) over the five-thousand-dollar price asked for a rare Sheraton sofa, a dealer trimmed the lady's sails without much trouble. He said, "What do you collect?" "Pressed glass," she replied. "What is the finest piece you have and what did you pay for it?" "A blue pressed pot, in fancy pattern, for two hundred dollars." "Aha," said the dealer. "This sofa, costing five hundred dollars originally, stands here, one hundred and twenty-five years after its making, at ten times the original price. And you think it's fantastic. Yet you paid two hundred times the original price for a piece of blue pressed glass that isn't over one hundred years old. What should be the price of this sofa, if marked up in line with your glass? One hundred thousand dollars! Think about that, madam. And think also that if you should break the sofa you could have it repaired without greatly impairing its value."

Yes, antiques prices are very funny things. Furniture prices for even the finest of antiques haven't increased, comparably, with the flamboyant kerosene lamps of the 1880s and 1890s. These, mistakenly called *Gone-with-the-Wind* lamps, are really selling at excessive prices in light of their age. The furniture made at

A, B and **C:** Cast-Iron Settees, 1850–60. **D:** Fine Victorian as Advertised, 1858. **E:** Victorian Sofa, 1854. **F:** Empire Sofas for the People, 1840–50. **G:** Victorian "Medallion" Sofa, 1880. **H:** Late Windsor Settee, 1850. **I:** Fine Victorian Rosewood Sofa. **J:** Grecian Ottoman, 1842. **K:** Cast-Iron Settee, 1850–60. **L:** Empire Sofa, 1856. **M:** Grecian Settee, 1835. **N:** Directoire Style Sofa, 1825–30.

the same time is still just junk, and much of it will remain junk until destroyed. More than one observer of today's antiques collecting scene is of the opinion that *Gone-with-the-Wind* lamps will return again to junk status, but this time with a woeful tale of poorly invested collecting money in their wake.

Windsor and Fancy Settees. Early Windsor settees of the Colonial period are quite scarce. One astute dealer told me that of six offered to him in the past ten years, he questioned five and bought one, only to discover it had three new legs and a new back rail. This is not so much a fact pointing to restoration as it is a fact pointing to scarcity of early Windsor settees in original condition.

These altogether lovely articles of furniture were used outdoors, on porches, piazzas, and in gardens. Often, when found "entire," the turned legs show decay, spindles are split and broken, and rails and arms need repair or replacement. You need not miss the enjoyment of an early Windsor settee just because you hate a restored piece. What should—and of course does—bother the thinking collector is that he might buy a piece as "original condition" only to discover he has purchased a restored piece at original condition price.

Later Windsor settees, dating from 1810 to 1850, are found with increasing frequency as the dating moves forward. Late Windsor settees, with an admixture of fancy settee styling, were made by the thousands for church and school benches. A Pennsylvania church in 1924 distributed some fifty of them to any parishioner wanting one, at two dollars each. They were purchased in 1850 as the original pews of the church. Today that same type of settee, scraped down to the bare wood, scrubbed, shellacked, and waxed, sells for twenty-five times that bargain price. Fitted with long cushions such settees are now used in informal living rooms, as farmhouse furniture, and rumpus-room equipment.

Fancy settees, in a variety that speaks well for the imagination of early chair factories, can be found in almost all of the better-class shops today. Pressed glass and knickknack shops seldom have them. At a recent antiques show at White Plains, New York, there was exhibited a corner settee of Sheraton influence. This settee was not built like a corner chair but was a right-angle settee, seating at least four people to a side. It had a fancy back, originally decorated, a rush seat, and turned legs. Structurally, it had been reinforced with strap iron at the right angle, probably because it had proved to be an awkward piece to move and, unless very carefully handled by two or three people, too much strain was placed on the angle joints.

In the shops today, and at almost every auction, late Windsor type and fancy settees of many kinds are on sale. Our pictures display plain-painted, fancy-painted, and stenciled examples. Some are even to be found painted in the original white with gold banding and stenciling. Some shops have scraped and scrubbed ones, finished in the natural wood. Seasoned collectors avoid newly painted settees, fearing the new paint may hide much restoration. What does this point to as a good pattern to follow? Buy your Windsor and fancy settees in as nearly original condition as possible, even though the paint is flaking off and only traces of decoration remain. Esther Stevens Brazer's little monographs on how to repaint and redecorate will tell you what to do next, and if you have a spark of adventure and a teaspoonful of talent you may even tackle the repaint job yourself. Many men and women have done just that and now enjoy antiques possessions that have something of themselves in the antiques. Of course you will have to entrust re-rushing to experts in that line, or to a man who can weave a good rope seat where the rush once was.

Empire and Victorian Sofas, Settees, and Seats. When steam power, labor-saving woodworking machinery, and the "production line" were introduced as America's answer to the question, "How can we make good furniture for all people at lower prices?" Directoire and Sheraton styles were still the fashion from Pittsburgh westward, northward, and southward. The kinds of furniture Duncan Phyfe and his fellow cabinetmakers were producing, largely by hand, in 1817 were duplicated at Pittsburgh and Cincinnati by machine production from 1827 to 1837. The Empire style, embraced by the "Phyfes" of the East at Boston, New York, Philadelphia, Baltimore, Washington, Arlington, Alexandria, Richmond, Charleston, and Savannah, after 1825 to 1830, did not take hold in the West until at least a decade later. But when it did take hold, it was made on a scale that sounds like the automobile production of Detroit a century later.

"Furniture and chairmaking in America," said an English commentator of the 1850s, "is what cotton manufacture is in certain districts of England. The factories are on an immense scale. In . . . Cincinnati there are factories where the saw, plane, lathe, and mortising *machines* do all the work. The great wonder is where all the furniture goes. You stand marveling at the huge proportions of the factories, and out pops a chair, newly put together, with rope attached, finding its way outside by pulleys, and then to the top floor for finishing; then follows another and another, in quick succession."

Mass production explains why we have so many near-Sheraton, near-Directoire, and Empire sofas in so many varieties of styles, surviving as antiques. They look like handmade cabinet jobs, but most of them are factory made. Amazingly, the variety available includes many rather graceful examples, some quite close to Sheraton or Directoire. Others are heavy, even massive; built, as one dealer has said, "like a five-ton truck."

In many factories the Empire styled sofas were not superseded at one fell swoop by the new "French" or "antique," but now called Victorian, sofas. Manufacturing furniture on a mass-production basis is first of all mass production—not just furniture production. The factories made furniture in "models." They had "lines" of furniture, often running to as many as two hundred and fifty items. Much Empire styled furniture was moving out of Cincinnati for the Far West at the very same time that so-called Victorian furniture, made in the same factories, was produced for Kentucky, Ohio, Michigan, and Indiana furniture stores. Furniture was made to suit the general demand of regions, not individual customers. The furniture store was the factory's customer. This phenomenon provides so vast a story that we can only touch upon it briefly here. Someday it may appear in a big, two-volume book. Only when that book is a fact can you know the whole of the amazing story of how America made good furniture for its ever swelling millions of people, and made everything from Directoire, Sheraton, and Greek Revival to Empire and "French Antique" in the same factories at the same time. In our files is the catalogue of one producer who also made Windsor chairs and Hepplewhite styled chairs along with what is called Victorian and Empire!

"Victorian" sofas of masterpiece quality were produced by Roux, Belter, and other custom cabinetmakers of New York, Philadelphia, Boston, and Baltimore. Perhaps every city and town of some consequence boasted at least one custom cabinet-maker who produced Victorian furniture with the same care his great-grandfather used in hand-fashioning the earlier styles of T. Chippendale. But such production, no matter how fine, was limited. It required factory operation to supply the enormous demand of all the people. The factories answered this demand by the simple process of producing expensive, medium-priced, and cheap Victorian.

Here are pictures exemplary of the Empire and Victorian sofas and settees you'll find in the antiques shops today. At what prices? Don't ask! As this is written the prices are so-and-so. When you see these words in type, and view in print the pictures which now lie on my desk, the price may be something other than so-and-so—maybe higher, maybe lower. Whatever they may be they'll reflect, not intrinsic values, but demand and supply.

CHAPTER IV

Tables, Stands, Sideboards, and Dining-room Cabinets

Seventeenth-Century and Early Eighteenth-Century Tables.
From late Tudor style through and beyond Queen Anne or, roughly, from 1620 to 1750, a grand lot of tables of pioneer and semi-formal quality were made in America. Pine, maple, and walnut woods were used. Turning, in some form or other, characterizes the legs. Names are gate-leg, high-low stretcher, butterfly, hutch, settle (dealt with in Chapter III), and walnut stretcher. There are others, but these are the ones still obtainable—early tables you can collect, although a high-low stretcher example will dent your bankroll in no amateurish manner! All of these tables seem to have been made generally in New England, and some in New York and Virginia.

The Pennsylvania Walnut Stretcher Table appears to be the exception to this rule. The Pennsylvania table is a variant of the William and Mary style. Its legs are beautifully turned, framed at the top in a skirt deep enough to contain drawers, generally two—one wide, one narrow. Finest examples have scalloped skirts. Legs are braced near the bottom with stretchers all around, or with turned stretchers joining front and back legs, and a middle stretcher spanning the two end stretchers midway between the legs. Such tables are known in sizes ranging from eight feet down to thirty inches long. They are believed to have been made from about 1685 to 1750. By 1725 they seem to have been made in great numbers. Even as late as 1925 these stretcher tables were staple stock items in most Pennsylvania antiques shops. Prices were low both in shops and at town and country auctions. Now they are scarce and high in price.

Often these tables were found in cellars to which they had been consigned as newer tables were used upstairs. Consequently, many of the original ball turnings at the bottoms of the legs

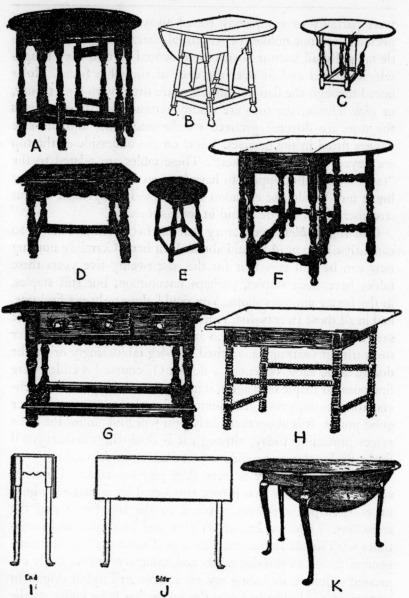

A and F: Gate-Leg Table with Spanish Feet, Gate-Leg with Turned Ball Feet.
B and C: American Canted-Leg Butterfly Table and English Straight-Leg. D and
E: Pennsylvania Walnut Table and Stand. G: Pennsylvania Stretcher Table,
Walnut, 1700–25. H: High-Low Stretcher Table, 1670–90. I and J: Simple Queen
Anne Table, Made as Late as 1820. K: Queen Anne Drop-Leaf Table, Walnut,
1710–50.

were partially or completely rotted away. These tables have a peculiar top, not unlike the structural characteristics of the settle table. Broad walnut boards are mounted on two deep flanges which parallel and fit over the ends of the table frame. Holes bored through the flanges and frame are fitted with long tenons, or pins. Hence, the tops are readily removable. Almost always the tops are dovetail grooved on the underside, and the side flanges fitted in the grooves. Joints on the underside of the top are keyed together with kerfs. These tables are related to the "tavern" table but appear to have been made almost wholly for home use. While not common now, these Pennsylvania walnut stretcher tables can be found in some shops.

Gate-leg Tables have a story that has been told and retold so often that little need be said about them here. Certainly nothing new can be said save that for the past twenty-five years these tables have been staples, perhaps uncommon, but still staples, in the better antiques shops. You could almost always find one, and in all those twenty-five years prices have fluctuated but little save in the boom years of 1928 and 1929. One Richmond dealer some fifteen years ago advertised gate-leg tables singly or by the dozen: $300 each, or $3,600 a dozen. Of course his tables were fine ones, of maple or walnut, with well-turned legs and stretchers, tongue-and-grove leaf joints, original drawers, and other good points. It is altogether likely you will find almost the same prices prevailing today, although it is doubtful whether you'll find a dealer able to provide a dozen tables on demand.

Butterfly Tables are scarcer than gate-leg tables. They are smaller tables, with two leaves, supported by a pair of wings, or wing-shaped members, pivoted to the top frame and the stretchers. They are known in pine and in maple, and sometimes with maple frame and pine top. They are about the same general dating as gate-leg tables and, contrary to previously expressed opinions, including my own, have an English origin. In respect of the butterfly table, the writer has been guilty of the very thing we have always cautioned other amateurs about—following the opinion of experts. For many years the experts have called the butterfly table a distinctly American development. It just isn't so. There were butterfly tables in late sixteenth- and early seventeenth-century England. They did not

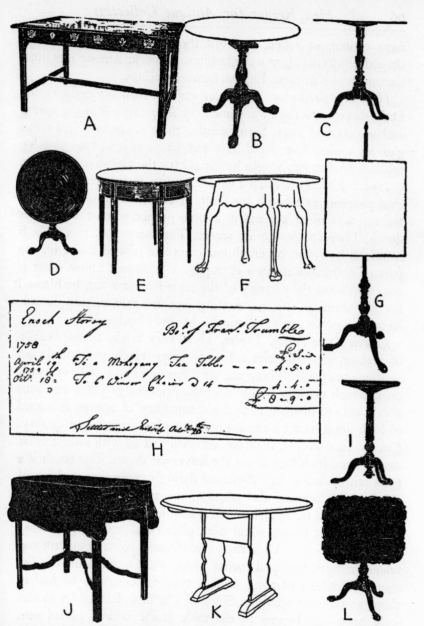

A: Chippendale Library Table. **B:** Chippendale Revolving Tilt-Top Tea Table. **C:** Queen Anne Tea Table or Stand. **D:** Chippendale Dish-Top Table. **E:** Hepplewhite Round Table. **F:** Queen Anne Solid-Top Table, 1740. **G:** Chippendale Pole-Screen. **H:** Bill for Furniture Dated 1758. **I:** Chippendale Candlestand. **J:** Chippendale Breakfast or "Pembroke" Table. **K:** Hutch Table. **L:** Chippendale Rectangular Piecrust Tilt-Top Table.

have canted, or raked, legs but they did have the butterfly-shaped brackets. They were fashioned of oak. Among our illustrations is one of these English butterfly tables.

High-low Stretcher Tables are scarcer than butterfly tables. Only three were found in some fifty shops visited in the spring and summer of 1945. Significantly, these shops also had some gate-leg tables. You could have purchased at least two gate-leg tables for what you would have paid for the high-low stretcher.

Hutch Tables are related to settle tables in that they served a dual purpose: as a hutch for flour, or even dough mixing, when the top was tilted up, and as a table proper when the top was down. They are now quite scarce. The scarcity of this table is matched, however, by an almost complete lack of desire on the part of collectors to own examples. We do not know what is responsible for the scarcity of the table but none can be blamed for not wanting one, or wanting one, for that matter. A collector's vagaries are emphatically his own business.

Queen Anne Period Tables. These very lovely tables, usually of walnut, exist in quite a few varieties which are still almost readily obtainable. There are very fine ones and country-made ones, which explains beforehand the price range you'll run into if you collect them. Queen Anne furniture, of course, is bound to look good because the cabriole leg gives it an air of quality. Queen Anne drop-leaf tables, especially those with semicircular drop leaves, look best when the leaves are down. The result is a table with cabriole legs displayed daringly, revealing nothing of the frame. There are also tables of this type with square leaves and some with triangular leaves. Then there are Queen Anne tea tables without leaves, some with plain tops, and others (rare) with dished tops. Also, there are Queen Anne style tilt-top tables, triangular-shaped corner tables, and Queen Anne candlestand tables. All of these various type tables are to be had in shops and also at auctions. Some of the drop-leaf tables in this style have legs hinged to the table frame which, pulled out, support the leaf. These are often used as dining tables. Another sort has fixed legs with pivoted or hinged flaps to support the leaves.

Chippendale Tables. You can buy little ones with narrow drop leaves, big ones with wide drop leaves, tilt tops, piecrust tilt

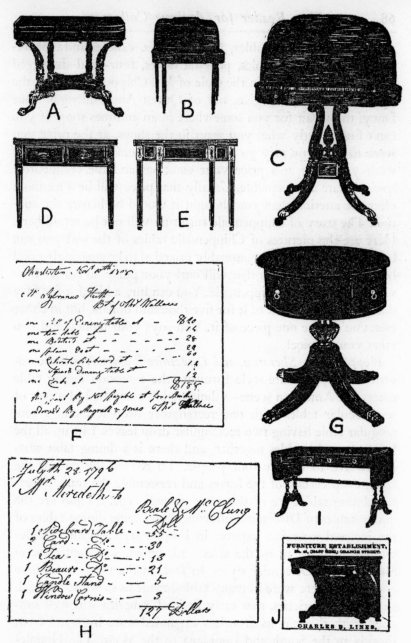

A: Directoire Side Table, 1810. B and C: Sheraton Style Side Table, 1800–10; Directoire Side Table by Duncan Phyfe. D and E: Hepplewhite Tables, 1785–1800. F: Furniture Bill, Charleston, 1808. G: Baltimore Drum Table, 1800. H: Furniture Bill, Philadelphia, 1796. I: Sheraton Sofa Table, 1810. J: Empire Console, Advertised 1850.

tops, tea and coffee tables, library tables, candlestands, breakfast tables, Chinese tables, pedestal tables, four- and six-legged
tables. If any of these, in the style of Mr. Chippendale—or in the
style he copied—Georgian, out of Queen Anne—intrigue your
fancy, they wait for you somewhere in an antiques shop. If you
can't find exactly what you want in the shops, at the price you
want to pay, you may go to the auction rooms and perhaps get
what you want at a price your emotions and the competitive
spirit dictate as acceptable. Usually that price will be a bit more
after the auction than you thought it would be before the auction. The story of Chippendale furniture will not be retold here.
Here are the pictures of Chippendale tables of the sort you can
buy today. Some are so reasonably priced as to be amazingly good
buys. Some rate prices that will curl your purse no matter how
well filled. That is Chippendale. You can buy a bit of it for fifty
dollars or a big chunk of it for five thousand dollars, but in either
case you'll have one piece of it. You pays your money and you
takes your choice!

Hepplewhite, Sheraton, and Directoire Tables. With the advent of Hepplewhite style furniture the extension dining table
enters the American scene—a dining table composed of a pair of
semicircular tables with one rectangular drop leaf and a rectangular table having two rectangular drop leaves. Lift up all the
leaves, run the tables together, and there is a dining table seating twelve to twenty-four people. To reduce the size of the
table, drop certain of the leaves and reassemble the train. Sheraton dining tables are of this same general type. So also are the
dining tables of Directoire influence. Next came dining tables of
the internal-extension variety, in Empire style. With Hepplewhite also came to us the sideboard, which was continued in
Sheraton and Directoire styles. In fact, in the three styles here
considered there were so many tables, made in so wide, fanciful,
and fruitful varieties, that early Federal America was well supplied with them as its frontiers expanded state by state, from
Florida to the South and Louisiana to the West. The Hepplewhite style persisted until about 1800. Sheraton began about
1795 and persisted, along with Directoire, until the 1830s.

In all these styles there are excellent opportunities for you
who want to collect a few tables or a lot of tables. There is the

A, B, and **C:** Empire Tables, Pictured from Early Advertisements, 1830–45.
D and **E:** Spool-Turned Tea Tables. **F:** Empire Eagle Console, 1825. **G:** Lazy
Susan Table. **H** and **L:** Two Whatnots. **I:** Early Victorian Sideboard, 1842. **J:**
Hunt-Board, Late Hepplewhite, about 1810. **K:** Victorian Table. **M:** Antique
Style (Victorian) Table, 1842.

sofa table with leaves at the sides, drawers to the front, and legs widely spaced. There are Hepplewhite Pembroke tables; there are Sheraton and Directoire sewing tables; there are card tables in all the styles. With this group of styles, the fold-over top table with a leaf that could be stood against the wall became common. We might add that the Hepplewhite style is marked by the classic, tapered square leg, often with inlay; Sheraton is marked by turned, reeded, and carved legs; and Directoire is marked by curved tapering legs which may be plain, reeded, inlaid, or carved. Sometimes Sheraton legs are twist carved or spiral turned. Most of the table types here pictured (unless otherwise captioned) were on sale in antiques shops, or passing through auction galleries, as this is written. If they are not in the shops now, others very much like them will be found there.

This furniture is well distributed now because it was well distributed when it was new. The Hepplewhite traveled some; the Sheraton and Directoire were made as far west as Cincinnati and certainly as far south as Charleston. In this period and considerably beyond it—perhaps to 1880—was made the kitchen or dining table with two very deep drop leaves and turned legs, often without reeding, and having as decoration only a few turned rings and a tapering curve toward the foot section. Woods used for this table were sometimes mahogany and sometimes walnut, but most commonly cherry. Between their "discovery" nowadays and their arrival at a place of sale something sometimes happens to these tables. A "lily-gilder," considering the desires of the people, the beauty he is about to add to the table, and particularly the value increase that will go in his pocket, puts reeding on the turned legs and sometimes around the edges of the leaves and table top. Seldom is this reeding as well done as on originally reeded leg tables. But the giveaway, if you study your subject, is that it is placed on tables that were not planned to be reeded, but just plain turned. Unless he reworks and reeds especially thick members, the lily-gilder in reducing somewhat the leg diameter of the basic type, over-slenderizes and gives away his trickery.

Some little idea of who made tables and other furniture of the Sheraton and Directoire types here considered, and where they made them, can be gathered from *The United States Directory*

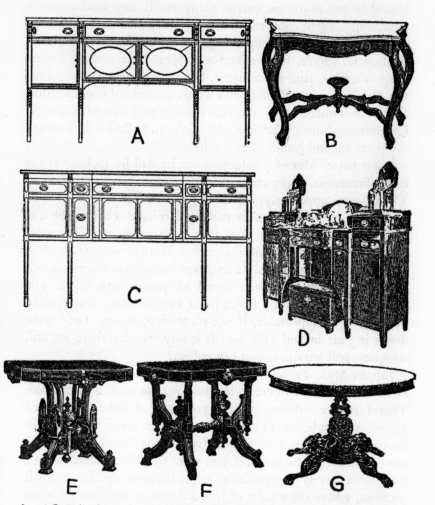

A and **C**: Pair of Hepplewhite Sideboards. **B**: Victorian Side Table, Marble Top.
D: Sheraton High Sideboard with Knife Boxes on Top and Cellarette Beneath.
E and **F**: "Eastlake" Tables, 1878. **G**: Empire Dining Table.

for the Use of Travelers and Merchants, published by Joshua
Shaw of Philadelphia in 1822. This ambitious little pocketbook,
bound in red morocco, carries many richly engraved pages of
advertising. Eight cabinetmakers of Philadelphia paid for advertising mention (but no engravings) in it. Five in New York, including D. Phyfe, were advertisers. John Dejernott of Peters-
burg, Virginia, paid for a listing, but the cabinetmakers of Boston, Baltimore, and Washington were coy and did not subscribe.
Cornelius Tooker of Fayetteville is listed as a cabinetmaker. At
Charleston, South Carolina, Deming and Bulkley, Richard
Gouldsmith, and James Main are listed.

A far better idea of production can be had by looking at the
early directories of the cities and towns of consequence in 1830.
There were, apparently, 1.7 cabinetmakers for every 1,000 of
population. All of them were making furniture—chairs, tables, et
cetera—and considerable of it in the Sheraton and Directoire
styles. The population of the nation in 1830 was 12,793,697.
That means approximately 21,748 cabinetmakers were at work
eight years after Mr. Shaw issued his pretty little book. The
Sheraton and Directoire tables made in 1830 must have totaled
up to quite a respectable, if not staggering, figure. They were
doing it year in and year out. Is it any wonder there are still
antiques—real antiques—you can collect?

Empire Style Tables. It is unnecessary to make polite but purposeful jabs at the Empire style whenever the name is mentioned.
Therefore, we will assume that you are (1) either prejudiced
against the style, or (2) prejudiced in its favor, or (3) you
haven't yet made up your mind. Here are the Empire style tables
now available in the shops, if you want to collect them. Few of
these tables are as yet appearing in the big auctions. Yet at small
auctions, where the effects of half a dozen or so households are
sold, or at the auctions disposing of the goods and chattels of
one household, these tables do crop up. Some of them are so
"pleasurable," as they say in the South, that prospective new
owners go into spirited bidding for them. Certain of the fold-
over top card tables make very useful consoles although there is
nothing of the true console about them. Some of the tilt-top
tables, while somewhat heavy in the base, are quite good. A
great many of these tables are veneered over a tulipwood or pine

CARVED BUFFET, OR SIDE-BOARD.

A: Victorian Buffet, 1853. B: Victorian Sideboard, Advertised 1852. C: Sheraton Cellarette on Reeded Legs. D: Dumbwaiter. E: Chippendale Cellarette on Stand. F: Empire Sideboard, 1840. G: Simple Sheraton Style Sideboard.

base excepting, of course, the tops, which are usually solid wood. These are the tables of the sort made by Meeks of New York in 1833, and by Mitchell & Rammelsberg of Cincinnati in 1843. The latter firm, by 1850, had a factory six stories high, 80 by 120 feet in size, employing two hundred and fifty people, equipped with special machinery for cutting veneers, repetitive manufacture of parts, and all the other mechanics of mass production. Some of this furniture is marked with manufacturers' labels although labels seldom remained on tables.

Victorian Tables. These tables, if they say anything to you in the pictures here shown, say about all that needs to be said. They represent the best Victorian tables now available in the shops that sell Victorian and also the worst Victorian—the latter-day styles in which the ideas of Eastlake are incorporated. Some makers of Victorian furniture, now of record, will no doubt one day be placed in the same hall of fame to which we have elevated our Mr. Phyfe. There will be rhapsodies in print over the work of men whose names are known only to patient researchers now delving into Victorian-furniture production. These names are found on labels pasted on bottoms of cabinet drawers, in little-known advertisements, and in city directories issued between 1842 and 1860. Already the names of Simon Belter and Alexander Roux have a bit of a halo over them. Fame is coming to others for the very simple reason that Victorian furniture is back to stay. Although its present vogue may go quiescent for a while, it will revive, and then collecting will go on with increased verve. It is now too late to get in on the ground floor, but here are pictures of the kind of Victorian tables that are yours for your floors now, if you want them.

Eastlake and Other Tables. Not because they deserve it, not because we wish to parade them in ironic mood, but because they are beginning to appear in some antiques shops, do we include these few examples of tables made between 1876 and 1896. To most collectors, comment can be compressed to one word. This is also the attitude of many antiques dealers. But now that the youngest of the breed is flirting with a half century of age, and the oldest is threescore and ten, they are edging into the vast pool of collectible antiques. It would be fun, as one dealer has said, to buy a vast quantity of the stuff for a little money, seal it up for twenty-five years or so, and then put it on the market. If there be any young chap who wants to do that, he can indulge in collecting these tables without having to live with them and, conceivably, he may make a pretty penny on the transaction if he has the patience to wait twenty-five to thirty years to cash in on his investment.

Sideboards. This important item of dining-room furniture was once nothing more than a side table. Chippendale designed only "side-board tables" in this category of furniture. Therefore, when you see a "Chippendale reproduction" sideboard in a modern furniture shop and are told it is authentic, you may be sure someone is trying to pull your leg. The brothers Adam began adding pedestals to the ends of a sideboard table and hence gave the piece cabinet qualities. Next, knife boxes were placed upon the pedestals. Adam's first idea was a series of three elements— two separate pedestals with urns, between which a free-standing table was placed. Shearer and other English cabinetmakers and designers made sideboards in one large piece. Then came Hepplewhite with his now well-known swell-front, serpentine-front, and round-front sideboards. In saying "Hepplewhite" we simply follow popular designation. Shearer, before Hepplewhite, made similar sideboards. Sheraton, after Hepplewhite, designed sideboards that are often called Hepplewhite. Presumably, the only sure clue to pure Hepplewhite styling is the concave end on the front of a sideboard. Sheraton and Shearer styles present this same section as convex. He who seeks a sideboard of the period 1760 to 1860 is not, however, so much interested in the fine points of style presented in *printed words* as he is in seeing what the styles are, and in knowing that he can hope to find a sideboard in the style desired.

Therefore, the Hepplewhite, Shearer influence, Sheraton, Directoire, Empire, Victorian, and "other" sideboards here pictured will serve more effectively than words to display the types of antique sideboards which now, at this writing, stand in shops waiting for custom. The captions under each tell what it is. They do not tell where you can buy it or the price asked. But take heart: from the random sampling of American antiques shops it is evident that sideboards of these types are on sale from coast to coast. Every year they come up at auction. And certain Eastern dealers, apparently, always have from three to six in stock. That means you can do big business—for buying a sideboard *is* big business—by mail, if you can't find what you seek where you are.

One form of sideboard that was given high place as an antique during the 1920s is that distinctly Southern piece, the hunt board, or hunting board. This is a simple piece, higher than a regular sideboard, and supplementary to it, designed to hold viands partaken of standing, whether as breakfast before a hunt or as a snack after the quarry had been killed. Hunt boards are known in cherry, walnut, mahogany, yellow pine, and tulipwood. Once they enjoyed an antiques popularity too considerably in excess of their real significance and usefulness. Which is to say, there was an element of downright snobbishness in the buying and selling. Now they seem again to have retired to their true status—a supplementary high sideboard small enough for a simple dining room or dining alcove furnished in the antique.

Knife Boxes. These graceful items in classical Greek, Egyptian, and Roman vase and amphora forms were designed to serve as decorative silverware chests. In some boxes the tops, when lifted, are found to be fastened to a rod which lifts up the silver that rests in felted slots. Others permit arrangement of the silver in tiers or terraces of slots. Some cases are made in the form of pedestals with sloping lids, and some in chest forms. These objects add quite an air of quality to the top of a sideboard. As one very smart (but not "clever," if you please, for there is a difference) decorator has said: "If you want to give an air of importance to a dining room that is evident the moment you enter, use a pair of knife boxes of appropriate style on the sideboard, and a pair of hurricane shades over a pair of silver or Sheffield candlesticks."

Wine Coolers and Cellarets. These objects may look like a barrel, box, drum, or keg on legs, a square or oblong casket of ornate design on feet, but they are nothing more nor less than early refrigerators of aristocratic quality. These dining-room cabinets, for keeping wine and other beverages cool, offer to the producers of modern electric refrigerating equipment a grand opportunity to sell an extra unit or two to many homes. Put a small compressor and a few ice trays in it, encase the whole in a metal box, place it in a period reproduction of a mahogany or walnut cellaret, and you have an item a great many people will want.

Sometimes the American manufacturer, so keen in many ways, is flagrantly obtuse in considering an idea beyond his immediate ken. In 1937 one of the great refrigerating-unit manufacturers was approached with an idea for housing a small, two-element electric stove and a two-drawer ice-cube refrigerator in a cabinet similar to one of the wine coolers here pictured. A drawer was to hold china, silver, and napery service for four. Under the lid were to be nested two block-tin skillets and two stewpans. They looked and looked at the idea. They considered it a "natural." But no, they wouldn't make it. Why? "Anything as good as this must have been thought of before and, if it was thought of and not made, it couldn't have been so good as this looks." When they were told that many steamboats had been thought of, and not a few made, before Robert Fulton put the elements together in a successful steamboat, their eyes glazed. A little flush of pink showed above the collar. It was time to get out—without selling the idea. Until the idea is brought out in concrete form, you'll have to chance finding a cellaret or wine cooler in an antiques shop or auction gallery. Five antiques shops out of every three hundred—one shop in sixty you visit—may have one in stock. The few here pictured were on sale in August 1945.

Other Stands. Wig stands, toilet stands, night stands, and allied pieces are properly boudoir and bedroom furniture and will be considered in another chapter. Here, however, should be mentioned such things as whatnots, dumb-waiters, music stands, periodical racks, and fretwork gimmicks. The dumb-waiter in the form of a tripod table stand, with a long shaft on which three table tops of gradually smaller diameter are placed in a tier, is an item of furniture that appeared about 1750. On it stood condiments, sweets, and relishes. The idea is found reflected in dining tables with an extra circular top that rotated before the diner. All that was necessary was a gentle tug, and the dish you wanted came 'round to you, without saying, "Please pass the parsnips." Lazy Susan is another name for these. They were popular in cottages and in boardinghouses, or so it is said. You may find dumb-waiters in mahogany, cherry, maple, and yellow pine. Also, they are known in cast iron! These are of the cast-iron craze period of 1845 to 1885 when you could buy settees, chairs, tables, and many other items of furniture in cast iron, and in cast iron combined with woven wire, woven strap iron, and wrought iron.

The standing shelves known as *étagères,* or whatnots, are to be found in various period styles. The most generally available are in the Empire and Victorian periods of fashion or style. Those illustrated are mostly in the latter category. Some are quite late. Production of these continued almost to 1900. But they are now in antiques shops as merchandise. Buy them if you like them, but with your eyes wide open as to their probable age.

CHAPTER V

Highboys and Lowboys

The names "highboy" and "lowboy" have become a part of our antiques nomenclature but are sometimes used without much regard for accuracy. Some people call a chest-on-frame a highboy and others call a highboy a chest-on-frame. According to the record, or as much record as we have available, the term "highboy" is an Americanism deriving from the English term "tallboy," designating a chest of drawers on a stand which is also fitted with drawers. The top chest and the lower frame were made separate and conceivably, but doubtfully, may have been used separately at times.

What we call a highboy is a piece of furniture of Dutch origin, apparently first made in the William and Mary style. A tablelike frame with turned legs, shaped skirting, drawers, and shaped stretchers was made with a molding around what would be the table top. This molding held in place a chest of drawers, usually composed of three drawers the full width of the chest, topped by two smaller drawers exactly half the width of the wide drawers. The top of this chest, in William and Mary pieces, is usually finished square, with a molding at front and sides. Not to be confused with the lower half of such "tallboys" is the true lowboy of the same style and period—a somewhat smaller replica of the tallboy stand but finished with a flat top and used as a dressing table, a side table, or dining-hall piece.

William and Mary highboys and lowboys usually have six legs—four across the front and two at the rear. These legs are turned in very pleasing forms, the chief varieties being the "cup" and the "trumpet." These two styles of turning are illustrated.

When the style now designated as "Queen Anne" entered the scene, the William and Mary type highboys and lowboys were made with four cabriole legs but with the same scalloped skirt-

ing on the lowboy and on the tallboy stand. The place where
the extra front legs had been placed in the William and Mary
style was often finished off with a small drop turning in the
Queen Anne style. Further refinements in the way of decoration included carving of the knees of the cabriole legs, shell
carving on the center drawers, and extra drawers. Hardware on
the William and Mary type pieces features drop handles. On the
Queen Anne style we find what are called "willow-pattern"
brasses—a style borrowed from the Chinese by the Dutch. Apparently both highboys and lowboys were also "borrowed"
from the Chinese. There are Chinese equivalents of both highboys and lowboys.

In the Queen Anne style there is also the chest-on-frame,
often miscalled highboy. The frame of these pieces is low, somewhat lower than a modern coffee table, and is merely a frame
upon which to stand a high chest containing from four to six or
more drawers. Later, this piece of furniture was made in one
piece, fitted with short legs. This is the so-called Queen Anne
bureau but actually a Queen Anne chest of drawers, unless it has
a slope-fall desk section. If it has that element, then it is a true
bureau.

The Queen Anne style highboy and lowboy, together with
the chest-on-frame, finally merged into the Georgian style. This
in turn merged into Chippendale—the last period in which, with
but few exceptions, the highboy and the lowboy were made.
With the advent of the Georgian style the highboy top begins
to display considerable ornamentation. The pillar-and-scroll and
broken-pediment tops, at first quite simple with a single turned
finial in the center, were finally carved in magnificent scrolls,
fretwork, and finials that jointly and severally are exquisite carvings and superlative dust catchers. In the Georgian period the
Chinese claw-and-ball and ball-and-claw foot was added. This
is not, as is often thought, a mark of the designer Thomas Chippendale. Chippendale did not show the ball-and-claw foot in his
design book. Rather, he showed the French upcurling foot.

Closely related to the highboy and chest-on-frame is the chest-
on-chest. This name almost completely describes the piece: a
low chest of drawers upon which stands another chest of drawers. These are known in Queen Anne, Georgian, Chippendale,

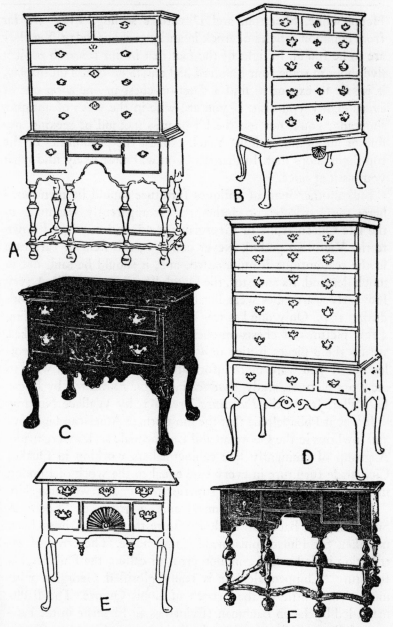

A: William and Mary Highboy with Trumpet-Turned Legs. **B:** Queen Anne Chest-on-Frame. **C:** Chippendale Lowboy. **D:** Queen Anne Highboy. **E:** Queen Anne Lowboy. **F:** William and Mary Lowboy with Cup-Turned Legs.

Hepplewhite, Sheraton, and Directoire styling. They are far from common articles of stock in antiques shops today. Yet they are to be found. In light of the fact that in our research project five shops in some four hundred had chests-on-chests on display, it is safe to expect to find a chest-on-chest in one shop out of every eighty you visit. If you are wise in the ways of antiques shopping, you'll not use the hit-or-miss method of seeking any fine or important antique. You'll exhaust the possibilities of the top-flight shops first. In that way you will most likely find what you want at once.

Still another item of antiques furniture should be mentioned here: the wardrobe, or clothespress. It apparently was made in the late Queen Anne or Georgian period, and continued down to the Victorian period. Never common, this item of furniture in the real antique is quite scarce and, it should be said, not in much demand. Its ancestor, the Dutch "*kas*," is rarer still. A very few early wardrobes were located in some four hundred shops during 1945. Only one kas was offered by a dealer. In including a few pictures of chests-on-chests, one wardrobe, and one kas, we do these pieces justice only in terms of availability to collectors. If you want more information about them, and want to see more pictures, study *American Antique Furniture*, by Edgar G. Miller, Jr., or the *Furniture Treasury*, by Wallace Nutting.

It was at Philadelphia that the most ornate American highboys and lowboys in the Georgian and Chippendale styles were made. A group of eminently fine cabinetmakers working in Quaker City made furniture in every case equal to the work of London masters and, in many cases, superior to London workmanship.

In Lancaster County, Pennsylvania, a group of "Ebenistes Suisse" named Bachman made furniture that has, at times, been mistaken for Philadelphia-made Chippendale. The error of attribution is tied to the common error of calling the Philadelphia furniture "Chippendale." It is really glorified Georgian with more than a little of the French of Louis Quinze. The Bachmans, led by Jacob Bachman (trained as an Ebeniste in the canton of Bern, Switzerland, and who emigrated to America in 1766), did work that displays elements of the French styles of Louis XIV, XV, and Provence. Perhaps the finest table in the superlatively fine Karolik Collection now in the Boston Museum

A: Block-Front Chest-on-Chest—shown as example only—not one found in shops in 1945. B: Dutch Kas. C: Hepplewhite High Chest. D: Queen Anne Highboy with Chinese Lacquer Decoration. E: Chippendale Wardrobe-on-Chest. F: Chippendale Chest-on-Chest. G: Chippendale Highboy.

of Fine Arts was made by Jacob Bachman. All the experts attributed it to the Philadelphia school and dated it between 1750 and 1760. It is Lancaster County, country-made, and the date is after 1766. Mr. Karolik states that he knows of no tea table to compare with it in terms of individual beauty.

Our pictures include the types and kinds of lowboys and highboys and chests-on-frames available to the amateur and professional collectors of today.

A really surprising number of very fine examples are still to be had. One need not wait for the dispersal at auction of a great collection to obtain either William and Mary, Queen Anne, Georgian, or Chippendale highboys, lowboys, or chests-on-frames. Obviously one shouldn't hunt for them in the general run of antiques shops, but this cannot be made a rule. Our research workers found a William and Mary highboy in a shop almost wholly devoted to Pennsylvania pioneer furniture and another in what must rightfully be called a junk shop. Yet, if one hankers for a highboy or yearns for a lowboy, the most logical place to seek—and find—is in the better antiques shops. The prices asked are not modest, if you measure modesty of price in dollars alone. But they are quite modest when measured in terms of the actual scarcity of the pieces.

We must forever keep in mind that William and Mary style furniture may date from 1690 or even earlier, and that what we call the Chippendale style came generally to an end about 1785. Also, we must remember that highboys and lowboys were not common furniture but furniture made for at least the well-to-do Americans during less than a century of time. Some of the highboys and lowboys could have been made for only the very well to do. This is to say that the pieces cost plenty of money when new.

Just how much the Goddards and the Townsends of Rhode Island charged for their block-front highboys and lowboys may never be common knowledge. But it is now common knowledge that the block-front style, a distinctly American variant of the Georgian style made between 1748 and 1780, is a masterpiece of design and, in the opinion of many connoisseurs, is superior to the ornate Philadelphia cabinet furniture of the same period. There is some true block-front furniture on the market. There is considerable near block-front, in which the blocking is shallow and carved from thinner boards. True block-front displays the blocking in bold relief. The near block-front was produced to the north and west of Rhode Island, by town and country cabinetmakers who appreciated the style but whose abilities fell short of producing the finer type of work. Or it may be their ability was sufficient but the pocketbooks of their clientele were not so well filled. At any rate, our pictures represent the quality and sorts of opportunities existing for you who want to collect highboys and lowboys. To all who are determined to seek them, good hunting!

CHAPTER VI

Desks, Bureaus, and Chests of Drawers

The first desk for general or home use was a box—a desk box. Desks, somewhat in the style of pulpits, lecterns, and other ecclesiastical furniture, were used by scholars and doctors in the fifteenth, sixteenth, and seventeenth centuries, but these need not concern us here. The American desk box—not to be confused with the Bible box—was a rectangular piece of cabinet-work with a sloping lid and fitted with a lock. Bible boxes sometimes had sloping lids, on which the Bible was placed for reading, but they had no locks. Bibles were not private, personal, and secret. They were not kept under lock and key. But desks held personal papers, writing materials, and letter sheets of foolscap. They rated the keep-out sign that is lock and key. The desk box is early, of a date ranging from 1630 to 1680. That is just another way of saying it is about as scarce an antique as you could decide to find. There was a revival of the desk box in the nineteenth century, when innumerable fine cases of bird's-eye maple, walnut, and mahogany were made, to serve as desks held on the lap or placed on a table. These were made with an angularly cut lid which, when opened, presented an unbroken sloping surface twice the folded dimension of the box. Under the writing surface there was space for papers. At top or bottom of the writing surface were compartments for inkwells, pens, and pencils. The early desk boxes come to light in shops and at auctions once in a blue moon. The nineteenth-century desk boxes can be found with little trouble, as they were made as late as 1900.

The desk box-on-frame seems to have entered the American scene about 1660. This, too, is a very scarce, or even rare, item. A table-like frame holding a large desk box seems to have been the first simple style. Then the frame was made with a drawer. Then the box was made with a drawer. Finally, the desk-box

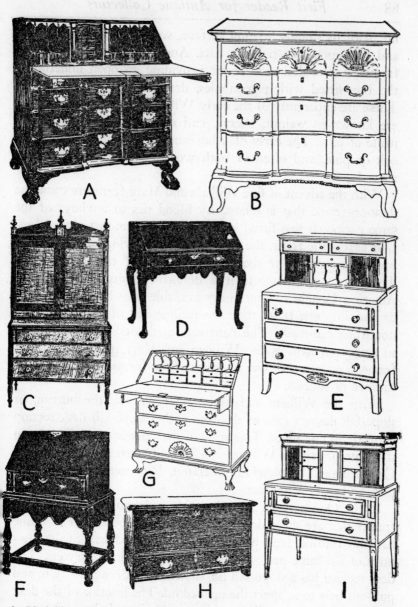

A: Block-Front Desk or Bureau. One Like It Reported in Dealer's Stock, 1945.
B: Block-Front Chest of Drawers, Offered by a Dealer in 1945. C: Sheraton
Bookcase Desk of Mahogany and Maple. D: Queen Anne Desk. E and I: Hepplewhite Tambour-Front Desks. (Tambour refers to the slatted fronts, which are
mounted on canvas, rolled out of sight.) F: William and Mary Desk-on-Frame,
1690–1700. G: Chippendale Slope-Fall Front Bureau, or Desk. H: Early Walnut
Chest with One Drawer.

lid, with its sloping writing surface, was made to fall outward and rest upon two pull-out bars. And there was the desk-on-frame! A real desk—the frame providing an open underbody, the box fitted with pigeonholes, drawers, cabinets, et cetera. These are apparently of the early William and Mary period and are known in walnut, cherry, and maple wood. A few were made of pine. The early desk boxes seem to have been made of oak or pine, and often of both woods. Sometimes they were carved.

With the advent of fine William and Mary furniture came the desk-on-frame that is related by blood ties to lowboys of the same period. It was fitted with six cup- or trumpet-turned legs, four across the front, the two center ones swinging outward to provide supports for the slope-fall front of the desk proper. These are quite rare and it is doubtful if any were made in America. Certain of those now available may have been early, or late, imports. If so, they are antique and of the period, but not American-made. The American-made desk-on-frame is not so scarce an item as the William and Mary gate-leg desk-on-frame. You can seek one or more of the former with every assurance of success.

With the William and Mary era came also the bureau, or slope-fall desk: a case of drawers with a slope-fall desk section all made in one piece. This style of desk persisted until 1860, in styles progressively William and Mary, Queen Anne, Georgian, Chippendale, Hepplewhite, Sheraton, Directoire, Federal, Empire, and early Victorian.

In the Queen Anne and Georgian styles there are desks-on-frames that are sheer delight in form and in beauty. The frame has four cabriole legs, with shaped skirting redolent of the lowboys of the same period, with from one to three drawers. The desk section has a slope-fall lid, sometimes a drawer or two, and pull-out bars to support the opened lid. The interior of the desk is fitted with drawers, little cabinets, and pigeonholes.

The bureau, or what most people mean by that term, is really a case of drawers. The purist will call only the slope-fall desk and case of drawers a bureau because the term "bureau" means "place where work is done." So, in calling the piece now generally and mistakenly called "bureau" a case of drawers, or low case of

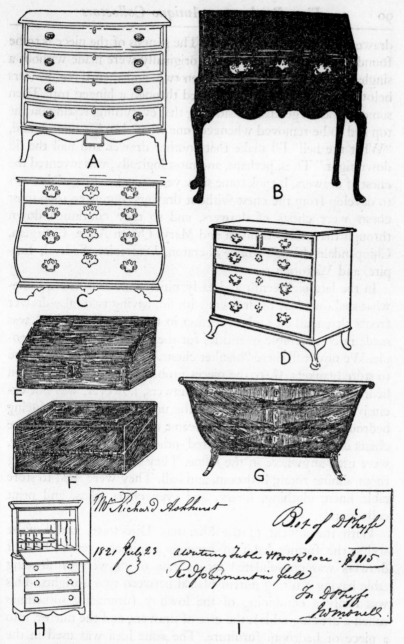

A: Hepplewhite Chest of Drawers. **B:** Queen Anne Desk-on-Frame, 1710–40.
C: Chippendale Bombé Chest of Drawers. **D:** Queen Anne Chest of Drawers.
E and **F:** Desk Boxes of 1692 and 1892. **G:** Directoire Chest of Drawers. **H:** Empire Desk, 1850–70. **I:** Duncan Phyfe Bill for a Writing Table and Bookcase, 1821.

drawers, we are on safe ground. The genesis of the piece is to be found in the early chests which originally were made without a single drawer, then with one, then two, and then three drawers below the "chest" section, reached through a hinged top. Then some unknown genius, considering that everything resting on the top had to be removed whenever one wanted to lift the lid, said, "What the hell! I'll make that another drawer and nail the lid down tight." Thus, perhaps, and most logically, was invented the chest of drawers. It took some sixty years for the chest of drawers to develop from the chest without drawers. But after 1690 most chests were chests of drawers, and so they continued down through the years—William and Mary, Queen Anne, Georgian, Chippendale, Hepplewhite, Sheraton, Directoire, Federal, Empire, and Victorian.

In the late eighteenth and early nineteenth centuries a somewhat shallow chest of drawers with lid, having two false drawer fronts that masked a chest section in the top of the piece, was made in considerable quantities for the use of the common people. We now call these "blanket chests." Perhaps they were used to store blankets. If so, the pieces probably were used mostly in bedrooms. The regular chest of drawers, however, was not exclusively a bedroom piece until the unholy habit of producing bedroom furniture in "suites" became the order of the day. The chests of drawers here considered, other than the blanket chest, were used anywhere in the home. They had entree to drawing room, dining room, bedroom, and hall. They were used to store table linen, clothing, finery, and even china, glass, and print collections.

With the advent of the Sheraton, Directoire, and Empire styles, the former habit of hanging a mirror over a chest of drawers was consolidated into a case of drawers or dressing table having a tilting mirror placed between two uprights. This was really a combining of the lowboy (originally sometimes called a dressing table), the case of drawers, and the mirror, into a piece of bedroom furniture. The same idea was used in the spool-turned era of cottage furniture and in the Victorian period.

Our pictures show desks, bureaus, and chests of drawers of the kinds you can procure today without too much hunting. Elsewhere in this volume there is a breakdown of the antiques-

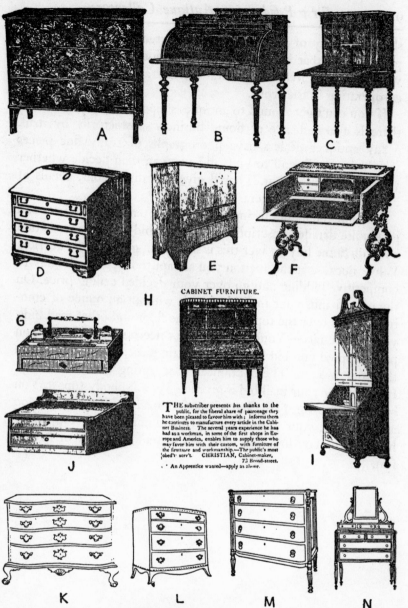

CABINET FURNITURE.

THE subscriber presents his thanks to the public, for the liberal share of patronage they have been pleased to favour him with; informs them he continues to manufacture every article in the Cabinet Business. The several years experience he has had as a workman, in some of the first shops in Europe and America, enables him to supply those who may favor him with their custom, with furniture of the first taste and workmanship.—The public's most obed't. serv't. CHRISTIAN, Cabinet-maker, 73 Broad-street.

∴ An Apprentice wanted—apply as above.

A: New England Painted Chest of Drawers, 1710. No Examples Found on Sale in 1945. **B:** Victorian Desk. **C:** Student's Desk, 1870. **D:** Sheraton Bureau or Desk, Advertised in 1830. **E:** Blanket Chest, Early Type. **F:** Victorian Desk on Iron Stand, 1850. **G:** Victorian Desk Box. **H:** Hepplewhite Roll-Top Desk, Advertised 1803. **I:** Chippendale Bureau-Bookcase as Pictured in 1840. **J:** Victorian Desk Box. **K, L, M,** and **N:** Chippendale, Hepplewhite, and Sheraton Chests of Drawers; Sheraton Dressing Table with Mirror.

shop inventory of August 1945, conducted by our research department. In that breakdown you will find the frequency with which antiques items of general interest appeared in the shops co-operating in the work.

If you can't get around to antiques shops as freely as you like, there is every chance of doing business satisfactorily by mail. Many antiques dealers have photographs of really fine pieces which they will send to you, and you can then decide whether you want them or not. They'll give you dimensions, details of condition, wood, et cetera.

Auction catalogues listing rare pieces often show pictures and give quite detailed descriptions. You can bid and buy at auction by mail. Some buyers aver this is safer than going to the auction. Why? Because at the auction you are apt to react emotionally to competitive bidding and go over your decided ceiling price. On the other hand, your mail bid stands without an ounce of emotion. If it is over the top bids from the floor and other mail bids, you get the piece. Your top bid is not necessarily the price you pay. Suppose you bid $500 for a certain piece. The last bid from the floor is $300. The auctioneer is accepting ten-dollar raises. Immediately your mail bid is given as $310. Nobody tops it. You get the piece for $310. But if another mail bidder has set $600 as his ceiling, your $500 bid is given and immediately topped by his at $510. You lose. He wins. It's just another way of having fun.

CHAPTER VII

Bedroom and Boudoir Furniture

The bedroom, as a social asset, really developed in the eighteenth century. In early New England, New York, Pennsylvania, and Virginia—and by early is meant seventeenth century—the settlers, and the lords and lesser officials sent over to regulate the settlers, placed beds wherever they pleased. Old inventories mention beds in halls, in keeping rooms, and in great rooms. Little bedroom furniture prior to the Queen Anne style or period is to be found in any antiques shops. Eighteenth-century beds, whether Queen Anne, Georgian, Chippendale, or Hepplewhite, are far from common in any shops. Sheraton, Directoire, and Empire period beds are not so scarce, and the closer we get to Empire the more frequently are they found.

Rope, button, or spool-turned beds appear quite frequently. And then we come to Victorian beds which, if you have room for them and can stand sleeping in one, are rather easily acquired. The pictures of the types of beds now available in antiques shops tell most of their own story. What they do not say, the captions do. Which leaves us in the happy position of needing to say no more about beds save this: in the Glossary there are several terms used in describing beds, and among our pictures in this chapter are some rather nice iron bedsteads.

Highboys and lowboys should not be classed as exclusively bedroom and boudoir furniture. These articles of furniture were as often used downstairs as upstairs. Hence we do not deal with them in this chapter. Neither will we consider here the chests, bureaus, desks, et cetera, which, used in bedrooms, were also used in many other rooms. Here, however, we will deal with the later objects, made specifically for bedroom and boudoir use. Most of these are nineteenth century. The dates range from 1801 to 1891, the last year spool-turned furniture appears in the catalogues of most nineteenth-century furniture manufacturers.

As this is written, we are surrounded by a deskful of bed-room-furniture catalogues. Some are dated in the 1850s and some in the 1890s. Items from all of these catalogues are on sale today as antiques. We are disposed to quote Shakespeare, or whoever it was, who said, "Nothing is either good or bad, but thinking makes it so." Many people think this late furniture is really good. That makes it so. By the same token, if all the connoisseurs and experts suddenly decided that Queen Anne furniture was bad, it wouldn't be long before it would be bad in the opinion of all collectors prone to follow the leaders.

Bedroom furniture in styles from Sheraton through to late Victorian, and spool turned, is here pictured and captioned with sufficient clarity so nothing more need be said about it. Everything that is pictured by type or kind was on sale as of the date of this writing. Richer, rarer, and more elaborate pieces that might well be called eighteenth-century bedroom furniture are always passing through auction galleries during the auction seasons. Very fine objects of the same general character can be found from time to time in the more exclusive shops. The demand for bedroom and boudoir furniture is not strong or steady. Many antiques dealers report that not one person in a hundred enters a shop looking for a bed or for bedroom furniture.

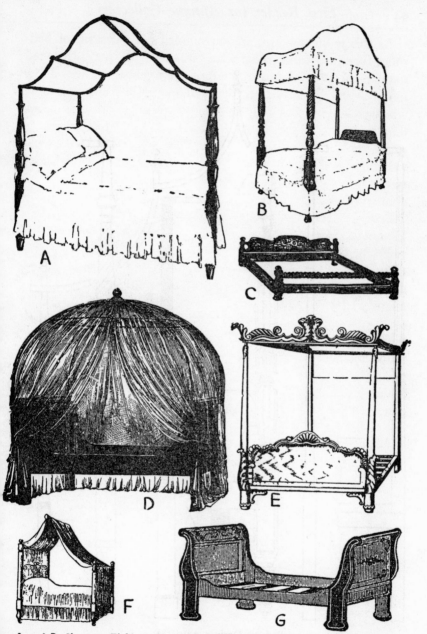

A and **B:** Sheraton Field or Canopy Beds. **C:** Trundle Bed, 1840–70. **D:** French Bed with Mosquito Canopy. **E:** Early "Antique" or Victorian Bed, 1842. **F:** Empire Canopy Bed. **G:** Empire Sleigh Bed.

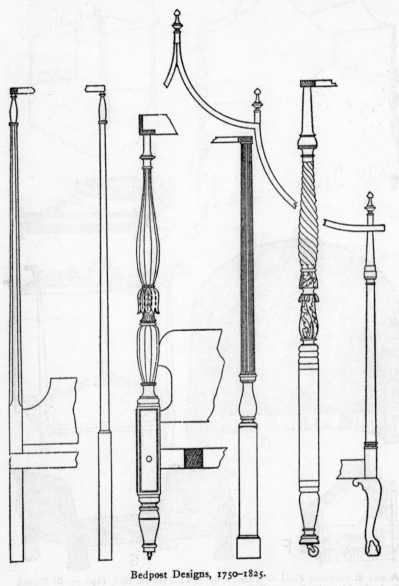

Bedpost Designs, 1750–1825.

A and B. Sheraton Field Bed. C and D. Sheraton Bed, 1790–95. D¹ French bed with Mosquito Canopy. E. Early "Acanthus," or Venetian Bed, 1825. F¹ Empire Canopy Bed. G¹ Empire Sleigh Bed.

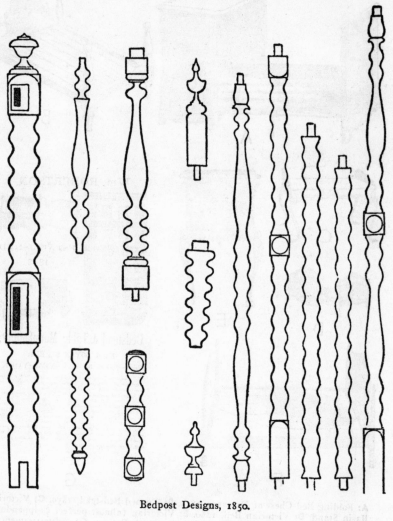

Bedpost Designs, 1850.

A: Folding Bed-Chest of Drawers, 1859. B: Turned Bedstead, 1859. C: Victorian Basin Stand. D: Victorian Bed, 1860. E: Victorian (almost perfect Chippendale) Night Stand, 1845. F: Spool Bed, Showing Sack Bottom. G: Advertisement of Bedstead Factory, Established 1843.

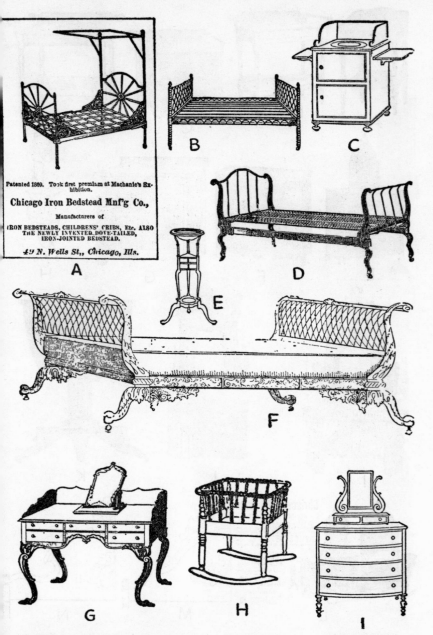

A

B

C

D

E

F

G

H

I

A, B, D, and **F:** Victorian Iron Beds, One with Cast "Spool" Posts. **C:** Empire Washstand. **E:** Walnut Basin Stand of 1760. **G:** Victorian Toilet Table. **H:** Cradle-Crib, Spool Turned. **I:** Sheraton Dressing Stand-on-Chest.

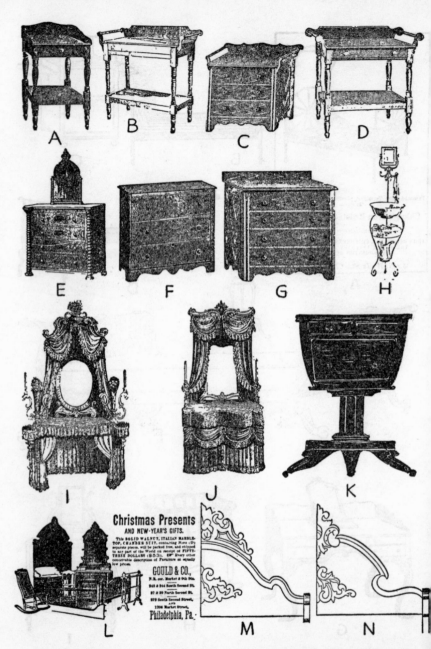

A, B, C, and D: Washstands from 1840 to 1880. E, F, and G: Chests of Drawers, 1840–80. H: Iron Basin Stand of 1860. I and J: Victorian Dressing Tables, 1845–50. K: Grecian Dressing Stand, 1840. L: Fifty-three Dollars would buy All This in 1874. M and N: Bedstead Headboard Patterns, 1870.

CHAPTER VIII

Clocks

The number of clocks of "near antiques" status still found in these United States is astonishing and amazing. That's because, originally, an amazing and astonishing number of these clocks were made and sold. Clocks were the first really mass-produced item of American manufacture. Conversely, the clockmakers of the nineteenth century reaped a rich reward when they mass produced good clocks for the people. The reward was rich because, up to the time they began manufacturing them for popular sale, clocks were luxuries. They turned them into staples. And thereby hangs a tale the telling of which, in respect of Connecticut clock manufacturers alone, makes a four-volume book!

In spite of the fact that many makers of the so-called grandfather clock were at work between 1750 and 1850, the production was limited and prices were high. Willard's great invention and patent, the banjo clock, was not, in its finer forms, a mass-production clock. Neither was it a cheap clock. Rather, it was a very fine timepiece in what has been called the most beautiful clock case ever conceived. With this many people agree. You can still buy a banjo clock by Willard, Phipps, Sawin & Dyar, Riggs, and other makers, but you might have to pay as much as you'd be asked for a tall case clock by one of the New England or Pennsylvania makers.

Riggs of Philadelphia made many modified banjo-style clocks for the Pennsylvania Railroad between 1850 and 1870. They also made the same clocks for general sale during the same period. Several of the type are pictured because they are to be found here and there in the shops. Fine banjos usually gravitate to the finer shops where they will be put into excellent running order and properly restored, if restoration is required. And often it is. These clocks are safe as a church when left on the wall, but when they begin to circulate as merchandise at this late

This and facing page: Double-Decked Pillar; O-G Moulding; Eagle Top, and Other Variants of the Basic Terry Mantle Clock Design Made from 1848 to 1888. Best Ones Have Eight-Day Brass Movements. Some Have Thirty-Hour Wooden Movements. Some Are Spring Driven. Some Have Alarm Attachments. The "Steeple" design clock with high peaked top is not a variant of the Terry Clock but a distinct innovation in its own right.

day, they lose bits of molding, pieces of gilding base, and other important features.

It is with the production of Eli Terry that clocks, now antique, are found in sufficient numbers to be generally available to any and all collectors. The Terry "pillar-and-scroll," or free-standing pillar clock, is every bit as lovely as a banjo. Only, it is a shelf clock, while the banjo is a wall clock. The banjo is a clock case of really "exclusive" design in that it successfully challenges attempts at variation. We have found only one banjo made as a shelf clock and that, believe it or not, was found in an antiques shop!

The Terry pillar-and-scroll design is not exclusive. American clockmakers proved it could be varied in so many ways and forms that they built entire lines of clocks around it. In fact, between 1836 and 1886 variants of the Terry-designed clock were made in no less than two hundred different forms. We are fortunate in being able to show quite a number of these taken directly from the catalogues of the makers. One of the catalogues was the very first issued by Seth Thomas. Others were issued between 1865 and 1880. More than half of the clocks in the 1880 catalogue are substantially the same clocks pictured in the earliest catalogue.

These are interesting facts for the collector to know. To the research worker in the field of Americana they are more than interesting—they are revealing. They say: "These clocks were made year after year, in successively increasing quantities, until the saturation point was reached." That spells millions of clocks, mass produced, at first sold by clock peddlers, then by shops, then by jewelry and department stores, and then given away as premiums.

The great story of American clockmaking is not yet published. It is, perhaps, half written, in the monumental manuscript recently prepared by Lockwood Barr. It may well be that the other half is already in print in some twenty-five or more books dealing wholly or partially with clocks. There is, however, one story you can read in words and in pictures, and that is the story told here. All of these clocks are items you can buy today. Some will hardly dent your purse (if you don't mind having the clock fixed to run again, and having the case repaired and re-

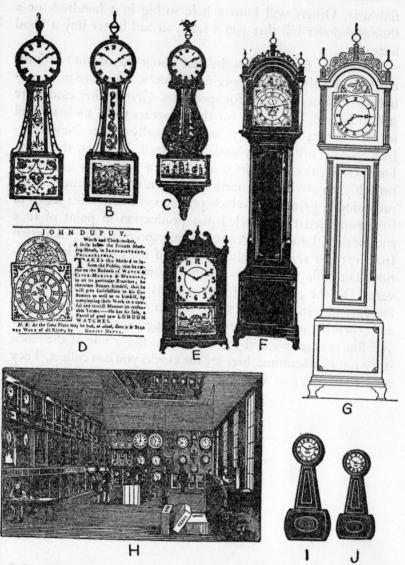

A, B, and C: Two Standard Banjo Clocks and a Lyre Banjo. D: Clockmaker's Advertisement, 1770. E: The Terry Pillar-and-Scroll Mantel, or Shelf Clock, from Which Some Two Hundred, All Different, Clock Designs Were Copied! F and G: Grandfather's Clocks. H: Interior of Beal's Clock Store, Boston, 1846. I and J: Late Banjo Clocks, 1857.

finished). Others will burn a hole so big in a hundred- or a thousand-dollar bill that you'll feel you had better buy a bond instead.

It is almost fruitless to write here about seventeenth-century clocks and early eighteenth-century clocks. They are now connoisseurs' pieces or items for specialists. Grandfather clocks are still to be had, but search for them appears to be most fruitful in the districts where they were originally made: New England, New York, Pennsylvania, Maryland, Virginia, the Carolinas, Ohio, West Virginia, and eastern Kentucky. There is probably no obvious connection between the phenomenon but, surprisingly, grandfather-clock production in America seems to have paralleled rifle-barreled gun production in point of time and locality. Lancaster, Pennsylvania, center of rifle production from 1750 to 1850, was also a center of tall case clock production. Did rifle lockmakers produce parts for clocks, or vice versa? Did the great firm of Brown & Sharp, originating as clockmakers and watchmakers, turn to tool and gauge making for Colt and others because they knew rifle making also? We do not know yet. But perhaps we will one day, when the whole of the clock story is told. Meantime, here are the clocks you can collect. They need a minimum of words to tell the rest of their story.

CHAPTER IX

Mirrors

If you are willing to settle for a Queen Anne or Georgian period mirror as the earliest type you seek, you can begin right there collecting mirrors and enjoy owning looking glasses made from about 1710 down to 1860. It is not beyond the realm of possibility that you will find mid-eighteenth-century mirrors in Iowa and Washington, or fine French- and Spanish-inspired mirrors in Louisiana, Texas, New Mexico, and California. Mirrors, in the eighteenth century, were precious things. Making the frames, however ornate, was easy. But to make a complete mirror required the mirror glass. That's where the rub came. Mirror glass was never common. Up to the time the Duke of Buckingham set up a plate-glass works at Vauxhall, England was dependent upon Italy for mirror glass. This reference is, of course, to plate glass, with slightly beveled edges, but made so flat that it was relatively free from distortion. Mirrors made of crown glass didn't make good looking glasses. The wavy lines and varying thicknesses of the glass were accentuated when silvered. The image reflected was a little on the odd side.

Queen Anne and Georgian mirrors are sometimes called Chippendale for no logical reason except that because mirrors were harder to get than new furniture, the Queen Anne and Georgian mirrors owned by well-to-do American colonists were retained even when they discarded other old furnishings. The earlier mirrors stayed on the walls and on the wall piers, even when new cabinet furniture entered the homes. Chippendale sometimes designed mirrors of fantastic and super-ornate framing, but he did not originate all the mirrors often designated as Chippendale today. Neither did Sheraton design the mirror of "tabernacle" form now called Sheraton by many people. The fact is, Sheraton displayed no mirrors in his pattern book. The columned mirror frame of mahogany, cherry, maple, or gilt, with painted panels and other decoration at top, is more likely an American adaptation of a French *trumeau* and should be called Federal mirror, or tabernacle mirror, or American trumeau. There is nothing "Sheraton" about it. This is the mirror that was made in tremendous quantities between 1790 and 1850, in sizes and at prices to fit every purse, even the flattest. You could, in 1820, buy a tabernacle or trumeau style mirror for one dollar, ten dollars, or one hundred dollars. In the cheaper ones the glass was of the crown variety and of course did not reflect an image without some distortion. The finer ones had flat plate glass. One seldom finds a tabernacle mirror with a beveled plate glass and, in the opinion of some experts, if the glass is beveled plate it is probably a later replacement and not the original glass.

Which leads directly to a very pertinent question: What is the "antique" part of an antique mirror? The frame, or the glass? Of course there are museum people who say that unless the mirror is original both as to frame and glass it is not truly of the period. This is perhaps strictly true in every sense, but it in no way can upset the common-sense observation that in museums mirrors are used as objects to complete a period showing, while in homes mirrors are usually used in company, and in solo, for a bit of self-admiration. For that, the best mirror glass is desirable. A fig for the original glass that makes your face look as though is were laddered vertically or horizontally, with bulges here and there, and giving a squint to your eyes! Further, it is the frame that was made by the cabinetmaker or artisan. It is the frame that makes the mirror of a period, and desirable as a collectible antique. Let who will quibble over it, early and late mirror makers bought their mirror glass from others, and not a few mirrors of the Hepplewhite, Directoire, and Federal periods were made as frames to accommodate older secondhand mirror glass panes.

Here are pictured the kinds of mirrors you can hope to find in antiques shops, or bid up in auction galleries. Each is captioned as briefly as possible. After 1820 the number of mirror makers in America increased by leaps and bounds. There were manufactories even in small towns and villages. America prior to 1800 was somewhat mirror starved. The mirror was both a luxury

LOOKING GLASSES.

B. CERMENATI,

Gilder, Looking-Glass & Picture Frame Manufacturer,

KEEPS constantly for sale at his Store in *Daniel-street*, four doors West of the Post-Office, Portsmouth, an assortment of
*LOOKING-GLASSES, PICTURES; SPY-GLASSES;
THERMOMETERS; PAINTS; PENCILS, &c.*

N. B. Old Looking-Glasses, Pictures, Ladies Needle-Work, &c. newly fram'd in the most modern style and at the shortest notice and as cheap as can be done elsewhere.
—ALSO—
Old Looking-Glasses new silvered, and Thermometers repaired.

Portsmouth, July 1812,

LOOKING-GLASS

WORCESTER MANUFACTORY.

WILLIAM WISWELL, Jr.

(Opposite the Centre Meeting House)

RESPECTFULLY informs the inhabitants of Worcester and vicinity, that he has on hand, at his old stand, a great assortment of, and is constantly manufacturing, *Looking Glasses; Portrait, Miniature, and Picture Frames*, of every size and description. Old Frames re-guilded, and all orders promptly attended to.

Traders in the vicinity of Worcester and elsewhere, will be supplied on the most reasonable terms.

Worcester, March 24, 1830.

A and **B:** Looking-Glass Advertising in 1812 and 1830. Most People Would Date the Eagle Mirror of 1830 before the Trumeau of 1812. **C, D, E,** and **F:** Queen Anne and Georgian Period Mirrors. The Type on the Right Is Often Called Chippendale. **G:** A Lady of Charleston Buys a Mirror for $6.00, 1822.

and an elegancy. But when mass production converted the former luxury into a staple, then the mirror was for everyone and everyone had not just one but up to half a dozen mirrors in the home. That's why we have so many of these Federal period mirrors left in spite of the outmoding process they were subject to in the Victorian era.

With the pictures of actual mirrors are included several early nineteenth-century mirror makers' advertisements. That of Wiswell of Worcester pictures an American adaptation of the French trumeau—and this is the style and type of mirror all America was buying right down to 1850. In 1790 this type of mirror was the latest conceit of Boston, New York, Philadelphia, and Charleston. In 1850 a trader on the upper reaches of the Missouri River could buy a little mirror in the same style, mass produced at St. Louis, and sold upriver by packet-boat furniture stores.

LOOKING-GLASSES,

An Elegant Assortment,

Of the most fashionable Kind, just imported from London, and

TO BE SOLD, by

ANDREW VAN BIBBER,

Who will agree to receive and have executed any Orders for the above Article, or CROWN WINDOW-GLASS, at the most celebrated Manufactories in England, with all possible dispatch, and according to any given dimensions or fashions.

A: Chippendale Mirror, 1765. B: Baltimore Looking-Glass Dealer's Advertisement, 1785. C: Empire Mirror, 1850. D: French Trumeau of Directoire Period, Ancestor of Our Federal or Tabernacle Mirror Styles. E: Georgian Mirror. This Type is very frequently Called Chippendale. F: Dressing Glass, 1790–1810. G: William and Mary Mirror, about 1700. H: Federal Mirror of 1815. I: Chippendale Mirror Frame.

CHAPTER X

Elegancies, Conceits, Fancies, and Fads

There are numerous categories of objective, or purposeful, collecting which deserve glorification in books or monographs. Certain of these are hereby started on that pathway by the gentle act of nudging them into prominence. Perhaps the least known yet most important collecting pursuit of all is the gathering of early commercial and industrial papers—documents of all sorts having to do with American commerce and industry. It sounds rather dry at first reading, but there is nothing fusty, for example, about the first catalogue issued by the Salisbury Furniture Company of West Randolph, Vermont, or the illustrated advertising of America's first manufacturer of glass Christmas balls. The early bills of F. B. Norton, pottery and stoneware manufacturer, were printed with completely priced lists of everything made. Many of the items are pictured on the bill. When a customer made a purchase, the pottery simply made a check mark on the bill beside the items sold, designated the quantity, extended the entry in ink, and there was a complete bill. Certainly it is still just a bill, but a bill revealing everything made by the pottery, dated as to time of purchase, and picturing much of what was made.

Not infrequently merchandise catalogues, bills, brochures, individual advertising sheets, broadsides, and posters tell more at one fell swoop than years of patient research expose about a company or a type of antique. A very great deal of what we know about the elegancies, conceits, fancies, and fads of other days derives from the still preserved material that was used to promote and to sell the objects, or from contemporaneous editorial comments about the things.

It was in 1854 that a New York newspaper, in commenting on a lot of "Egyptian Curiosities," including several mummies then on display, gives us a clue to when fancy glass paperweights were first sold in stores. Says the paper: "Here [from ancient Egypt] are glass objects with flowers and other elements in them, very much like the paper holders now being offered in the shops." Advertisements rescued by chance tell us about glass bells for "Wardian" cases, Christmas-tree ornaments, wax and hair work, special lamps, fine clocks, and give us information about them which, more often than not, upset both amateur conjectures and expert opinions.

The furniture catalogues of the Walter Heywood Chair Company of Fitchburg, Massachusetts, established in 1826, and of the J. W. Mason Furniture Company, New York, established in 1844, picture, as new goods, much of what today is, or passes as, antique. The Edward Bassford catalogues depict the wooden-wares, japanned wares, and ironwares offered by this firm, and on the back cover of the forty-eighth annual catalogue (issued in 1884) appears the advertisement of James Graham of 19 East Fourteenth Street, New York, offering antiques! Mr. Graham had this to say about antiques: "I am constantly receiving from Europe all kinds of Rare Antiques in Furniture." He pictures Hepplewhite chairs, Adam chairs, Queen Anne roundabout chairs, Adam tables, and Sèvres and Dresden china.

In 1857 George F. Nesbitt & Company, lithographers of New York, issued a four-page paper called *Little Scissors Pictorial*. In it they picture seventy-one clipper-ship advertising cards in colors. Until a copy of this promotion piece was found nobody knew how many cards for clipper-ship lines this firm issued, although the cards were—and are—avidly collected.

The various scrap paper drives staged during the war years 1941–45 accomplished the salvage of millions of pounds of paper and also the complete destruction of countless priceless commercial documents. It is a great pity that every town and village did not appoint a historic monitor to examine the salvage before it was sent to the pulp mills. It is an even greater pity that an administration so patently wise in its own pattern for cultural-historic propaganda—and with poets and aesthetes at work in the many extra and emergency agencies—did not issue just one pamphlet for the American people dealing with what kinds of scrap paper to save. Instead, perhaps, the paper and the brains needed for such a project were spent on writing American culture pamphlets for the edification of the Siamese.

Quite conceivably the dear old lady of Charleston, South Carolina, who put some one hundred old valentines in original envelopes into the paper salvage drive got quite a little thrill out of her patriotic gesture. Her thrill would have turned to a chill had she known she threw away three hundred dollars in just one of those valentines. Happily, that valentine was rescued. It is now owned by a stamp collector who, in turn, is gloating over the fact that on the envelope is a genuine, used Charleston carrier's stamp.

It is in these early documents, catalogues, et cetera, that we find the story of America getting somewhere in obtaining luxuries by the simple process of converting luxuries into staples. Our first complete bathrooms were miniature Greek temples, constructed and plumbed at considerable expense. Within ten years all the fixtures required for a bathroom were available to anyone having running water and sanitary facilities. It may seem a far cry from having a bathroom to desiring other elegancies, conceits, and fancies, but it isn't and wasn't. Putting one obvious luxury into a home has always broadened the desire for other luxuries. The bathroom, hot-water supply, refrigeration, and central heating were true harbingers of luxury for the many instead of the few. In very early days only the top-drawer people could afford luxuries. In America, almost everybody wanted luxuries and, if we couldn't afford them as luxuries, we mass produced them into staples that we could afford.

Of course there are experts in antiques who, within the narrow fields of their own experience, will scoff at this. Most of the scoffing is a defense device—a smoke screen thrown up until they can re-orient their ponderous thought processes into new channels. Then, some years later, they'll blithely announce that it is all true and, perhaps, that they have made the original discovery. All these facets of collecting show why the amateur can have loads and loads of fun within the pursuits he marks out as his own. It is not without some misgivings that we stake out the following collectibles as worthy of inclusion in this chapter. If the list doesn't include what you fancy, we are a dope, to you. So, if what you fancy isn't here, we can only beg your pardon

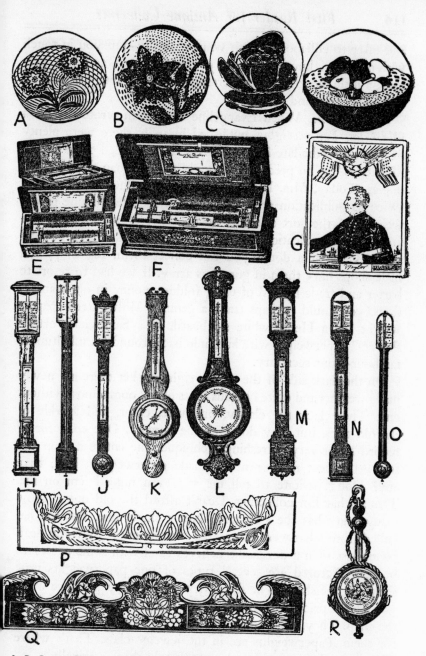

A, B, C, and **D:** Paperweights, Now Almost in the Category of Jewels. **E** and **F:** Music Boxes, 1865, 1888. **G:** Transparency of Zachary Taylor. **H** to **O:** Barometers by Tagliabue, New York, 1840–76. **P** and **Q:** Venetian Blind Cornices, 1835. **R:** Fancy Barometer, 1853.

and offer to collaborate with you personally—put you in touch with others we know who have your same fancy—and then, perhaps, a little monograph concerning your joint fancy can someday be written and published.

Paperweights. When Evangeline Bergstrom wrote the book *Old Glass Paperweights*, published in 1940, there were plenty of dopesters (the late Harry Koopman once called them "white Mahatmas") who predicted it would sell less than five hundred copies. Today, Mrs. Bergstrom's book is selling at more than twice its publication price of ten dollars, while genuine paperweights of the sort she tells about and pictures in full color are in the classification, price-wise, of precious stones. Beyond any shadow of a doubt you can collect them. Big shops and little shops have them in gorgeous array. If we had to resort to barter and trade instead of using folding money in our transactions, you could perhaps trade a genuine Millville rose paperweight for a Hepplewhite sideboard, or a Sandwich "manyflowers" paperweight with latticinio background for a Baltimore tambour-front secretary.

On the dark side of the paperweight market there are newly made weights and quite obvious fakes of old ones almost without end. These lack the clarity, brilliance, color, and sparkle of the old ones, but they do catch the unwary. One collector of record has a very refreshing technique. She enters a shop and says, "I collect fake or newly made paperweights. D'ye have any? Don't hesitate to tell me and even unload 'em on me. That's what I'm collecting. I can't afford the old ones." How many fakes has she collected? Not a single one. But she has culled from what were considered "wrong ones" by many dealers no less than a dozen she believes (and with some cause) to be real. Pictured are several types of fine paperweights now shown in the shops. The shock that is yours to experience when you ask the price shall remain exclusively your own. Don't blame the shop. They, too, are shocked at the prices they have to pay for them. Paperweights are in the jewelry class. That's where they made their start. Jewelry stores sold them originally.

Music Boxes. If you think they're only Swiss, you have a nice little surprise coming to you. The Swiss type with a cylinder full of tiny prickets and a comb of steel reeds is but

A, B, and C: Pianoette and Music Boxes, 1870-1880. D and E: Painted Bellows and Mechanical Blower. F, G, H, I, J, and K: Fancy Thermometers, 1830-76. L, M, and N: Plain and Fancy Venetian Blinds, 1830-50. O, P, and Q: Wardian Case, and Nests of Glasses.

one type of music box. There is an American-made type with melodeon reeds, a miniature bellows, and rolls of pricked paper. And there is also an American-made type that played from perforated flat metal discs. There are few music-box collectors as such. Most buyers just want one or, at most, two examples. And most buyers want them not merely as antiques but as music boxes —perhaps as escape from radio programs or radio commercials. For free, we remark to radio advertisers, "try some spot broadcasts based upon Early American music played on Early American musical instruments. You'll be delighted with the *quality* of the audience that listens." If you seek music boxes, seek for them not only in antiques shops; visit also the secondhand stores making no pretense at antiques selling. Quite frequently in these shops, especially those buying and selling household goods of the current and past few decades, you'll find music boxes of good quality in working order. The mechanical organs of American make are something else again. They're scarcer than the Swiss music boxes and, because paper was a part of their mechanism, they haven't survived in quantities as have the Swiss type of all-metal mechanical construction.

Here are pictures representative of the types of music boxes you can hope to find. The pictures are straight from the catalogues of the makers and vendors, 1855 to 1885. It should be remembered that the American "Regina" and other music boxes were made until the Victrola and Grafonola—those first luxury record players—captured the market. Now early Victrolas, Grafonolas, and their records, if not antiques, are collectors' items of considerable importance.

Scientific Antiques. Here is a beautiful japanned and gold-stenciled bellows with a bit of hand-painted scenery. The price is so-and-so. Here is a mechanical blower mounted on a hand-hold of mahogany. The working parts are of fine brass. It's rotary in action and it sends out a continuous blast of air as you turn the crank. The price is four times the price of the bellows. It's a scientific antique. So are globes—terrestrial and celestial; orreries; sundial guns; vieu optique machines and all the other gadgets. In spite of the fact that our pictures are mostly from dealers' catalogues, these objects are to be found in antiques shops today. None of them is a cheap antique, and they were not

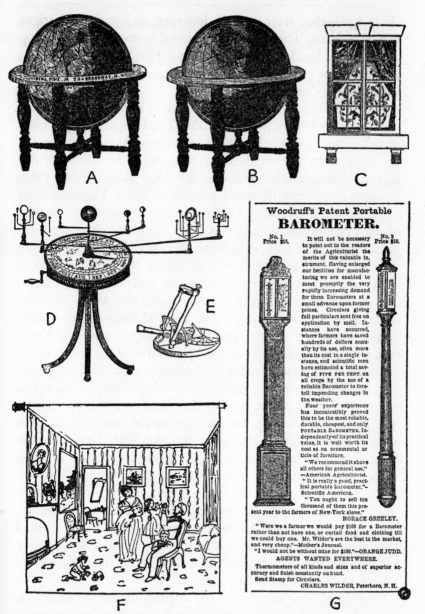

A and **B:** Celestial and Terrestrial Globes, 1840. **D:** Orrery, 1840. **E:** Sun Dial Gun, 1840. **C** and **F:** Painted Window Shades, 1855. **G:** Barometer Advertisement, 1864.

cheap when they were new. If, however, such antiques intrigue you, take heart. They can be purchased in more than one shop out of every hundred, and if you cannot find them in the shops you visit you can transact your business very satisfactorily by mail with the shops that do have them.

Venetian Blinds. Invented in France as the jalousie, in 1765, these were the luxury window shades of early Federal days. They were far more popular here than in England. We began importing them from France after the Revolution. By 1810 we had several Venetian blind factories. By 1840 almost every town boasting over three thousand population had a Venetian blind manufactory. This luxury became a staple by the simple process of mass production. While it is quite true that not many complete old Venetian blinds survive, the carved valences or tops, some quite ornate and others depicting the great American eagle, are now collectors' items to be found in many shops.

Painted Window Shades. These entered the American scene as a new luxury about 1830. The Holland linen shade, or curtain on a roller, was then beginning to compete with the Venetian blind. It couldn't compete "plain" but it certainly could compete when made "fancy." Dressing up the Holland shade was merely a matter of painting it with landscapes, seascapes, and conversation pieces, with fruits, flowers, and fancy scrolls. The colors were transparent. In daytime the drawn shade made a transparent picture in the room. At night, with the room lights lit, it simply shrieked quality to the passer-by. A few of these shades have survived. To find even one in an antiques shop requires more than a little hunting, but collectors who really want them are willing to do the hunting. One collector said recently, "I want historic painted window shades. When I find them, I have them mounted on canvas in stretcher frames. To me they are pictures worthy of preservation and better than the general run of so-called American primitives."

Wardian Cases. These were the original idea of the terrarium or garden under glass, sold by many flower shops in the 1920s. Dr. Ward invented the device as a means of transporting exotic plants to England, about 1845. By 1850 a Wardian case, placed upon a fancy table, was a conceit of the wealthy. Various ferns, sedums, and succulent evergreens were planted in good earth

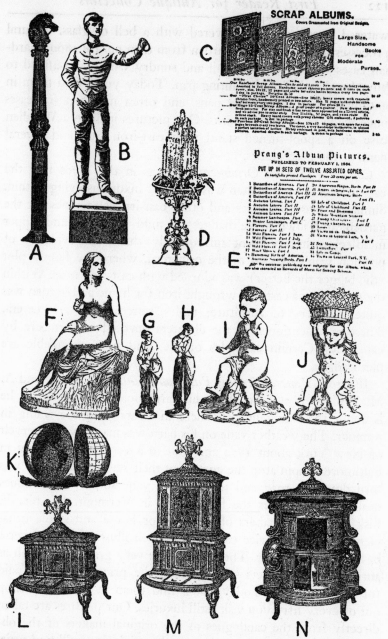

A and **B**: Hitching Posts, 1880. **C** and **E**: Scrap Albums, and Prang Card Advertisement. **D**: Fairy Fountain, 1872. **F** to **J**: Parian Statuary, 1852. **K**: Segmented Globe, 1874. **L**, **M**, and **N**: Parlor Stoves, 1850–80.

watered once, and then covered with a bell of glass. Natural processes took care of the garden from then on. By 1860 Wardian cases were available to all and sundry who could afford to buy the glass bell and planting pan. Today you'll find them in antiques shops, minus the pans, and often mistaken for cases once made to hold waxworks. Our pictures include a Wardian case on a spool-turned stand with cast-iron base and several nests of the glass globes.

Cast-iron Garden Ornaments. It was in the 1870s that the cast-iron deer on the lawn was a sign of luxurious living within. Similarly, Brevoort vases and other cast-iron elegancies for the garden and lawn were badges of mild opulence and upper middleclass luxury. Not infrequently this same evidence of position was extended to the cemetery, where the family plot (the bigger the better) was adorned with cast-iron urns. Within the category of cast and wrought iron for home and garden was quite a gallery of furniture: tables, settees, chairs, et cetera. These are mentioned in the chapters devoted to furniture by categories. Certain examples of the kind now obtainable are pictured.

Weather Vanes, Hitching Posts, and Fountains. My friend A. M. Willcox is as keen about his farmhouse in Vermont as he is about the skiing he gets there in winter and the riding in summer. The weather vane on his barn was made by Westervelt of New York about 1870 and sold to a very swank family in Baltimore to spin atop the cupola on their stable. The stable was torn down in 1937 and the weather vane sold to an antiques dealer. Now it flies the four winds in Vermont. Westervelt, Fisk, and other makers of luxuries for house and stable ornamentation, issued price catalogues which illustrated their wares in the grand manner. The prices were very grand too. Even as antiques these objects seldom reach the prices originally paid for the elegancies. Today you'll find them in about one shop out of every fifty you visit—still luxuries. Our pictures are taken directly from the catalogues of the original makers of the objects. Hence they are as antique as the originals you'll find waiting for you if you collect such things.

Albums. There is now a vogue of card collecting. Several thousand collectors are buying old scrap albums pasted full o

A, B, and **C:** Iron Flower Stands. **D:** Bedroom Refrigerator. **E:** "Brevoort" Vase.
F, G, and **H:** Iron Settees, 1855–70. **I, J, K,** and **L:** Weather Vanes, 1870–80.

lithographed advertising cards issued by manufacturers to promote the sale of their goods and wares, and by retailers of all sorts of commodities. Also, there are collectors of the sets of cards that were once a part of every package of cigarettes. About 1856 Prang, of Boston, made albums to hold cards. If this sounds something like the souvenir post-card collecting vogue of 1900–10, your hearing is playing you no tricks. Prang's cards, reproducing scenes painted by that great American artist, Winslow Homer, are now selling at rather fancy prices. Merely to whet your acquisitive instinct, here are pictures of albums, made for advertising cards of the sort you can buy today. Some dealers can offer you a bushel basket full of cards. Others will not bat an eye when they offer you 25,000—all different. But your own eyes may blink a few times when you hear the price of the basketful, or the 25,000.

Rogers Groups and Other Statuary. When the New York Historical Society stages an exhibit of objects, the objects exhibited certainly have achieved importance. When this great institution exhibited the plaster statuary groups made and sold by John Rogers, from the 1870s to the 1890s, the stamp of antiquarian approval was finally put upon them. Yet as early as 1926 there was a collecting vogue for these groups. Rogers groups are American social history in as nearly the concrete as a secret hard-plaster formula can make them. Interestingly enough, these groups are no longer to be found in every nook-and-corner antiques shop. It may well be that the size militates against many shops bothering with them. Or the possibility of damage in transit may discourage much interstate trade. But whatever the reason, you'll not find these late statuary groups common articles in antiques. You can find them, however, even though the better shops will not touch them.

West Statuary Company of Chicago, in the late 1880s and 1890s, produced statuary that was in direct imitation of John Rogers's work, and in the catalogue (issued without date but apparently about 1888) of this firm they state that the statues are like those of Rogers in style and quality. The West Company also imported Parian and other pottery and china statuary from Europe. During their years of operation they probably

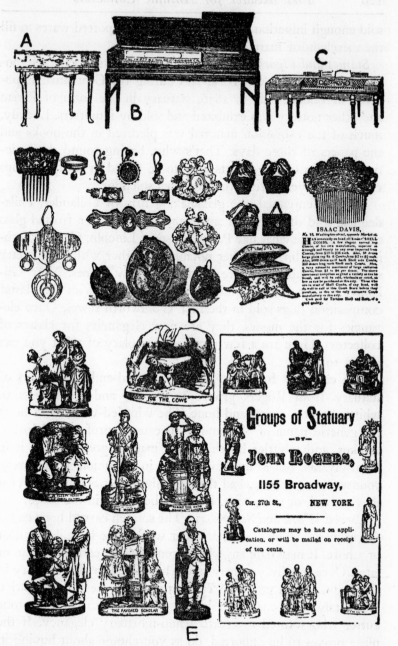

A: Early Staarstruck. **B:** Pianoforte, 1780. **C:** Pianoforte, 1840. **D:** Jewelry Elegancies, 1825–80. **E:** John Rogers' Advertisement and Eight of His Statues.

sold enough imitation Rogers statuary and imported wares to fill the merchandise mart.

Statues and Figurines. During the great Crystal Palace Exposition of 1853 at New York, and during the Centennial Exposition at Philadelphia in 1876, statuary in the form of Parian and other pottery was exhibited and sold by importers. Luckily, much of the exhibition material was pictured in the books and the papers of those days. That's why, having found these pictures, certain of the objects now to be found in antiques shops can be displayed here in their original splendor.

At the Centennial, the glassmaking firm of Gillander, Philadelphia, sold thousands of small statuary items in a frosted glass that looks somewhat like Parian. Busts of Lincoln, Grant, Washington, Franklin, and other notables, together with very pretty sentimental subjects, were carried to many homes. Now Gillander glass is to be found in the shops, along with the plaster composition dogs sold in the first Woolworth stores. Once elegancies for the masses, they are now elegancies for classes of collectors. Here are a few pictures exemplary of what you can expect to find.

You can sally forth and find a thousand-and-one objects of statuary from Rogers groups to Parian, and from glass to whittled wood, stone, and bone. The whittled-wood stuff bears the generic name of "Schimmel" because a professional loafer, drinker, and whittler by that name made a great deal of it in Pennsylvania. But at least every state in the union, if not every county in every state, had the equivalent of a Schimmel. What they carved, or some of it, is still to be found in the shops.

Carved Work and Scrimshaw. The scratch carved bone called "scrimshaw" is, of course, amateur work done by sailors, afloat or ashore. It may date anywhere from 1760 or earlier to 1840 or later. Occasionally you may find a bit of real marble statuary in the shops. When you do, step lightly, it may be an importation from Italy, or it may be a bit of work by a native tombstone cutter who wanted to create a non-mortuary elegancy. If the piece proves to be imported, do as you choose about buying it. But if it is cut from native stone, grab it. One day, and not far distant, American stone carvings will be as good to own as a table or a chair of the Phyfe period.

Top: Victorian Piano; Bass Melodeon, 1860; Melodeon, 1850.
Bottom: Coverlet Patterns, 1810–40.

Transparencies. About 1840 a new conceit, a "transparency," the original name of which is now obscure, took hold of American imagination. This was a thin panel of porcelain upon which portraits, scenes, genre subjects, flowers, fruits, et cetera, were impressed. When held up to the light, lo, there appeared a perfect representation of a mezzotint. The impression upon the substance varied in depth so that the passage of light formed the finished picture. These are really quite lovely things; one wonders why the art has not been revived and the sheets made from plastic. Frequently the scenes were colored. These objects were used in two ways of record: one, as panels in lampshades; two, as decoration to hang in front of a window. The single example illustrated is a portrait of Zachary Taylor, twelfth president.

Jewelry and Allied Items. If costume jewelry were a new thing, which it isn't, we might believe some of the costume-jewelry advertising which states that this or that conceit is new. There were rings and bracelets made for our grandmothers when they were girls which were nothing more or less than charm rings and charm bracelets. Wedgwood made medium, small, and tiny medallions for the jewelry trade. Near silver, silver, and plated gold jewelry of really exquisite workmanship was sold between 1840 and 1880. Real gold jewelry for men and women was not exactly rare in the American scene from 1750. Many buttons of early vintage (and since many buttons were "pressed" we are not far out of line in using the term "vintage") fall rightfully into the category of jewelry. After 1850 there were buttons of glass, fashioned in the form of miniature paperweights of the sort that bring jewelry prices today. Pocketbooks, reticules, handbags, writing implements such as gold and silver and painted tin pen cases, rejoicing in the name of "kalendam," were sold in many jewelers' shops. So also were carved dress combs, chatelaines, clips, spectacles, and snuffboxes of precious and semi-precious metals. Some items in these various categories, still to be found here and there in antiques shops, are pictured. Really fine antique jewelry is not discussed and not pictured here because it is still jewelry-store merchandise and not general antiques shop stock. But it can be had if you want it, and there are shops which specialize in it.

Luxury Stoves and Fireplace Equipment. When, five years

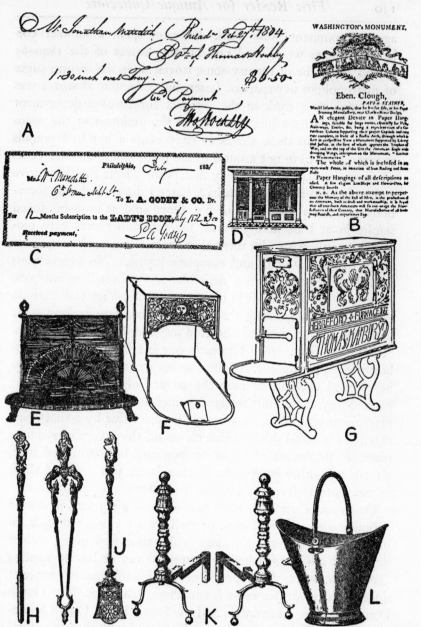

A: Bill for Oval Tray, 1804. **B:** Wallpaper Elegancy, Advertised, 1800. **C:** Mr. Godey Gets a Subscriber, 1831. **D:** Greek Temple Bathroom, 1840. **E, F,** and **G:** Franklin Stoves, 1810 and 1765; Pennsylvania Ten-Plate Stove, 1765. **H, I, J:** Fire Tools, 1846. **K:** Andirons, 1810. **L:** Coal Scuttle, 1875.

ago, a prominent New York decorator spent a summer collecting unique wood- and coal-burning stoves of the 1840–65 period, his cache of twenty-some stoves made the feature pages of metropolitan newspapers. Later, his collection of stoves was sold quick as a wink in the antiques corner of a department store. It is perhaps just as well that the junkmen of the 1900s who bought up these stoves at sixty cents a hundred pounds as scrap iron were not around to see them selling at sixty cents a pound. In 1942 I paid ninety dollars for a little Franklin stove and wondered if I had been had. Later I discovered that somebody had been had, but not me. Once sold as mass-produced staples in at least luxury form, the cast-iron stoves here pictured, or others so like them that there is no need to quibble about it, are now full and complete luxuries. No longer mass produced, they are scarce, desirable, and collected as antiques. Most of them were made in the early and mid-Victorian periods. Some were made during the reign of heavy Empire, and some date from Directoire and Sheraton inspired days—1810 to 1830. A few date from 1765. The early one is a Pennsylvania wood-burning ten-plate stove. All these stoves are fancy castings. They bear raised decoration upon the surface of the iron plates or parts. Many were built to stand immediately in front of a fireplace, connected directly with the fireplace flue by a short pipe through the metal shield which closed off the cavern of the fireplace. If you want andirons of iron and brass-trimmed iron, screens and other equipment for fireplaces, you can find them in the shops today. Dates range from about 1790 to 1850.

Quilts and Coverlets. Here we bite into a segment of textile antiques with enough facets, or shall we say enough threads, to occupy a collector full time and double time. Bedcovers, such as quilts and coverlets, whether pattern woven or having applied decoration, were the concern of the distaff side of America since the days of Jamestown and Plymouth Rock. The Dutch Dames of New Amsterdam and the Swedish and Dutch housewives on the Delaware were also concerned with these comforting elegancies. When woven, the early counterpointes, or counterpanes, displayed a raised diamond pattern from which the name "counterpointe" derives. In the less meticulous form of weaving, a heavy "towling," or coarse tow-linen thread, was used.

Top: Decorative Stoves, 1848–75. **Bottom:** Hooked Rug Patterns, 1870–90.

In the finer counterpointes, all fine threads were used. Thus essentially the same heavy cord as used in candlewicks was used in some counterpointe weaving in the seventeenth and eighteenth centuries. We have seen pattern-woven coverlets of linen using almost the same heavy tow-linen thread. Woolen coverlets, pattern woven in colors, usually two, and contrasting, but sometimes in three and even four colors, seem to have come into general use early in the nineteenth century. Many patterns, a host of which are displayed in that excellent book *Heirlooms from Old Looms*, published by the Coverlet Guild, were in general use. Coverlet weaving was carried on by individual weavers and factories, by itinerant weavers, and by workhouses, or prisons. Often the non-prison-woven coverlets are signed and dated, not infrequently bearing the name of the customer, or the person for whom the coverlet was woven. Most of these coverlets are of wool, or wool and cotton, or wool and linen. Some few were woven in light weight, of linen and cotton and all linen. The latter have some vestiges of the counterpointe pattern in their background.

Patch quilts is a name generally applied to pattern-appliquéd quilts and to actual patchwork quilts without sufficient differentiation. The pattern-appliquéd quilts are emphatically not patch quilts. They are made up of geometric patterns cut from the whole cloth (not rags, tags, and scraps), and they are needle-worked so finely that, on the reverse, plain, or all-white side, they carry the "pattern" in stitches alone. Patch quilts, actually made from "patches," are to be classed in several levels. There was the friendship quilt, made up of patches but not actual scraps, each prepared by a friend, and finally assembled as a quilt. And then there was the quilt made up of odds and ends of fancy fabrics—silks, velvets, lace, calico, et cetera—in triangular, parallelogram, rhomboid, and every other hit-or-miss geometrical pattern, feather- and cross-stitched together and stuffed with a blanket, cotton, or some other warmth-inducing material. These are, properly, "Crazy Quilts."

Hooked Rugs, according to William Winthrop Kent, represent a type of homecraft textile work carried to America by Swedish and Scottish settlers. Apparently the gentle art of hooking was a North Country practice. It is essentially a form

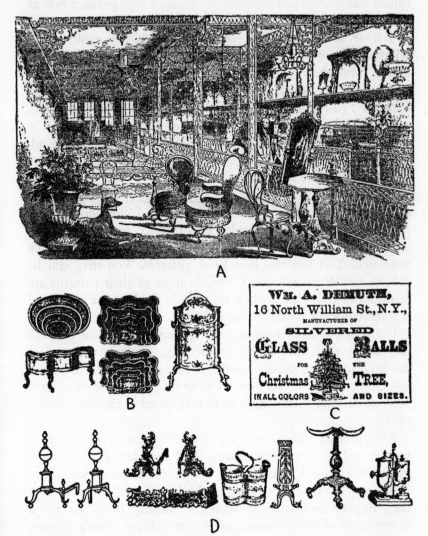

A: Iron Elegancies on Sale, 1854. **B:** Tray, Food-Warmer, and Coal Vase of Japannery. **C:** Christmas Balls, 1870. **D:** Andirons, 1810; Fire Tools, 1850; Wine Cooler; Bootjack; Footrest, and Coffee Urn, 1850.

of pulled tufting, achieved with bands of fabric rather than with tufted yarns. America enjoyed the hooked rug, perhaps first as a bedspread, and finally put it on the floor. But between bed and floor the hooked rug served for a while as table cover, window-sill cover, and mantel-shelf mat. It would seem also that at times chair seats were made in the hooked-rug technique.

All America became mad about hooked rugs when in 1870 Edward Frost began stenciling designs on burlap, or sacking, selling the finished product as a hooked-rug pattern. He made several hundred designs which were sold all over New England. Pond, of Biddeford, Maine, entered the business and then, at Dayton, Ohio, the Ross Company entered the scene about 1885. The latter firm did for the great Midwest what Frost and Pond did for New England—made good, easy-to-follow hooked-rug patterns available to all people. This resulted in the making of so many hooked rugs in the home that the output cannot be estimated. You can still buy Frost patterns. You may still be able to buy Ross patterns. Certainly most of their patterns are reproduced today in hooked rugs made in the same way, and not infrequently mistaken for old ones.

Collecting hooked rugs may be an engaging pursuit but, for the most part, it isn't antiques collecting. The vast majority of the hooked rugs available today are of twentieth-century making. Some of those you buy on your next excursion may have been made after these words were first typed in the late autumn of 1945.

Embroidered Pictures are a real elegancy today, just as they were a real elegancy when made. And very few of them were made. We would consider the era to cover many years, say from 1675 to 1835. They are in the British tradition, whether they display an American scene, a "fishing lady," or are a direct copy of some famous picture or element from a picture. The "fishing-lady" type is so called because it depicts a genre scene—a storytelling scene in which the lady is about to do some fishing and is equipped with angling tools. This type of embroidered picture was popular with the women and girls of eighteenth-century New England; with those having sufficient energy and patience to tackle the almost interminable job of embroidering a picture.

We can show here only pictures of hooked rugs and a few pattern-woven coverlet designs within this group of elegancies. But all of them, including even the rare embroidered pictures, can be found occasionally in most antiques shops of the better sort.

Boxes: Fancy and Painted. In old gardens boxwood was often planted in what was called a labyrinthine maze. That's the kind of Cretan puzzle we are in now in respect of fancy and painted boxes. It seems that some of these boxes were made in every American home between 1800 and 1850. It is likely that no two were alike. That is why we must confine this discussion to professionally made boxes designed for sale in shops.

Our files of Early American advertising contain no less than two hundred advertisements of fancy-box makers at work in 1820–50, and a similar number of advertisements by fancy stores having such boxes on sale. They were covered with fancy and colored papers, fancy paper tape, gilt, paper frills, colored engravings, and lithographic pictures. They were made to hold handkerchiefs, ribbons, bands, gloves, and toiletries; to pack gifts, candy, and comfits. Some experts aver they are not bandboxes if made of paper or card. They say the original bandboxes were made of thin band-sawed sheets of wood. But our authority says they were called bandboxes no matter of what they were made—if they were made to hold "bands."

There was a factory in New York State that made—shall we say millions, and be on the safe side?—tiny wooden boxes for pill manufacturers. There were others who made big ones for hatters and milliners. And then there were importers of Swiss-made painted bandboxes of oval shape, now popularly called Pennsylvania German brides' boxes. It is much to be doubted that a single one of these boxes was made in America. Making them involved a great deal of painting, not by stencil, but free-hand. Yet they sold at very low prices.

America even in 1820 had a scarcity of laboring hands. We could make bandboxes, quick-decorate them with fancy paper, and sell at a low price at a profit. But not hand-decorated brides' boxes. It was far cheaper to import them from countries where there was plenty of labor and where living costs and standards were 'way under ours. It is believed that the Swedes and

Dutch first brought the hand-painted bandboxes to America. There is plenty of evidence that this is true—and the evidence is not here but is, or was, in the Netherlands and in Sweden. Many of the boxes made in those countries, almost counterparts of the boxes found here, still remained in private and public collections before the war.

The date of these early boxes most likely is after 1750. The nineteenth-century imports seem to have come in after the War of 1812 and continued until about 1850. During that same period many pewter screw-top perfume bottles, of Swiss glass decorated in colored enamels, were imported. These, from 1915 to at least 1935, were often bought and sold as Stiegel glass. Some dealers are still of the belief that they are Stiegel. When such belief is held, the price asked for the bottles is high. When the dealer knows his glassware, the price is low. The moral is: buy from dealers who know their stock!

Musical Instruments. This is not the place to indulge in a historical discourse on how the piano of today evolved from harpsichord, dulcimer, and other keyboard instruments. Neither can we even scratch the surface of the story of pipe organ into melodeon, or how the music of the cathedral was put into the cottage parlor.

But what we can say is this: An early pianoforte, or harpsichord, is a thing of beauty as a piece of cabinet furniture. That it also provides music is a plus factor. Seek you a rather high table to place back of a sofa that is facing a fireplace? Then consider one of the five-foot-long yet narrow pianofortes of the 1785–1830 period. They have the mechanism hidden in a skirting ranging from eleven to fifteen inches deep. They stand on slender legs—in Hepplewhite, Sheraton, or Directoire style. There is a folding cover that goes over the keyboard and presto! it's a table; perhaps the very thing you've wanted.

Among our pictures is one that may give you pause—a Queen Anne "Staarstuck," a Clavecin à Queue—harpsichord to you. This instrument, as you read this, may be in private hands. But as it is written the writer wishes his purse were large enough to capture and own it. Imagine, it is a corner piece!

If a Queen Anne Staarstuck, invented and styled in the Netherlands, is to be found but once in a decade, there are compensations. Six antiques dealers in three hundred—one in fifty—reported one or more early pianofortes in stock. A word of warning must be injected here. When you buy such an instrument ask, "Is its mechanism in playing order, and is it tuned?" If the answer is yes—and it is true—that explains the price. It costs considerable money to put an early musical instrument of this kind into playing condition. Some, with wooden frames for the strings, must be tuned too often for comfort. Professional harpsichord players carry a tuner with them on tour. He tunes the instrument daily.

So maybe you'd better buy a melodeon? Go to it. You're apt to find a melodeon almost anywhere. We suspect that some millions of them were made and sold between 1835 and 1855. Some have lyre-shaped ends and other characteristics of early Federal cabinetwork. They're wind instruments—you pump the bellows pedal with your foot as you play with your hands. We have seen three-, four-, and five-octave melodeons, in good to fair working order, double in price in two years. What's happened? Two things. More Americans are again playing some sort of musical instrument and more Americans are collecting antiques. Also, a considerable number of melodeons, closed up tight, are serving as side tables.

Did you ever hear of a "spinet desk"—a desk-like piece converted from a "Colonial" spinet? Most spinet desks are converted from Empire style pianofortes and melodeons made in 1845–55. That's how Colonial they are. The question is asked and answered merely to pave the way for this admonition: don't buy such desks. They're neither flesh, fish, fowl, nor vegetable. Which is to say, they should be out of this world.

Our pictures show what kinds of musical instruments you can find in antiques shops in this day and age. If you will leaf through the advertising pages of any city or town directory before 1860, it's an even bet you'll find an advertisement by a pianoforte or melodeon manufacturer. These instruments in the nineteenth century were sold in stores, by postmasters, by traveling salesmen, and peddled over the countryside on wagons. They were sold from canal-boats stores and steamboat stores. They had them in San Francisco in 1849—and all over America they were in churches, schools, halls, and homes.

CHAPTER XI

Silver and Sheffield Plate

Collecting American silver is a delightful and satisfying pursuit. Sheffield plate, made in England, was imported to America in quantities sufficient to make it American by adoption. The Sheffield was imported mostly between 1790 and 1840. The silver was made here between 1680 and 1850. Thus the Sheffield you can collect covers approximately a half century of activity while the silver covers almost two centuries of time.

Today you can buy American silver made in the seventeenth century, or the eighteenth century, or the nineteenth century. The less demanding you are in respect of the period of making, the larger is the pool of silverware you can draw from in your collecting. Few general antiques shops have silver of any period prior to 1800 in stock. Silver has the habit of gravitating to silver shops—stores specializing in this most precious of specialties. Many antiques shops have American silver of the nineteenth century, say after 1810. About half of the antique or near-antique silver now extant was made after 1810. This may sound a bit confusing. If it does, we must consider that the growth of our nation after 1810 had considerable of the spectacular in it. Our frontiers were expanding at a rate that amazed the rest of the world. Cities grew up almost overnight. Money was made in manufacture, in speculation, in farming. Everybody was as good as anybody and, if they had the wherewithal, could own anything they fancied. The fancies were many and varied, and included silver.

This was not generally the case in Colonial days. From the very beginning of silver-making in the colonies down to 1800 the roster of silversmiths totals in all some two thousand names. In the year 1830 there were, approximately, 2,286 silversmiths at work. Most of these silversmiths made more silver in one year than the early silversmiths made in two, five, or even ten years. They had faster techniques, better tools, and more help. It might

American Silver, and Silver Advertising, 1801–50.

also be added they had more customers and less trouble getting the precious white metal. They could, if they so desired, make silver from ready-at-hand United States silver coins. One silversmith of 1830 had a saying, "A silver dollar makes a teaspoon."

The early silversmiths and their marks are fairly well tabulated. You can identify almost any marked silver made before 1800 by referring to the several volumes that have been published on the subject. On the other hand, very little has been done as yet about our nineteenth-century silversmiths. It is a job that needs doing, but it poses a problem of almost mountainous dimensions.

Philadelphia silversmiths from 1800 to 1850 are covered in Maurice Brix's *Philadelphia Silversmiths and Allied Artificers, 1682–1850. Maryland Silversmiths, 1750–1830*, by J. Hall Pleasants, contains twenty-nine years of nineteenth-century information. *Silversmiths of Delaware, 1700–1850*, by Jessie Harrington, and *South Carolina Silversmiths, 1690–1860*, by Milby Burton, are also informative in respect of nineteenth-century silversmiths of these several states. George B. and Minnie Warren Cutten's works on the silversmiths of New York State and Utica give us valuable data. *Early Ohio Silversmiths and Pewterers, 1787–1847*, by Rhea Mansfield Knittle, published in 1943, contains nineteenth-century silversmith records of the Buckeye State. From there we must turn to the various city and town directories, published between 1800 and 1850, and laboriously check every name in every directory to which is added the enlightening information "silversmith." Nice work for long evenings, if you can find the directories. Luckily, these directories, if scarce, are not rare. You can buy them or borrow them. And to them you must go if you want to know who made silver in your locality.

To the connoisseurs of today most nineteenth-century American silver is beyond the pale of interest. To the connoisseurs of 1960 our nineteenth-century silver may well be an item of intense interest. The silver isn't at all bad in design; it follows generally the designs then prevalent in pottery and china. There are silver tea sets of 1840 that look much like the china and pottery tea sets of the same period. Trays and salvers are somewhat in the form of the china platters decorated with historic views. There are silver cream pitchers of form comparable to the "silver

American Silver, 1750–90.

resist" lusterware of the period. Somehow our nineteenth-century silversmiths clung to the styles born in what we have called the Federal period in American furniture. They made very nice things. Some of the water pitchers have a form not unlike the glass pitchers made at Pittsburgh and at Sandwich. This is the silver of the nineteenth century you can collect. But identification of mark, place, et cetera, must be largely your own job.

We have heard of a collector of nineteenth-century American silver who is specializing in spoons. She would like to have spoons from every town in the United States, made by the silversmiths of that town. We had the pleasure of standing beside her as she culled over a cache of some hundred silver spoons in one antiques shop. Swiftly she turned them over and looked at the marks. One after the other went back into the drawer, but no less than a dozen went into her bag—at one dollar each! Later she whispered to me, "If you are wise you can buy early nineteenth-century silver for less than new sterling costs in jewelry stores." She is having fun collecting. If she persists in her nineteenth-century silver spoon collecting she will one day have an important collection, not only of silver but of nineteenth-century American silversmiths' marks.

Our pictures for this chapter are presented in several groups. One group deals with silver made in America prior to 1800. There may be some pieces of later date in this group but not enough to be concerned about. We cannot date silver accurately without precise knowledge of when the silversmiths made it. They didn't date their work. Hence we must approximate, by consideration of style and pattern, plus our knowledge of the period of years the smith was at work. Another group shows silver of the nineteenth century. Groups 3 and 4 are wholly Sheffield plate. Group 5 is American electroplated silver.

Sheffield plate is so vast a subject for study that one should begin by reading Frederick Bradbury's *History of Old Sheffield Plate*. But most amateur collectors are more interested in the objects they desire than in the categorical history of manufacture from first to last. It is, however, because we were interested in certain phases of Sheffield-plate history that we can display the pictures in Group 3. Each and every picture is lifted bodily from priced catalogues of Sheffield plate that were sent to America

Sheffield Plate.

for the use of importing houses. Sheffield firms of note issue these catalogues: James Dixon & Sons; and Love, Silverside, Darby & Co. Some idea of the magnitude of the Sheffield-plate business may be gathered from the fact that a catalogue issued by Theops-Richards & Company (1813–14), now in the possession of the Metropolitan Museum, bears the serial number 46,752!

"Where to buy it" and "what to buy" are the two major questions asked by the collector which this book can attempt to answer in words and pictures. The other double-barreled question, "What shall I pay—what is it worth?" is the one we duck answering. But not with the greatest of ease! Every day our office mail contains queries from somebody, somewhere, and almost invariably the gist of the query is, "What is it worth? And where can I sell it?" Some people are of the naïve opinion that because you write a book you should become an agent for the sale of antiques. Once, when we were very young, we tried to accommodate a correspondent. She had a painting and a piece of silver. We asked her to send photos and set a price. She did. We showed the photos and quoted the price to a dealer. He said, "Tell her to send it." We did. Back came the reply, "I think it is worth more." A new price was set. The dealer said O.K. once more. Again the owner thought the things were really worth more than she had asked the second time. The dealer got mad at me. I got mad at the lady. She got mad at me, suspected me of trying to cheat her—in fact, I was little short of being a crook.

When I told her that she had solicited my services unbid, that her two prices had been met and refused by her, her only reply was: "Don't think I don't know you are trying to make something out of this for yourself, and take advantage of me. Now that I know what the things are worth, I shall get every penny of it." One year later I happened to be in the town from whence the query had come. In an antiques shop I saw the very picture and the very piece of silver she had offered for sale. What price? The dealer gave me a price comparable to the first price the original owner had asked. Upon remarking that they must have been purchased for less than that, the dealer smiled. "Yes," he replied, "these were brought in by a very smart owner who was a bit too smart for her own good. She was offered a good price for them by a New York man but she tried to raise him. The

Sheffield Plate of the Kind Generally Available Today in Antiques and Specialty Shops.

agent in New York refused to do anything further for her. Then she discovered she couldn't get near the price offered and she just had to sell to me."

If we have any admonition it is, "Don't be coy" or "Don't play too smart for what you know." The latter is a colloquial expression picked up in a backwoods Pennsylvania town. Far too many owners of antiques have placed excessive emotional values and age on their own things. It is high time we stop thinking late Empire style is "Colonial" and that any piece is over two hundred years old just because a great-grandmother once owned it.

If you have old silver or old Sheffield, and want to sell it, offer it to the specialized dealers in silver and Sheffield or run an advertisement in the classified columns of such magazines as *American Collector, Hobbies, Antiques,* or the magazine of the Americana Foundation. If what you have interests the readers, you'll have action. But don't say "best offer takes it." Smart people shy away from such advertising. They know you are running a kind of auction, and that finally you may not accept the best offer. You may change your mind, keep the things, and put a new value upon them—perhaps 50 per cent above the best offer you have received. No auction gallery can operate that way. Most individuals soon discover they can't operate that way either.

The silver that collectors consider true silver is, of course, solid silver. American silversmiths of the seventeenth and eighteenth centuries followed, as best they could, the silver standard established by law in England. During and after the Revolution, and until we established "sterling" as the American standard, our silversmiths considered coin silver as "pure." Sterling, as a name, is said to derive from the "easterlings" who, in the fourteenth century, were given the task of refining the silver mined in England. About 1350 the term sterling was used to designate refined silver fit for coin. The word sterling was not stamped on silver plate. That sentence, because of the confusion still current in respect of silver terms, requires explanation. Silver plate did not, and should not now, mean plated silver. It means plate made of pure silver, and includes salvers, dishes, trays, pots, cans,

American Electroplated Silver, 1845-80.

beakers, and other vessels, eating tools and all other pure silver objects.

"Sheffield plate" was so called by law because it was not true silver plate, but plate with a center of copper or sometimes of white metal. This quite sensible composite metal, made legally and under strict control for well over a century in England, did, however, result from skulduggery on the part of early silversmiths who put a core of tin between two sheets of silver and still called their product solid plate. Sheffield was made into practically all objects generally used with the exception of knives, forks, and spoons. There are Sheffield salvers, trays, candlesticks, tea and coffee pots, inkwells, communion flagons and cups, altar wares, and a host of other objects now almost readily available to collectors of this lovely ware. It is all of English production and has the copper core between the inner and outer, or upper and lower, layers of pure silver—a sandwich of two layers of silver in sheet form with a sheet of copper between. The two plates of silver, together, are about as thick as the copper filling. This percentage of silver was usually maintained in Sheffield wire, which was rolled from bars of copper wrapped with a layer of pure silver and then drawn, as wire, for finishing the edges of some Sheffield wares, or worked into baskets and other elegancies. When not finished with a wire edging, the edges and rims of Sheffield wares were lapped, or rolled, to cover the copper core with a sheet of silver.

America did not produce Sheffield plate, but at about the same time the makers of Sheffield were turning to electroplating (C. 1845) many silverware manufactories in this country began the making of electroplated wares. Certain of these early makers are still in business. Other of our silversmiths did not enter the plated-silver field but applied mass-production methods to the manufacture of solid-silver wares. Rogers Brothers is a shining example of the former and the Gorham Company is one of the early American firms that has continued to produce solid silver. Gorham, of course, has stamped its silver "sterling" for many decades.

Early English silver of the seventeenth and eighteenth centuries, and not a little made in the early nineteenth century, was contemporaneously sold in this country. Tremendous quantities

Bill for American Silverware, 1822.

of this silver have been imported by antiques dealers during the past forty years. Collectors of early English silver are in the happy position—thanks to the remarkably complete records of the goldsmiths' and silversmiths' guilds and companies of Britain —of knowing who made it and when. There are hallmarks on English silver which indicate maker, place, and year—a practice not followed by our Colonial silversmiths and not mandatory in our Federal era.

One other kind of silver that is distinctly American, and yet not of North America, deserves passing mention. We refer to Peruvian silver, mined in America and fabricated by European workmen who had emigrated to Peru. Some of this silver may have been made by native workmen trained by Spanish silver-smiths. Basins, bowls, cooking utensils, and even chamber pots were made of silver in Peru. Some of it has a sheen almost like highly polished pewter—and is almost as heavy as pewter because it is not hammered as thin as most English and North American silver.

American plated silver, and solid silver made after 1830 are not to be despised now by any active or coming collector. Neither is it out of order to have your early but worn plated silver replated. It is wiser to buy it old and worn and have the replating done by a good plater to your order than to buy replated old wares of American make.

Silver, Sheffield plate, and plated silver! Here are the pictures. Under them are captions intended to be helpful. There is no effort at history making, or compressing a hundred-page mono-graph into ten. Read such books as those mentioned in the text, or the following listed volumes. Read them before you collect and as you collect old silver, Sheffield plate, and American plated silver.

American Silversmiths & Their Marks, by Stephen G. C. Ensko.
Early American Silver, by C. Louise Avery.
Historic Silver of the Colonies and Its Makers, by Francis Hill Bigelow.
American Silversmiths, by Ernest Currier.
The Book of Old Silver, by Seymour Wyler

CHAPTER XII

Pewter and Britannia

Pewter has been made in America since early in the seventeenth century. It is still made, although it is doubtful whether the early pewterers would recognize the metal, or the alloy, we designate as commercial pewter today. They might, however, envy its quality. The finest pewter also was a metal unknown to our own earliest pewterers. They worked, mostly, with a metal alloy of soft, sad quality. Sad, of course, meaning "heavy" and not "lugubrious." Some experts aver that no pewter with lead in it has been discovered at the assay table. Nonetheless by the seventeenth century the original right or true pewter had been cheapened with lead and other low-melting metals. The original pewter alloy was of tin and copper—80 to 90 per cent tin and 10 to 20 per cent copper—essentially a white bronze, almost the same as that of the Chinese. Tutenag was another name for it.

There is no seventeenth-century American pewter available to collectors. This is not to say there is not a single piece of it around. There is some, but it isn't in antiques shops. All that collectors can hope to find is eighteenth- and nineteenth-century pewter—the cheap ware made between 1740 and 1840. After 1840 it became Britannia, at least in terms of popularity—a harder, whiter, tougher, and more brittle metal, fashioned into utensils in factories and sold everywhere in stores. Some of it was silver plated and otherwise dressed up to look aristocratic. And it did just that. Made in the same general styles followed by silverware manufacturers, Britannia ware was available everywhere, and purchased by everyone.

Most collectible pewter is of a date after 1760. Rarity is no longer a matter of date but a matter of object and maker. Perhaps the most sought after pewter today, and certainly the highest priced pewter in America, was made by the Lancaster, Pennsylvania, pewterer John Christopher Heyne, who worked

1754–1785. His ware is marked "ICH" and "ICH LANCAS-TER." Heyne was a master tinsmith who took over a trading post, founded in Lancaster, 1744, and operated it for a number of years. He married the widow of Christopher Steinman, who had a young son. This son succeeded to the Heyne business. The firm is still in operation as the Steinman Hardware Company.

Heyne's marked pewter is now excessively rare. Not over half a dozen pieces of record have been tabulated. Heyne pewter is therefore tops in rarity—and price—with little more than its rarity, to give it its high, exalted position. Yet Heyne made a great deal of pewter and tinware. And that statement is not conjecture. The account books are preserved. We can know exactly what this man sold, from pewter to pins, during his years of operation. His was a store of many resources. In going over the books we discovered he had sold a "bowle of Shangaree," a "Wine-sling," a "garden hoa," and some "horse furniture" to an ancestor. His sales of pewter and tinware were considerable. What happened to his stuff? Well, for one thing, there was a revolutionary war. Lancaster was a center of rifle and rifle-ball making during that war. Lead was rather scarce. Pewter, in the form of housewares, abounded. More than one British and Hessian soldier carried pewter, in the form of a rifle ball, home in his hide.

One error we sometimes make is in thinking the revealed history of a certain pewterer (or any other craftsman) is evidence that that artisan was unique. What happened in respect of Heyne's pewter happened in respect of the work of other pewterers. If *all* the pewter of an early craftsman was destroyed, we have no concrete record of the man or his mark. Yet many town records contain names of taxables designated as pewterers or tinsmiths, none of whose pewter has survived. Of course, says the pundit, collecting names of obscure pewterers isn't collecting pewter. But a pundit did the original guessing about I.C.H. pewter when a beautiful flagon so marked was offered for sale, and his guess was about as wide of the mark as that of an amateur guessing the distance in miles to the constellation Lyra.

One of America's great collections of pewter has been in process of disposal over a period of several years. Many dealers have enriched their stocks from this fount, and not a little of the

Top: Very Early Pewterer's Bill, 1759.
Bottom: Philadelphia Pewterer's Advertisement, 1765, and Britannia Advertisement, 1856.

pewter has already passed through auction rooms even though the collection from which it came is far from dispersed. How good your chances are of getting a modest collection of pewter together may be judged from the fact that one dealer who answered the voluminous questionnaire we sent to some three hundred shops did it by returning a sixteen-page list of pewter he had in stock! In addition, he had suggested "Collections" representative of American pewter of the eighteenth and nineteenth centuries, for museums and shrines to purchase en bloc.

Do you live in or come from a city or town founded before 1750? If so, there is a better than an even chance there was a pewterer at work there, and perhaps two, or even a score of them. That means you have a good chance of collecting hometown pewter. Also, if you like, you can collect only plates of a certain size, by as many different pewterers as your resources permit.

American pewter is to be had in the form of platters, plates, dishes, bowls, flagons, cans, beakers, flasks, mugs, ladles, spoons, et cetera.

Pewter marks, as used by our American craftsmen, are of wide scope and varied design. We know of one collector who has this project in mind: buying only damaged, incomplete, and badly battered pieces, so long as the pewterer's mark is intact. The marks are to be cut out, in the form of badges of uniform size, in order to create a collection of American pewterers' touch marks.

That isn't nearly so destructive a project as the one started by a young lad who in 1858 wanted to collect the newfangled postage stamps that Uncle Sam was putting on mail. His father forbade his removing stamps from letters. So the lad began collecting furniture makers' labels off the antiques (only they were then just old furniture) in his father's and his grandmother's homes! The rascal had pulled off half a dozen before he was stopped, perhaps by the judicious application of a razor strop at precisely the right place. He kept his collection in the family Bible. There it stayed. And that is how we have learned that one Michael Lund, a Swedish cabinetmaker of Pennsylvania, made walnut chairs in the Queen Anne style as late as 1753.

If you want to know all about American pewter, read and

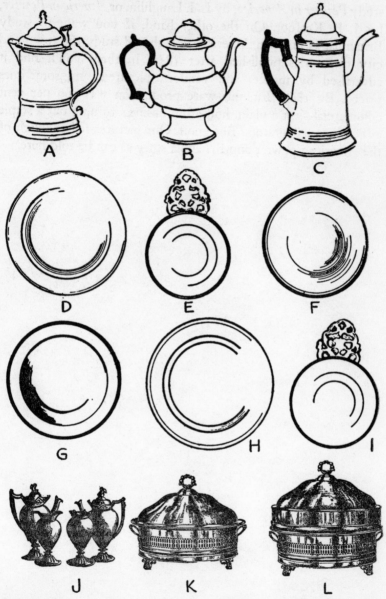

A, B, and C: Pewter Flagon and Two Teapots. D, E, and F: Pewter Porringer and Plates. G, H, and I: Pewter Basin, Plate, and Porringer. J: Britannia Ware, 1865. K and L: Britannia Chafing Dishes, 1884.

study *Pewter in America*, by L. I. Laughlin, or *American Pewter*, by J. B. Kerfoot. On the other hand, if you want to study Britannia, as made in America, you should study the town and city directories published after 1840. In them you'll find it advertised by makers and vendors, pictured, and sometimes priced. By 1860 Britannia-ware production was 100 per cent commercial—just a plain, humdrum business turning out a staple as common as potatoes. But good. Our pictures tell as much of the American pewter and Britannia story as can be told here.

CHAPTER XIII

Lamps and Candlesticks

Someone has said (perhaps merely to make a joke, or perhaps to hide a great deal of wisdom under the cloud of humor) that, in America, "our first lamp was a crude copy of the Roman lamp, hung on a string to lower into a cook-pot to see what was cooking, without dropping candle grease into the pot." It may sound silly, but the statement is substantially true. The betty lamp, apparently our first oil- (or fat) burning lamp, is said to have been used primarily for cook-pot peering. While the betty lamp is far from the classic Roman lamp in form, it is one with it in principle. Made of copper, sheet iron, tin, and any other metal the tinker could use, betty lamps were made for strictly utilitarian purposes. It is much to be doubted whether any household used them instead of candles, or in preference to candles, for general lighting purposes.

The use of candles called for candlesticks to hold the burning tapers. These were a common item of household equipment, every home having from a few to a few dozen candlesticks. They were made of iron, tin, stone, pottery, wood, glass, brass, silver, and pewter. Many of these have survived the years. Some—now considered antiques—haven't survived very long. This because candlesticks have been made continuously down through the years and are still made, of practically all the substances mentioned above. By their styles shall ye know them, excepting the outright fakes of brass. And to detect those requires experience of the sort this *First Reader* cannot impart.

The pictures of candlesticks, candelabra, and other taper-holding devices here displayed are the kinds you can now find in many antiques shops. You'll not find all kinds in all shops for several reasons. The better shops will not stock some of them. The smaller shops cannot afford to stock fine brass and silver candlesticks. When they find them they strive at once to turn them over quickly, either to an advanced collector or to another dealer.

All Sheffield-plate candlesticks are, of course, British-made and most of them bear identifying marks. Eighteenth-century silver candlesticks of American make are identifiable if marked; identification of the nineteenth-century made candlesticks of silver or silver plate (and there were hundreds of thousands made) will pose you something of a problem. This because few nineteenth-century silversmiths have as yet been tabulated. You'll not find in any books on American silver the name of Mrs. Luckey of Pittsburgh, a lady silversmith who worked in the western Pennsylvania city between 1830 and 1840. Similarly, thousands of silversmiths working between 1801 and 1850 in almost every city and town in America are yet to be tabulated and their marks studied and pictured.

Early American lamps are largely Federal period items. By lamps is meant specifically an oil-burning device with wick or other means of combustion, to provide a bright flame useful as a light. The equivalent of a lamp was the candlestick in hurricane or other type of shade, and also the open-flame, oil-burning, twin-wick pewter arrangement that had the wicks set between two magnifying lenses. But these are steps toward the true lamp, whether in the form of an oil-burning device with reservoir pegged to fit into a candlestick socket, or a lamp constructed as a lighting unit without reference to adaptation to any other form of lighting fixture.

The history of better lighting really begins with the invention of the Argand burner in 1780 and the various improvements thereon; with the invention of illuminating gas and the establishment of central gas generators and piping through city streets to homes after 1820; and with the discovery of petroleum in Pennsylvania in 1859. This is not to suggest that lamp history had three separate and distinct beginnings but to point out the three great discoveries that boomed lamp making and, in succession, gave the candle another push toward oblivion as a home-lighting device. By 1810 there was an American lamp factory turning out lamps on a mass-production basis. By 1825 there were at least half a hundred lamp factories in operation.

Very few early lamps, from the Argand burners of 1780 to

Mrs. Shields   Philad.ᵃ Jan.ᵞ 20ᵗʰ 1804

Bᵗ of Sam.ˡ F Bradford

1 Pair Mantle Lamps —— $120 —

X.ᵈ Payment in full
for S. F Bradford
Thoˢ Rogers

Mrˢ Roth   Bought of Abm̄ Van W. Syn
January 30th 1824,

1 Vase Lamp $12.c
Feby 10 Received the above in full
Abm̄ Van W Syn

Mr Smith   Boston, Sept 3, 1835.

Bought of Alfred Welles & Co.

LAMP AND FURNISHING WAREROOMS, 82 WASHINGTON STREET,
Manufacturers of Silver Ware, and Importers of Plated Ware, Cutlery, Watches, Military Goods, &c.

1	Entry Lamp	$5 40
1	Peg Lamp	2 50
	Japᵈ Side "	3 50
	" Hang Astral $11, 5 0

Recᵈ payᵗ Alfred Welles & Cᵒ

Bills for Lamps, 1804, 1824, 1835.

the camphene-burning lamps of America, 1800 to 1840, are now articles of general stock in antiques shops. Don't ask why. It may be that in spite of early general availability of lamps, most people got rid of their old ones as soon as new, better, and cheaper ones were made. The camphene-burning lamp was not an entirely safe device. At times these lamps exploded, causing fires. Early issues of the *Scientific American* are filled with new safety-lamp inventions, some of which brought the inventors considerable fortunes. Our pictures show the lamps you can buy today, and a number of advertisements of lamps dating from 1800 to 1840.

Antiques lamp buying has taken a weird trend in recent years. The kerosene-burning lamps of the 1880–1900 period are selling at prices that would give the original makers—and the stores that once sold them—either heart failure or ulcers. Lamps which once sold for $1.98 now sell at from $20 to $40. Student lamps, made in the 1880s and 1890s and then selling from $2.50 to $7.50, now sell at from $35 to $150. As one dealer said to me, "This is the craziest business imaginable! I had some really good early lamps at bargain prices and a few monstrosities my grandfather bought at wholesale in 1893 and couldn't sell. I wish he'd bought a carload of the monstrosities and stored them all in the cellar. I could sell them now at about one dollar on every five cents of original investment. That's five times better than 6 per cent interest, compounded semi-annually."

Gone-with-the-Wind lamps is what they call them. Yet only the very earliest models could have been in Scarlett O'Hara's last mansion. Few of these lamps were made before 1885. But after that year production began to hum. By 1890 it was a business that had representation—and stock—in several stores in every village and town. In cities there were lamp emporiums and lamp departments in furniture stores, crockery and china stores, and department stores. The lamps, now the rage, were then, also, a rage. Oil-burning lamps, mind you, a rage in the era of gas! It was crazy then, and it is crazy now. Yet I have bought several of the lamps. You, perhaps, have done the same thing. The woman who takes care of my mimeographing and addressing has a *Gone-with-the-Wind* lamp on her desk. Another of our researchers has two in her home. Modern department stores

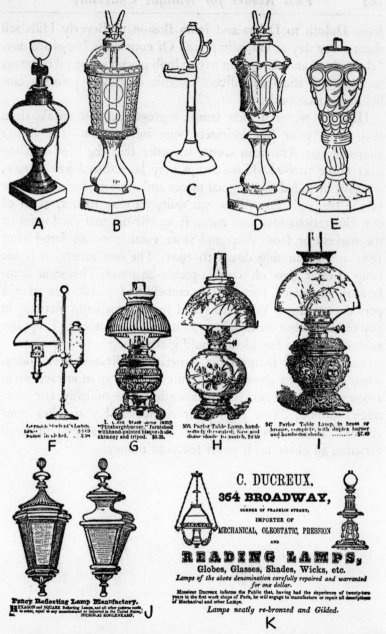

A, B, C, D, and E: Safety Lamps of 1850; Early "Betty" Lamp with Pewter Stand and Glass Oil Font. F, G, H, and I: Look at the Lamps of 1890 and the prices! J and K: Lamp Advertising, 1833 and 1853.

from Duluth to Dallas and from Boston to Beverly Hills sell them every day at fantastic prices. Of course the lamps are now "electrified" and some even have a bulb placed in the oil reservoir to show off the "magnificent" scenic or flower painting embellishing that basin.

Here are pictured these lamps, segregated, so to speak, from their now poor but infinitely superior relations—the earlier lamps of our American scene. In order that the head-swelling over *Gone-with-the-Wind* lamps may be reduced just a trifle, we have included the original prices and descriptions with a few of the lamp pictures. This was quite an easy matter, as all of our illustrations save one come from the original catalogues of the makers or from shop and store catalogues—all dated after 1882 and continuing down to 1901. The one exception is the lamp of clear glass, blown in a pickle-jar mold. That same flamboyant, embossed rose design embellished pickle jars of the period 1880–1900. We have failed to find this lamp pictured in any catalogue but we now bow in its direction, not as a lamp, but as an example of late blown-mold glassmaking.

These are the lamps most American collectors seek today. They constitute a showing not unlike a midway of attractions at a country fair. Again, all we can add is the midway (or race-track) phrase, "You pays your money and you takes your choice." What you fancy in these lamps, in several hundred varieties, all different, is yours for your money!

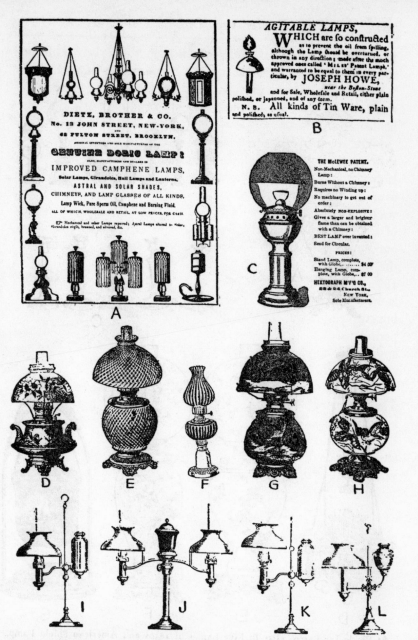

A, B, and **C:** Lamp Advertising, 1854, 1800, and 1884. **D, E, F, G,** and **H:** Five Lamps of 1890, Highest Price $6.50—in 1890! **I, J, K,** and **L:** Student Lamps, 1872.

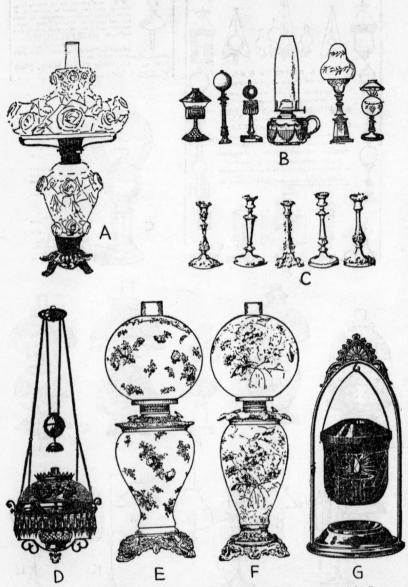

A: Pickle-Jar Lamp, 1890. **B:** Five Lamps of 1850s and American Shield Lamp, 1880. **C:** Sheffield Candlesticks, 1810–40. **D, E,** and **F:** Three Lamps of 1890–1900. **G:** Gothic Wax Light, 1892.

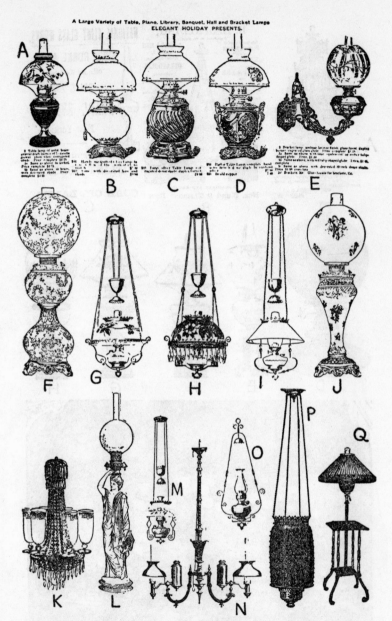

A, B, C, D, and E: Gone-with-the-Wind Applies to the Prices at Least, 1891.
F, G, H, I, and J: Hanging Lamps and Parlor Lamps, 1896–1900. K to Q: Over
a Century of Light: Chandelier, 1770; Figure Lamp, 1850; Hanging "Student"
and Hall Lamps, 1870–98; Table Lamp, 1900.

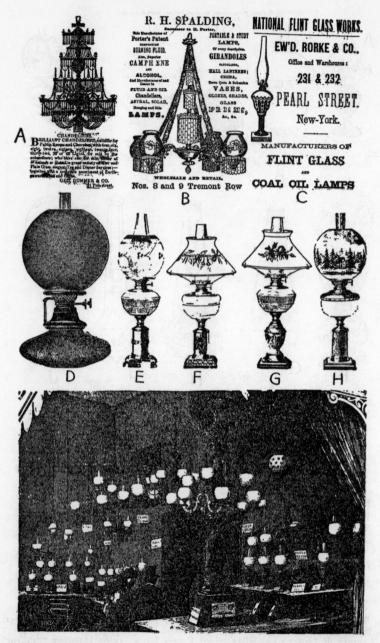

A, B, and **C:** Chandeliers of 1824 and 1854; Lamp Advertisement, 1860. **D, E, F, G,** and **H:** Plain Lamp for Home Decorating, 1900; Four Decorated Lamps, 1888; Tucker's American Lamps Win First Prize, Paris Exposition, 1867.

CHAPTER XIV

Pottery and China

In the year 1830 America had in round numbers some 12,700,000 inhabitants. To supply the pottery and stoneware demands of that population, between five hundred and fifty and six hundred potteries were in operation. Some of these potteries had but one kiln for the firing of wares. Others had two, three, four, and even six kilns. Wares made included cake pots, butter churns, milk bowls, water jars, jugs, bottles, preserving jars, flowerpots, cream pots, pie dishes, ovenwares, spittoons, stove tubes, soap dishes, pitchers, ewers, bean and pudding pots, and baking dishes.

Some fearful and wonderful things were made by potters when the whim took them or when a customer or group of customers demanded something special in offhand work. A great deal of what is called gray stoneware, decorated with a little or a lot of curlicue work in cobalt blue, was made. Earthenware, or red clay pottery, decorated with a few twists of white slip forming crude tulips, birds, flowers, et cetera, was made. Almost all of the objects made in stoneware were made also in earthenware. And almost all of what was made, categorically, is still to be found in antiques shops from coast to coast. So much of everything was made by American potters during the first fifty years of the nineteenth century that examples of about every item they made have survived in considerable numbers.

A certain amount of this pottery, especially the stoneware, is marked. Frequently the marking is impressed in the ware somewhere upon the face and, at times, on the bottom. Also, it is found marked with stamps, in blue, and on rare occasions the marking is brush-traced in blue. Some of the jugs are embellished with lovely tulips, scratch-outlined, and colored blue. Certain pro-Germanic experts would have you believe these are Pennsylvania-made jugs. Our researchers traced most of them to New York State and western New England potteries. A few potters seem to have persisted in marking certain of their jugs with a crude scratched or painted representation of a bearded man. Colloquially these were named "pope's head" or "pope's nose" jugs. They are a late survival of the Dutch Bellarmine jugs which caricatured Cardinal Bellarmino. Again these seem to be of New York State and New England production.

The geographic distribution of potteries seems to have been almost in line with population density, at least until transportation facilities by land and water permitted shipping the production cheaply and expeditiously. With the advent of canals, steamboats, and railroads, potters, no less than furniture makers, could extend their distribution and hence extend themselves in production. More than one arkload of pottery came down the Erie Canal to Albany and down the Hudson to New York. Norwich pottery moved by boat as far south as Baltimore and Charleston. Some idea of pottery and stoneware production may be gathered from the few original lists and advertisements pictured in this section along with the wares. The potteries of Bennington were started in 1793 by Captain John Norton, who had guarded Major André at the time of that unfortunate officer's execution as a spy. By 1795 the Bennington pottery had two kilns. The pottery expanded further under the management of sons and grandsons until finally, in 1845, Julius Norton took in a partner named Christopher Fenton.

Partner Fenton left Norton in 1847 and founded his own "United States Pottery." Fenton was not a master potter but he was a typical exemplar of American ingenuity. He "thought to produce," and he projected his thinking into the concrete. So well did he plan, design, and employ good men that he has been called the American Wedgwood. Fenton's pottery made hound-handled pitchers, cow creamers, curly-maned lions, coachman bottles, Toby jugs, reclining deer, Parian wares, and a vast amount of what is called scroddled ware, Rockingham ware, and flint ware, before it failed in 1858.

In the research work for this book we unearthed advertising by at least fifty potteries operating between 1800 and 1850 which, unfortunately, we cannot produce here. But what can be said as a contribution to the knowledge of the amateur col-

Top: Hound-Handled Pitcher, 1830, and Gaudy Dutch Plate.
Bottom: Pottery Advertising, Lancaster, Pennsylvania, and Geddes, New York, 1850.

lector is that stoneware was made in such quantities that apparently this ware was America's favorite household pottery; that scratch and cobalt-blue colored stoneware is the earliest, and that cobalt-blue decorated ware, without scratching, is the later ware. Thus we find Early American stoneware made in the tradition of the stoneware of England perhaps best exemplified in the George Rex (G.R.) jugs. These jugs are now scarce, but you should find at least one in, say, every fiftieth antiques shop. The more complete and well stocked the shop, the greater the chances of finding one.

Earthenware, in the manner of early Staffordshire pottery, with slip decoration, seems to have been a favorite with the potters of Pennsylvania. Tulips and birds, lifted almost bodily from early Staffordshire ware, embellish the Pennsylvania product. The Staffordshire dates from 1670 to 1720. The Pennsylvania ware dates from about 1750 to 1900. Yes, you read that quite correctly. Some of it dates from 1920—faked wares in imitation of the old, but made to sell at "antiques" prices. Certain of this production, it is alleged, derived from Honey Brook, Pennsylvania. Certainly it comes from that neighborhood. No less than fifty pieces of it have been sold in the past several years and have brought real antiques prices. Perhaps this happened only because it came from famed collections, upon whom the fakes were unloaded by a little clique of Pennsylvania "runners" and "traders" in antiques.

Almost no early Pennsylvania slip-decorated or the even scarcer sgraffito ware (decoration scratched through a coating of one colored clay to a base of clay of another color) of the late eighteenth and early nineteenth centuries will today be found in antiques shops. Most of the dated pieces are in museums and private collections and bear dates in the 1800s—down to 1850. The earliest known piece of slip ware attributed to a Pennsylvania potter is dated 1733. This was formerly in the Danner Museum at Manheim, Pennsylvania, but may now be in the museum at Hershey, Pennsylvania. When we say "attributed" we mean deliberately to question its Pennsylvania source. It is a barber's basin with a notch to fit the customer's neck. It bears the inscription "*Putz und Balwir mich heibsh und fein das ich gefal der leibste mein, 1733* [Clean and shave me nicely and fine

Worcester, _____ 18

M

Bought of **F. B. NORTON & CO.,**

MANUFACTURERS AND DEALERS IN

STONE WARE OF ALL KINDS,

WASHINGTON SQUARE, WORCESTER, MASS.

F. B. NORTON. | All Orders by mail promptly attended to. | F. HANCOCK.

JUGS.

	Per Dozen.
Doz. 4 Gallon, - -	$9,00
" 3 " - -	7,00
" 2 " - -	5,00
" 1 " - -	3,00
" 1-2 " - -	2,00
" 1-4 " - -	1,25
" 1-8 " - -	0,75

COVERED CREAM POTS.

Doz. 4 Gallon, - -	$10,00
" 3 " - -	8,00
" 2 " - -	6,00
" 1 " - -	4,00

CHURNS.

Doz. 6 Gallon, - -	$12,00
" 5 " - -	11,00
" 4 " - -	9,00
" 3 " - -	7,00
" 2 " - -	5,00

COVERED PRESERVE JARS.

Doz. 4 Gallon, - -	$9,00
" 3 " - -	7,50
" 2 " - -	6,00
" 1½ " - -	4,75
" 1 " - -	4,00
" 1-2 " - -	2,25
" 1-4 " - -	1,50

CORK TOMATO JARS.

Doz. 1-2 Gallon, - -	$2,25
" 1-4 " - -	1,50

Pudding Pots, Doz. 1 Gallon,	$3,00
" " " ½ "	2,00
Bean Pots, " 1 "	3,00
" " " ½ "	2,00

BUTTER POTS, COVERED.

	Per Dozen.
Doz. 6 Gallon. - -	$15,00
" 5 " - -	12,00
" 4 " - -	10,00
" 3 " - -	8,00
" 2 " - -	6,00
" 1 1-2 " - -	5,00
" 1 " - -	4,00
" 1-2 " - -	3,40

COVERED CAKE POTS.

Doz. 4 Gallon, - -	$10,00
" 3 " - -	8,00
" 2 " - -	6,00
" 1 " - -	4,00

PITCHERS.

Doz. 2 Gallon, - -	$5,00
" 1 1-2 " - -	4,00
" 1 " - -	3,00
" 1-2 " - -	2,00
" 1-4 " - -	1,25

FLOWER POTS.

Doz. 4 Gallon, - -	$9,00
" 3 " - -	7,00
" 2 " - -	5,00
" 1 " - -	3,00
" 1-2 " - -	2,00
" 1-4 " - -	1,50
" 1-8 " - -	1,00
Stove Tubes, Doz. 1st size,	6,50
" " " 2d "	4,50
" " " 3d "	3,00
Spittoons, Doz. 1st size,	7,00
" " 2d " -	5,00
" " 3d "	3,00
Beer Bottles, per doz. net	0,75
Soap Dishes, " "	1,50
Water Kegs, per gallon,	33 1-3

Received Payment,

Billhead, Norton Pottery, 1850.

so that I'll please my loved one]." In our opinion this basin is Swiss. The lettering upon it is done in a manner completely foreign to the style of the German immigrants who were beginning to enter Penn's Haven in great numbers by 1733, but it is in the style of Swiss slip ware of that period.

Another interesting light upon this Pennsylvania pottery is that certain of the very finest pieces are lettered in English, not German. A magnificent sgraffito dish, dated 1762, perhaps the finest piece of the ware ever found, is inscribed in English all around the rim of the plate. But enough has been said about a ware which in its finer forms is off the antiques market and which in its coarser forms it is well to avoid altogether if it shows any signs of newness. If you'd like other authority on the non-Germanic source of Pennsylvania pottery and the decorations appearing upon it, read the chapters on American pottery in Warren Cox's *Pottery and Porcelain*. He explodes the myth in a few well-chosen paragraphs.

Tucker, and Tucker & Hemphill of Philadelphia, 1825 to 1840, made an excellent near-porcelain of the soft paste variety, beautifully decorated in the French taste. Which is to say, Tucker porcelain is decorated with painted scenes, with colorful flowers in clusters, and gold banded. It reflects the taste and style of its period of manufacture. Tucker porcelain achieved a considerable distribution during the years of its production. It was sold in New England, Ohio, and down the Ohio River Valley. Some of it was sold in Natchez and New Orleans. No doubt St. Louis dealers also sold it as the newest American-made china in 1836.

There is still considerable Oriental export porcelain, or "Lowestoft," to be found in the shops. Mantel garnitures in this ware are rather rare, but teacups, saucers, service plates, tea caddies, and even teapots are to be found. On the day this is written, two Lowestoft teacups with matching saucers were found on sale in a Greenwich Village antiques shop whose stock at first glance seemed to be only pressed glass.

English chinaware, historic blue china, Liverpool historic pitchers, and even early Staffordshire slip-decorated wares are still to be had. So, also, are the statuary bottles made by Denby & Codnor Park at the Bournes Pottery, Derbyshire, by Doulton & Watts' Lambeth Pottery, and other nineteenth-century Eng-

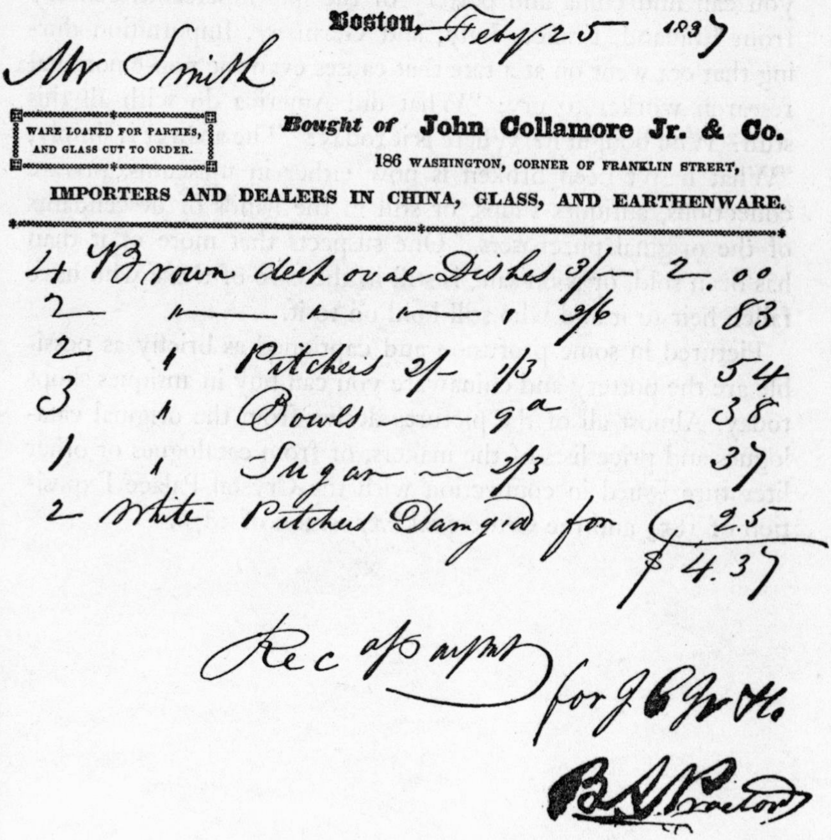

Boston, Feby 25 1837

Mr Smith

WARE LOANED FOR PARTIES,
AND GLASS CUT TO ORDER.

Bought of John Collamore Jr. & Co.

186 WASHINGTON, CORNER OF FRANKLIN STREET,

IMPORTERS AND DEALERS IN CHINA, GLASS, AND EARTHENWARE.

4	Brown deep oval Dishes	3/—		2	00
2	,, ,, ,, ,,	1	3/6		83
2	,, Pitchers	2/—	1/3		54
3	,, Bowls	—	9ᵃ		38
1	,, Sugar	—	2/3		37
2	White Pitchers Damg'd for			25	
				$4	37

Rec⁴ ⁰⁄ ₚₐyₘₜ ₛor J C Jr & Co.

B A Crawford

Bill for China and Pottery, 1837.

lish potters. Staffordshire cottages, ornaments and busts, Toby jugs, Parian, Wedgwood, Spode, and a score of other eighteenth- and nineteenth-century potted wares are represented on the shelves and in the cases of antiques shops from Maine to California, and from Duluth to New Orleans. In these same shops you can find china and pottery of the mid-nineteenth century from England, France, Italy, and Germany. Importation during that era went on at a rate that causes even the non-emotional research worker to cry: "What did America do with all this stuff? Who bought it? Where is it today?" The answer is simply, "What hasn't been broken is now either in museums, private collections, antiques shops, or still in the hands of descendants of the original purchasers." One suspects that more of it than has been sold, or is on sale, is still in the care of those who have fallen heir to it and who still hold on to it.

Pictured in some profusion and captioned as briefly as possible are the pottery and chinaware you can buy in antiques shops today. Almost all of the pictures derive from the original catalogues and price lists of the makers, or from catalogues or other literature issued in connection with the Crystal Palace Exposition of 1853 and the Centennial Exposition of 1876.

BOSTON, *Jany 4th* 183 5

Mrs Smith

Bought of **SAMUEL B. PIERCE & CO.**

IMPORTERS OF CROCKERY, CHINA & GLASS WARE,

NOS. 11, 12, 13, & 14, UNION STREET.

1½ df Bro Plates	/ —	150
2 ″ ″ Cupplate	3/9	92
1 ″ ″ Coffees		150
1 Cov^d Chamber		88
~~½ df Cut Tumblrs~~		~~2.00~~
2 ″ plain printed do	6/	280
1 China Sugar		87
1 ″ Stone Nappie		42
6 Bro Dishes	1/3	125
Recd Payt		$9.34

Saml B. Pierce & Co

Bill for China and Pottery, 1835.

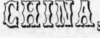

DAVIS COLLAMORE,

IMPORTER OF

CHINA, GLASS,

AND

CROCKERY WARE,

NO. 447 BROADWAY,

Near Grand Street, NEW YORK.

Particular attention is given to the selection of the purest quality of

FRENCH CHINA,

Blue Canton China, by Set or Piece.

In the department of Glass Ware will be found the most complete variety of forms, in cut and engraved, from the very celebrated Prize Medal Manufactory of the

BROOKLYN FLINT GLASS COMPANY.

N. B.—GLASS CUT TO ORDER AND CHINA PAINTED TO PATTERN.

Advertisement of 1855, Mentioning French China and Blue Canton China.

HENRY B. GLEASON & C?

(SUCCESSORS TO J. H. LUDLOW & Co.)

264 KING St. CHARLESTON, S.C.

Famous China Store of 1836.

Top: Bill for a Set of French China at $40, 1830.
Bottom: Haviland Vases, 1853.

A, B, C, D, E, and F: Queensware of 1840; Advertising Pitcher from Van Heusen,
Albany, 1855; Two Copeland Pitchers, 1853. G, H, and I: Historic Liverpool
Ware. J, K, L, and M: Three Pitchers from Bennington and an Urn by Copeland,
1853. N, O, P, Q, and R: Gaudy Dutch Ware.

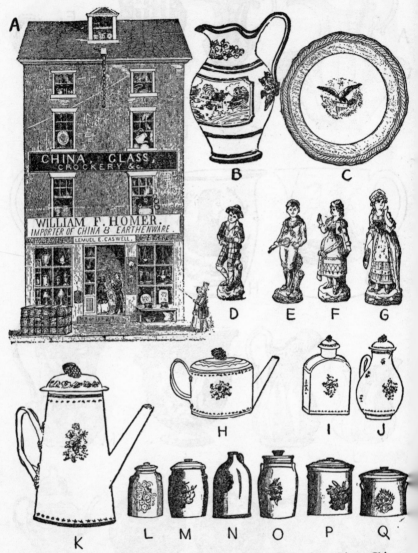

A: A "China Hall" of 1855. B: Tucker Pitcher, 1840. C: President Pierce China, 1853. D, E, F, and G: Bisque Figurines, 1886. H, I, J, and K: Oriental Export Porcelain, or "Lowestoft." L, M, N, O, P, and Q: Ft. Edwards Stoneware, 1885.

A, B, C, D, E, F, G, H, and **I:** Victorian Majolica. Plentiful Today Because It Was Sold to Millions, 1870–85, at These Low Prices. **J, K,** and **L:** Cheap French Ware and Fine Sèvres, 1850–80. **M, N, O, P,** and **Q:** "George Rex" Jug, 1785; New York Stoneware; Pope's Nose Jug, 1835–40. **R, S, T,** and **U:** Historic China —Staffordshire.

CHAPTER XV

Blown Glasswares, Bottles, and Flasks

In 1914 Frederick William Hunter wrote and published a book titled *Stiegel Glass*. That book was published in a limited edition at $10. Ten years later the secondhand price of the book was $125. American interest in early blown glass was responsible for this increase in the value of Mr. Hunter's book—an increase in interest marked by the fallacious belief that all old glass with a large pontil mark, wavy lines, and minute flint specks, whether clear and transparent or in any shade of amber, amethyst, blue, or purple, was Stiegel glass.

Since then we have learned a lot. And recently, to consolidate our learning, that definitive work, *American Glass*, by George S. and Helen McKearin, was published. This book, worth any number of times the original price of Hunter's monograph on Stiegel, is obtainable for half the sum and, pictorially alone, is a moving history of American glass from the beginning in 1629 to 1876.

Because glass was made at many glasshouses in eighteenth-century America, and because even the output of a small glass furnace runs to a hundred thousand or so pieces a year, we can enjoy a mass of surviving glassware that includes just about everything a collector's heart could desire. In fact, to make a general collection of glassware is to dissipate one's collecting effort over too wide a field. You can specialize in wineglasses, goblets, decanters, plates, sugar bowls, cream pitchers, milk bowls, water pitchers, or liquor flasks, and set yourself a pursuit that will have something to feed upon as long as your interest holds. There are at least a score of kinds of bottles you can collect even before you get into the realm of nineteenth-century mold-blown or blown-mold liquor flasks. When you look at the flasks, there are at least threescore specializing possibilities. You can collect colors, types, shapes, portrait-bust, scenic, marked,

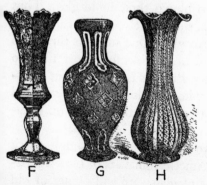

A, B, C, and **D:** Advertising by New England Glass Company, 1829; Bay State Glass Company, 1854; T. W. Dyott, 1831. **E:** Your Grandmother Had Such Novelty Blown Glass of 1880s. **F, G,** and **H:** One Clichy and Two Maes (Paris) Vases, 1853 and Cut-Glass Advertising by M'Cord & Shiner, 1828.

or monumental flasks. You can collect Washington, Franklin, president, statesmen, railroad, or steamboat flasks. You can collect bitters bottles, or—— But why go on? Even if you wanted to collect only flasks bearing the portrait bust of Andrew Jackson, or flasks showing misspelling or misplaced lettering, you could start collecting and end up with a pretty lot of flasks.

Collecting glass made by specific Early American glass factories is, to my mind, a rather fatuous form of collecting. To pretend knowledge of the difference between Stiegel, Amelung, and Zanesville, or early Sandwich blown glass, is but to invite the just rewards of self-deception—being done good. So for the sake of your collecting peace of mind and your bankroll, don't pretend to knowledge. Seek it. Or, better still, just collect old glass because you like it. To do that, all you'll need is knowledge enough to discern the difference between really old glass and its modern counterpart, whether made in Mexico, Czechoslovakia, France, or Spain. It takes years of handling old glass, keen observation, and infinite capacity for taking pains to be a glass expert. On the other hand, a happy degree of connoisseurship can be achieved by simple appreciation plus a knowledge that can differentiate between the real and the fake.

The McKearins devote well over a quarter of the pages of their 622-page book, with innumerable illustrations, to free-blown and pattern-molded bottles and flasks. Close to 20 per cent of their book is devoted to blown three-mold glass. Thus these two kinds of glass make up, subjectively, almost half of the greatest tome extant on American glass. One suspects these two kinds of glass engage the interest of considerably more than 50 per cent of the collectors of glass. But this is said without reference to pressed-glass collectors who, in this case, are considered a separate company even though some of them may, on occasion, don high hats and step into the field of blown glass.

It is entirely impossible here to deal with even so simple a task as that of listing all the known American makers of blown glasswares. Any and every collector of glassware and owner of old glassware should study the one book herein mentioned—the McKearin masterpiece. Let that be your guide and monitor. All that you can know or need to know as an amateur collector is there. But what that book doesn't tell you can be told here in a

A

GLASS MANUFACTORY.

THE PROPRIETORS
Of the Pittsburgh Glass Works,

HAVING procured a sufficient number of the most approved European Glass Manufacturers, and having on hand a large flock of the best Materials, on which their workmen are now employed, have the pleasure of assuring the public, that window glass of a superior quality and of any size, from 7 by 9, to 18 by 24 inches, carefully packed in boxes containing 100 feet ea h, may be had at the shortest notice. Glass of larger sizes for other purposes, may also be had, such as for pictures, coach glasses, clock faces, &c. Bottles of all kinds and of any quantity may also be had, together with pocket flasks, pickling jars, apothecary's shop furniture, or other hollow ware—the whole at least 25 per cent. lower than articles of the same quality brought from any of the sea ports of the United States. A liberal allowance will be made on sale of large quantities. Orders from merchants and others will be punctually attended to on application to JAMES O'HARA or ISAAC CRAIG, or at the Store of Messrs. PRATHER and SMILIE, in Market-Street, Pittsburgh.

B

CUT AND PLAIN GLASS.

JACKSON & BAGGOTT beg leave to inform their friends, and the public in general, that they have opened the store 36 Maidenlane, (four doors below Nassau-street, on the south side), for the sale of Cut and Plain Glass, of the best quality and newest patterns, which they are determined to sell on such terms as shall ensure them a share of the public patronage. They respectfully invite private families, store-keepers, and those desirous of exporting to the southern states, to call at their store. Orders taken at the store, Maiden-lane, at No. 76 Chatham-st. or at the manufactory, Grand-street, Bowery.

N.B. Dinner and Sideboard Sets, Decanters, Bowls, Celery Dishes, Goblets, Tumblers, Wines, &c. &c. cut to any pattern, and at the shortest notice

C

Pittsburgh—Manufacturers in 1836.

BAKEWELLS & CO.

Pittsburgh Flint Glass Manufactory,

Corner of Grant street and Monongahela wharf,

PITTSBURGH.

Manufacture Plain, Pressed, and Cut Flint Glass Ware of every description—which they offer for sale at their works, together with a general assortment of *Castor Frames, Vials, Green Glass Ware, &c.*

[☞ See Statistics.]

CURLING, ROBERTSON & CO.

MANUFACTURERS OF

CUT, PRESSED, AND PLAIN

Flint Glass,

No. 7, Market street, Pittsburgh.

ROBINSON, ANDERSON & CO.

Flint Glass Manufacturers,

STOURBRIDGE FLINT GLASS WORKS,

Kensington, opposite the Gas Works, Pittsburgh.

Thomas Robinson,
Alex. M. Anderson,
John Robinson, Jr.

A: Ballroom in Mansion of Stiegel, the Glassmaker, of Manheim, Lancaster, Pennsylvania, 1762. **B, C,** and **D:** Pittsburgh Glass Advertising, 1800 and 1836; Cut-glass Factory, 1819.

very few more words. It is simply this: You can buy Stiegel "type" blue-glass saltcellars, sugar bowls, and creamers; you can buy Amelung "type," Zanesville, and other Ohio glass; you can find free-blown and mold-blown and even cut glass from Sandwich and Pittsburgh, and you can find bottles and flasks in right fair profusion in the shops today. Excessively rare glass is continually passing through the auction galleries. Also, this rare stuff can be found in the better shops. Further, you can use your head (if you have a lot of patience) and collect various kinds of sets of glassware, even though piece number five may be found a thousand miles from piece number three.

Late in the year 1945 a collector purchased a two-bottle castor frame of Sheffield plate from a Connecticut dealer. All he did was measure the diameter of the bottle holes and ask the price. I said, "What do you propose to do with that?" His reply was indicative of the patient and wise collector of antiques. Said he, "Why, I found two blown-mold castor bottles a year or so ago, minus stoppers and minus the castor frame. I paid seventy-five cents each for them. Then I sought for a pair of stoppers that fitted the bottles. Those I found after several months. They cost me twenty-five cents each. Now I have found the castor frame and, in finding it, I have completed my antique. From here on it will be on the table at dinner, with oil in one bottle and vinegar in the other. Total cost, less than $10." That's collecting with the head as well as with the heart.

Our pictures display in some small measure the kinds of glassware you can collect today—free-blown and mold-blown glass of the eighteenth and nineteenth centuries. Many of these pictures come from the McKearin book. Others come from glassblowers' catalogues, and others are made from photographs of items that are generally to be found in antiques shops. At least 25 per cent of the pictures are of historic flasks. At least 20 per cent are of blown three-mold glass. That is approximately the status of antiques shops glassware stock, percentagewise, excepting, of course, pressed glass. And with the pictures we come to the end of the glassware story. But again the admonition: If you collect old glass, or have old glass, or want to study American glass, get yourself a copy of *American Glass*. Between this chapter and that book there is all the difference between a first reader and a postgraduate course.

A: Mr. Dyott Sells One-Half Dozen Bitters; the Bottles Today Worth Three Times the Total Bill per Each! B, C, D, and E: Amelung "Type" Jars and Stiegel "Type" Cream Jugs. F, G, H, I, and J: Bohemian Glass as Imported in 1850s.

A: Blown Mold Bowl. **B, F, D,** and **H:** Candy Jars of Blown Glass, 1835-90. **C:** Enameled Glass. **E** and **G:** Fancy Blown Glass of 1880, Now Much Collected. **I:** Venetian Blown Glass of 1888—Then Selling at Ten Cents.

Blown-mold Decanters, bowls, dishes, hats, and salts, 1760–1850.

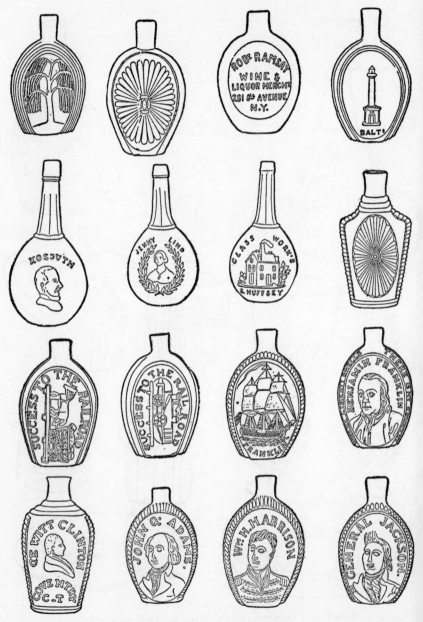

American Historic Glass Flasks.

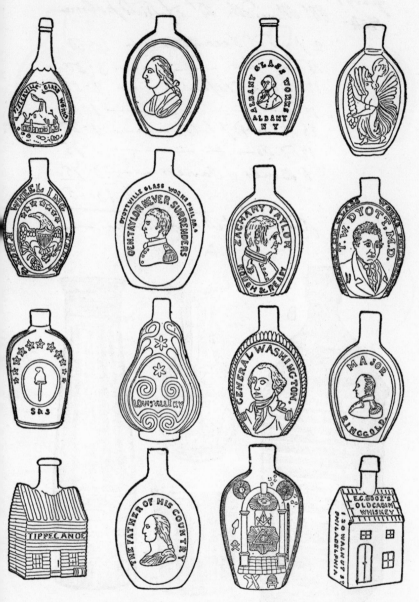

Historic Flasks, Some Scarce, Some Rare.

febry 1
1804 — Mr Merridth Bt of Richd palmer

2 pair of decanters — — — 4=50
18 tumbles — — — — — 3·00
12 wine glasses — — — — 2·00
12 Ditto — — — — — 1·00
24 Blue Ed plats — — — 1=25
12 Ditto — — — — — 0·75
6 Bowls & Sarsers — — — 0·75
                          $ 13·25

Recd in full Richd palmer —

A

A: Bill for Glassware, 1804. B, D, and E: Bitters Bottle, Jelly Glass, and Olive
Bottle, as Originally Used, 1865–75. Empties Are Now Collected as Antiques. C:
Clichy Glass, Imported in 1850s.

A and B: Clichy Toilet Bottles and Vases, 1855. C, D, E, and F: Jersey "Type" Mug and Pitcher; Stiegel "Type" Salt Cellars. G, H, and I: Blown Sugar and Celery Bowls; Blue Stiegel "Type" Sugar Bowl. J and K: Clichy Glass, Imported in 1850s.

CHAPTER XVI

Pressed Glass

The history of pressed glass in America begins with the discovery, if not the invention, of the process in 1827 by Deming Jarves at the Sandwich glassworks of the Boston & Sandwich Glass Company. Because most of the publicity about Sandwich has had to do with pressed glass, many beginning collectors assume that the Sandwich factory made only pressed glass. This, of course, is not the case. Sandwich produced free-blown and blown-mold wares of various kinds before Jarves introduced pressing techniques, and continued to produce blown glass after pressing methods were in full operation.

Sandwich pressed glass is, of course, the first American pressed glass and, in the opinion of many, is our finest pressed glass. Certainly Sandwich pressed cup plates, especially those of historic pattern, are today classed with rich and rare stuffs. The larger pieces of lacy Sandwich, from saltcellars to bowls and from condiment dishes to pitchers, are now so universally acknowledged as desirable antiques that even the most exclusive shops give them shelf room. Sandwich glass lamps, combining blown and pressed elements, and pressed Sandwich candlesticks are held in high esteem. A pair of Sandwich "dolphin" candlesticks has, on more than one occasion, topped the price of a pair of coin-silver candlesticks of the same period. But please do not misread that statement. It is as antiques that the topping has been done. When orginally sold the dolphin candlesticks were cheap wares, within the purse limits of almost everyone, while silver was silver and worth its average dollar or more per ounce.

You can collect Sandwich pressed glass today, and you can collect Sandwich blown glass. It is easier to identify the pressed Sandwich because, thanks to the indefatigable work of Ruth Webb Lee in her grand book *Sandwich Glass*, a great deal of the original Sandwich pressed glass is pictured and identified. In

Our "FIFTH AVENUE SWELL" Assortment.
The Cream of all "50-Cent Sellers."

Our "HALF DOLLAR Pitcher Assortment."

OUR "CRYSTAL TABLE OUTFIT."

Pressed Glass from a Catalogue of 1886.

saying you can collect it, a reservation must be made. You can collect it if you are willing to pay the price. This once cheap ware for the American people, made at a mass-production glass factory between the years 1827 and 1887, now stands at the pinnacle of all collected pressed glass. It stands miles high on that pinnacle because, from the time of its first making at Sandwich and the end of its making at Sandwich, scores of other glass factories were making pressed glass in such volume that what is left of it is still, figuratively speaking, a pile that is miles high. And it is *that* pressed glass, not Sandwich pressed glass, that you find here, there, and everywhere.

It is all very well to render anthems of praise to pressed glass and to assert that it is a superfine and Early American antique. But in so doing both expert and collector should also keep in mind that pressed glass was the cheapest glass ever made; it was about the commonest of common merchandise ever offered the American public, and it was sold in its greatest quantity between 1880 and 1900.

Which is not to say it was vulgar. By common we mean universally available at a price within reach of all people. In the research project for this and other books on American antiques, we sought for original catalogue entries and illustrations of many things, including pressed glass. Pressed glass apparently was featured in illustrated catalogues issued by Western glassmakers by or shortly after 1850. These catalogues are now quite scarce, bespeaking a perhaps somewhat limited distribution. Catalogues of pressed glass appearing after 1865 were apparently printed in greater numbers since they have survived in greater numbers. But it is the catalogues of great wholesale houses such as Butler Brothers, and popular mail-order houses such as Ehrich which, issued between 1875 and 1890, reveal the most interesting data about pressed glass. These firms devoted page after page to pressed glass, featuring, in the Butler catalogues, five-cent specials and even penny items, along with the "sets" and combinations to sell at from twenty-five cents up to eighty-eight-piece sets at five dollars.

Many patrons of antiques collecting have had the happy idea of chalking out a province, or back yard, in which they plan to reign as the supreme authority. They make splendid contri-

"OUR DOT"

TABLE SET.

A Rapid Mover,

TO RUN AT

25 Cents per Set.

This is a new set, and it is one that for the price will warrant a large sale. The set comprises sugar bowl and cover, cream pitcher, buttter dish and cover, and spoon holder.
......Order here. Put up 24 sets in a bbl. Sold only by bbl. (Bbl. 35 cts.) Price 15 cts. per set.

Our

"TOWN

TALK"

TABLE SET.

A big beauty to rush at about 35 or 40 cents per set, and one that will give great satisfaction wherever sold. The pieces are all large, well finished, and of the handsome Optic pattern.
......Order here. Put up 24 sets in bbl. Sold only by bbl. (Bbl. 35 cts.) Price, 19 cts. per Set.

Our

"FAVORITE"

TABLE SET.

A 25-Cent Wonder!

This well known and favorite pattern was one formerly sold by us in colored glass, but we now offer it in pure crystal at a price low enough to admit of your *retailing the entire set of 4 pieces for* ....Order here. **Price, 16 Cents per Set**
25 cents. Put up 24 sets in a bbl. Sold only by bbl. (Bbl. 35 cts.)

OUR

"Jewel"

TABLE SET.

A "Gem" at a low price.

This set we ran last season with a sale of more than half a thousand packages. It is a beautiful high grade set of the cut diamond pattern, such as will prove a "*quick mover*"

Our "FASHION" Hand-Engraved Set.

A Rare Offering for a "Dollar."

"HIGH ART"

WARE.

Catalogue Page of Pressed Glass, 1886.

198 of Antique Collectors

butions in certain phases of research; elevate the object or objects of their interest to a high pinnacle; and then, unhappily, some of these collectors-historians gasp in amazement, pique, and sometimes with outright animosity at anything or any fact deemed likely to topple their chosen goods from the high place they have built for them.

If there be any such collectors in the realm of pressed glass they should now use the time-honored feminine technique of not looking at either the following words about, or pictures of, pressed glass.

This because we have made but very few drawings of the pressed glass now in shops, nor do we reproduce a single drawing from other books on pressed glass. Rather, we reproduce only original pictures from Ehrich, Butler, and other catalogues, issued between 1875 and 1890. If space permitted we could have tripled the display without stretching the pictorial resources of these catalogues in respect of pressed glass. Note that the text which here and there is included with the pictures reveals prices, terms, and shipping standards. Low prices prevailed, and by the barrel you should order your supply!

In 1849 Apsley Pellatt, in his *Curiosities of Glass Making*, stated that pressed glassmaking had been introduced into England from America. He said further that the glass lost much of its brilliancy in pressing, hence it was used chiefly to make cheap articles, but that the process of rewarming, or "fire polishing," after pressing had somewhat remedied the defect. In the Butler Brothers catalogues of 1887 and 1888 we find the statement: "This glass fire polished" or "polished in the glory-hole." It is termed brilliant, sparkling, and bright. It was, and it is.

Emotional people resent, somehow, the fact that this glass was so cheap it was used for premiums in early tea stores. They seem to take it as a personal affront when told that it was sold in the early Woolworth stores and even in the "three-and-nine-cent" stores. By the same token, they do not seem to resent being told, for example, that chairs very close to the styles favored by Duncan Phyfe were once offered as premiums; that Currier & Ives and other now highly regarded prints were given away as premiums; and that Connecticut clocks of the sorts collected today were once offered as premiums. If there be a collector of

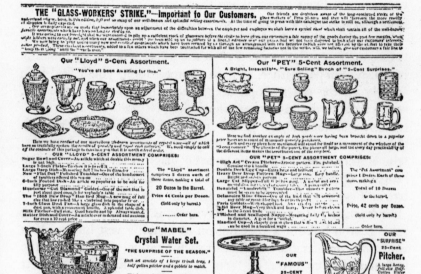

Glass-Workers' Strike, News to Pressed Glass Buyers, 1888.

pressed glass who loses interest in his American ware when he discovers it once was glassware of the people and for the people, then that collector had better quit, or collect pressed glass by Stouvenel, Clichy, and Lalique. These latter kinds are really rare in America.

The only antiques shops not having *some* pressed glass in stock today are the shops that can't find it. Fine early Sandwich pressed glass—in white and colors—is now a standard stock item in even the finest shops, when they can get it. Some Sandwich cup plates are now so rare they stand on a parity with the hand-blown glass of much earlier periods. But run-of-the-mill pressed glass, made mostly between 1870 and 1890, will not be found in exclusive shops. Rather, as if in compensation, you'll find it in nearly all the other shops. Some shops have nothing else but, and prefer to do business at wholesale.

You will not find that grand pressed-glass pattern "Westward-Ho!" or animal-head pieces with great frequency wherever you go. Rather, you'll find just pressed glass in an almost endless variety of patterns. From there on you will be strictly on your own. Trying to find a specific piece in a specific pattern, if not like hunting for a needle in a haystack, is certainly like hunting in a button box for a coat button to match a vest button. You must do considerable hunting. In such hunting, one suspects, the pressed-glass collector of "sets in patterns" finds the greatest fun. There is so much to cull, and every shop save the fine ones is sure to have some of the glass through which to cull. Our own research warrants the assumption that a well-filled, run-of-the-mill kind of antiques shop will yield as high as one piece of common pressed glass for every square foot of floor space. In such a shop, 20 by 50 feet, you should find about one thousand pieces of pressed glass. If you run into a one-thousand-square-foot shop without a single piece, chances are the next shop of the same size will have two thousand pieces. That's the way "averaging" works out.

When applying modern techniques of fact-finding in antiques research we can make many interesting discoveries about early products, their distribution, and their degree of consumer-acceptance. What is needed in such research is a well-ordered random sample of the advertising of the shops and stores of a

THE "PRIZE" CREAMER.

A

The above is a sample of the "Prize" line of the National Glass Co., it being the design which took first honors and the $500 cash prize in the open to all contest which closed June 1, 1900.

THE "REWARD" CREAMER.

B

This is a sample of one of the six new lines the National Glass Co. are showing, and gives signs of becoming one of their leaders this season.

Pressed
Glassware.

Full Lines of

TABLE
WARE.

"Harvard"
"Virginia"
"Atlanta"
"Oxford"
"Manhattan"
"Albany"
"Princeton."

Tumblers, Goblets,
Beer Mugs, Lamps, etc.

Tarentum Glass Co.,

TARENTUM, PA.

New York Office: 24 Park Place, D. R. Marshall.

C

Fine "Star" Lemonade Set, 6 tumblers, 1 ½-gal. pitcher and glass tray (plain edge), decorations in amber and in blue; has a most beautiful effect. Very cheap, $2.25 per set.

D

Fine Colored Glass Lemonade Set, consisting of 6 tumblers, 1 ½-gal. pitcher and one glass tray, $1.00.

E

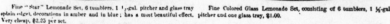

A and **B:** Prize Pressed Glass of 1900 and 1901. **C:** Tarentum Glass Advertisement, 1896. **D** and **E:** Cheap in 1886—Antique in 1946.

given period—a sample revealing what factories were producing what, and where, and when, and lo! by putting two and two together you have what must have been the exact commercial situation. Research workers have the healthy habit of keeping their emotions at home. They look at facts with an open mind. They admit of no basic differences between the people of one decade and the people of another. Thus our researchers are stretching neither imagination nor fact when they assume that because pressed glass was offered in almost every wholesale catalogue they studied, it must have been sold everywhere. They know that anything universally offered by wholesalers year after year was universally bought—and resold at retail—year after year. Nothing collected today, excepting only buttons, match covers, and postage stamps, appears to have been produced in the quantity enjoyed by pressed glass. It was once as cheap as a Currier & Ives print, as cheap as a "Boston Massacre" engraved by Paul Revere, as cheap as an HL hinge, when these several antiques were also new and made in quantities.

Now it is collected, and collecting must go on within the mass of pressed glass that has survived the years. Now, also, it is being faked, as are some Currier & Ives prints and other antiques. The faking of pressed glass, deplorable and reprehensible though it may be, is proof of one thing—pressed glass *is* a collector's item.

Now, if you want the whole amazing, perplexing, and astounding story of pressed glass you must study Ruth Webb Lee's books, *Sandwich Glass* and *Early American Pressed Glass*. You may, just as a wise beginning, start with her *Handbook of Early American Pressed Glass*. These books are rich in pictures and the text does a good job of explaining. If you want to collect pressed glass, step blithely forth and collect. Your pressed glass is waiting for you if you want to collect it, unmindful of the laughs and sneers of others. There is a secret about this laughing and sneering that should be understood by all amateur collectors. All collectors were once hazed by the laughs and sneers of their fellow men. But the collectors went right ahead collecting. When they noticed another original thinker collecting what he liked, they laughed and sneered in turn, even as the

Wholesale Page of Pressed Glass, 1887.

sophomore in every school, hazed as a freshman, dishes out hazing to the freshmen under him. There the simile ends. In collecting, he who sneers most and laughs loudest at what another collects usually winds up by collecting the same thing, or lauding the object to the skies.

Catalogue page, 1886, Showing Three Patterns.

Catalogue page, 1886, Showing Seven Patterns.

Goblets, Tumblers, Pitchers, and Bowl of the 1880s.

This is a *brand new assortment*, comprising a "*high grade*" *quality of ware* suitable for the *swell aristocracy*. *Every piece* mentioned here is *fully and elegantly fire polished* and full finished throughout. It only needs to be shown to be sold, and an order from you for a single barrel will be but the commencement of a large business on these exquisite pieces.

Pressed Glass for Everyone, Elegantly Fire-Polished, 1886.

Our "DRUMMER" 5-Cent Assortment.
An Assortment of Brilliant Beauties. All "Self=Selling" 5=Cent Wonders.

This is of the richest of Crystal Glass, and each piece will stand for itself at a genuine bargain seeker's prize. The ware is all *thoroughly "full finished."* Each piece having been separately fire polished in the "Glory Hole" of a factory universally famed for this work in this department. The pieces, while all of high grade quality and finish, are yet very large, and will positively sell at sight wherever shown.

OUR "DRUMMER ASSORTMENT"

Heavy Brilliant Dot Mug with Woven Handle—A dazzling pattern, full size with heavy outside projecting dots......

Fancy High Toned Butter Dish and Cover—A 6-inch fancy butter dish with castle-top cover complete. ....

Large 7-inch Fan Plate with Handle—A gem that will sell for a "dime" just as readily as for 5 cents..............

Large Comport on Foot—A brilliant reverse diamond pattern 4½ inch comport on a high foot. A rapid mover.........

Large, Beautiful Diamond Goblet—A superb artistic pattern, full finished throughout.............

Mustard or Horseradish Dish and Cover—A beautiful Arabian pattern, full size and full finish.............

Large Milk or Cream Pitcher—A refreshing pattern of the reverse diamond order.............

Artistic Cut Diamond Tumbler—Full and exact imitation of the cut glass pattern. A gem...............

Large 8-inch Leaf Pickle Dish with Stem Handle—A very handsome and artistic pattern and one that will attract immediate attention.............

Extra Size Easy Handled Mug—A free, easy handling pattern of an artistic brilliant design...............

Large 7-inch Diamond Plate—A dazzling table ornament that will sell "off hand".............

Full Size Sugar Bowl and Cover—Another piece of the above handsome pattern. Put it in sight and it will sell itself.....

Our "PREMIUM" 10-Cent Assortment.
All "Fire Polished Gems" In Crystal Glass.

Five-and-Ten-Cent Assortments, 1887.

OUR NEW "QUARTER LEADER" PITCHER.

"The king of 25-cent Leaders."

This pitcher is an extra large and heavy half gallon size. It is a handsome pattern and will "go off a rushing," at the price. 2 doz. in bbl. Sold only by bbl.
Price $1.84 Doz.

OUR "OPALESCENT BEAUTY" LAMP.

"To Sell at 75c Complete."

Consisting of a beautiful opalescent lamp ("now all the rage"), with a *globe chimney* of the same artistic opalescent threaded ribbed ware, and best brass burner and wick, complete. It stands 16 inches high.

Put up 1 dozen lamps (complete) in a barrel.
(Sold only by barrel.)
Price, $4.90 per Doz.

Goblets—One Kind Only in a Barrel.

38c. Doz.   39c. Doz.   40c. Doz.   55c. Doz.

No. Bbls.   Price per doz.

...Our "Plain Pattern" Goblets—*A bang up 5 center.* This well-known and desirable pattern is a splendid seller. Put up 10 doz. in a bbl. Sold only by the bbl. 38

.....Our "Plain Flute" Goblet *A regular every day and Sunday favorite,* and one that will give satisfaction. 10 doz. in bbl; sold only by bbl. 39

.....Our "Brilliant Goblet—*A popular selling goblet,* one that will *reflect credit* on the seller. 10 doz. in barrel. Sold only by bbl. 40

.....Our Heavy Hotel Goblet—*A giant of strength.* The well-known staple massive, plain, heavy hote. goblet that can be thrown against a house without breaking. Put up 7 doz. in bbl. Sold only by bbl............. 55

....Special Bargain—With the beginning of every season we have a number of styles of goblets left over which we cannot duplicate, and yet the quantity is not sufficient to warrant us in listing them. We therefore "close them out" at this nominal price. They are all first quality, in excellent condition, and ones which have never been sold at so low a rate in a regular way. We offer them while they last at.... 38

N. B.—Goblets sold only by barrel. Barrels 35c. each. Each kind of goblet is packed separately.

Pressed Glass, Good and Cheap, 1880s.

A: "Polar Star" Offered by Wanamaker, 1887. **B:** "Hobnail" Offered by Wanamaker, 1880s.

DESPLAINES ASSORTMENT.

THIS SET IS MADE OF THE VERY FINEST QUALITY OF PRESSED GLASS. The convex panel design bring out all the fire and brilliancy so characteristic of high grade crystal glass. The pattern is the newest produced this year. It is exceedingly heavy and beautiful, and the tops of the salt and pepper shakers are of SOLID SILVER. A new but massive design which will attract the eye of the most particular.

We can furnish the following assortments:				$1.16
No. 27534	Water Set.	Price		.89
No. 27536	Berry Set.	Price		.78
No. 27538	Glass Tea Set.	Price		2.13
No. 27537	18-Piece Set.	Price		

For the number and style of pieces included in above sets see page 631.

No. 2T538 Assortment of 37 pieces, including:

1 Water Pitcher (½ Gallon)	1 Butter Dish	12 Nappies	1 Vinegar Cruet
12 Tumblers	1 Spoon Holder	1 Celery Tray	1 Salt Shaker
1 Cream Pitcher	1 Sugar Bowl	1 Jelly Glass	1 Pepper Shaker
	1 Berry Dish	1 Syrup Jug	1 Fruit Stand

Packed complete in box. Shipping weight, 40 pounds. Price....$2.96

WEST MOORELAND ASSORTMENT.

THOSE WHO ARE NOT EXPERTS IN GLASSWARE WOULD READILY BELIEVE THAT THIS DESIGN IS OF THE REAL CUT GLASS. It is elegantly polished and of good practical size. The ball's eye and cut glass design brings out the fire and brilliancy of this crystal glass. The top of the sugar bowl fits the scallops of the base, giving a very neat appearance.

We can furnish the following assortments:				$1.12
No. 27540	Water Set.	Price		.86
No. 27541	Berry Set.	Price		.74
No. 27542	Glass Tea Set.	Price		2.16
No. 27543	18-Piece Set.	Price		

For the number and style of pieces included in above sets see page 631.

No. 27544 Assortment of 42 pieces, including:

1 Water Pitcher (½ Gallon)	1 Butter Dish	12 Nappies	1 Salt Shaker
12 Tumblers	1 Spoon Holder	1 Celery Glass	1 Pepper Shaker
1 Cream Jug	1 Sugar Bowl	1 Syrup Jug	6 Custard Glasses
	1 Berry Dish	1 Vinegar Cruet	1 Toothpick Holder

Packed complete in box. Shipping weight, 40 pounds. Price....$3.18

OUR RAINBOW ASSORTMENT.

OUR RAINBOW PATTERN IS AN EXCELLENT IMITATION OF CUT GLASS, made of the very best quality of crystal full fire, polished, highly finished. This assortment is not the cheap grade generally offered by many other dealers, but is the best class of glassware made.

We can furnish the following assortments:				$1.16
No. 27546	Water Set.	Price		.90
No. 27547	Berry Set.	Price		.78
No. 27548	Glass Tea Set.	Price		2.20
No. 27549	18-Piece Set.	Price		

For the number and style of pieces included in above sets see page 631.

No. 2T550 Assortment of 47 pieces, including:

1 Water Pitcher (½ Gallon)	1 Butter Dish	12 Nappies	1 Salt Shaker
12 Tumblers	1 Spoon Holder	1 Celery Tray	1 Pepper Shaker
1 Cream Pitcher	1 Sugar Bowl	1 Syrup Jug	12 Custard Glasses
	1 Berry Dish	1 Vinegar Cruet	

Packed complete in box. Shipping weight, 40 pounds. Price....$3.99

Sears, Roebuck Offered Pressed Glass in 1900.

Tarentum Glass Co.

TARENTUM, PA.

1898.   **1898.**

New Line.

    Over 100 Pieces.

"Cornell"

    Pattern.

"Cornell" Pressed Glass Pattern by Tarentum, 1898.

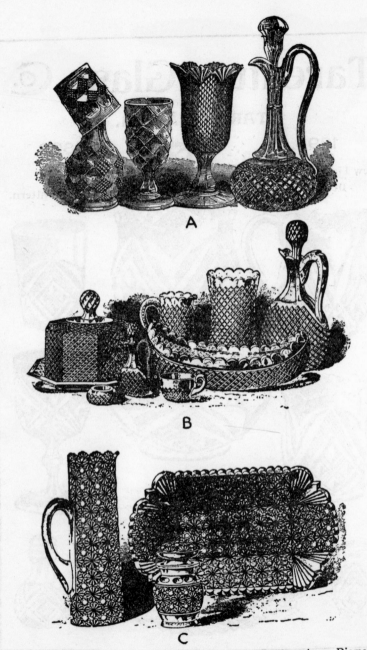

A: Fine Pressed Glass by Stouvenel, New York, 1852. **B:** "Strawberry Diamond" offered by Wanamaker, 1887. **C:** "Russian" sold by Wanamaker in 1880s.

Wholesale page of Pressed Glass, 1887.

CHAPTER XVII

Paintings, Engravings, and Lithographs

Here is where we should say, "Dear Reader, bear with us, for we are in deep trouble." You see we know considerable about the subjects of this chapter, or think we do, and yet we are simply stymied about pictures. Early American paintings, reduced to black-and-white line drawings, are beyond our narrow bounds of facility with pen and pencil. When it comes to engravings, the situation grows worse. When we get to lithographs, we are simply sunk. If it weren't for the fact that Messrs. Currier & Ives reproduced a few of their prints as line cuts in an advertising folder, we'd have almost none of them to show here. Some of the engravings, which of course are in line or stipple, lend themselves to the kind of reproduction we must use here. And then, in the case of the pictures—the paintings—happily some of the *original* concepts exist in a form we can reproduce even though the paintings made from them cannot be shown.

This latter situation literally screams a big story to a research-minded delver into the American scene. Since you are reading this chapter about pictorial antiques, perhaps you'd like to know just what this scream is about. Here, then, is the story:

Most of the paintings which now rejoice in the wrong name "American Primitive" are really American pioneer amateur art executed by men, women and children between the years 1830 and 1860. To educate this great crew of amateur artists, that is, to give them a few lessons, a few hints, and a little pictorial instruction, there were itinerant teachers, fly-by-night drawing schools, and drawing instruction books and packs of drawing cards. Also, many issues of *Gleason's Drawing Room Companion* and similar illustrated weeklies carried black-and-white cuts of scenes, people, events, and homely, folksy subjects. Most of the amateurs went to work, as the saying goes, copying their paintings from drawing books and illustrated weekly pictures. The

Top: Early woodcut view of Chagrin Falls, Ohio.
Bottom: Penn's Treaty, Favorite Subject with Amateur Artists, 1830–70. Many Paintings Copied from This Woodcut.

longer we study the paintings that crop up from time to time and the more we study the drawing books and weeklies, the more evidence we get of the copying habit.

In the Museum of Modern Art, New York, there is—well, call it a magnificent American Primitive genre of a "Quilting Party." It is a good, amateurishly painted picture of a very interesting subject. It bespeaks the American scene because it *is* an American scene. The picture is painted in oil colors on a wood panel 13¼ by 25¼ inches. Experts date it between 1840 and 1850. Unfortunately for the experts, the dating falls to pieces when we discover the picture first appeared in *Gleason's Pictorial Drawing Room Companion*, October 21, 1854. Gleason's comment was, "The artist has presented a characteristic and expressive picture of country life in West Virginia—a quilting party convened at the house of a villager." The name of the artist is not given. The Gleason picture, however, is the original and the amateur oil painting is the copy. So, even if we cannot show the oil painting—now nobly hung in a great museum—we can show you the Gleason original.

Similarly, we can display a number of other painting studies of American scenery from various drawing books. Paintings of these studies were made, not in lone examples but perhaps by the dozen, the score, or even the hundred. There is as much chance of finding one in Kentucky, or Missouri, as there is of finding one in Pennsylvania, New Jersey, or New Hampshire.

Primitive portraits are, of course, not in this category of copied things. These are often the work of itinerant likeness painters who roamed the country, often with a lot of partially finished bust paintings in which they'd paint a likeness as to face and thus have a finished picture for you in a few hours. Also, they may be the work of local artists who stayed in one place for years, eking out a living if a poor painter, and reveling in fair luxury if a good painter. Such men are known to have painted portraits for ten, fifteen, or twenty-five dollars. Some received as much as one hundred dollars for a portrait in the 1840s. If the population of a town or city was more than three thousand in 1840, the chances are there was at least one portrait painter and one historic and fancy painter at work there as permanent craftsmen. If the town enjoyed a wealth above the average, there

Top: On the Mississippi, Currier & Ives.
Bottom: Mississippi Steamboat Race, Currier & Ives, 1870.

were more painters. In 1830 there were approximately .25 portrait painters per one thousand of population at work in the nation. New York, with two hundred and two thousand population, had fifty-one; Lancaster, Pennsylvania, with eight thousand population, had two portrait painters.

Within the past fifteen years antiquers have found quite a number of small portraits, not miniatures, but water colors on paper, around or under 9 by 12 inches, and oil paintings on thin panels of wood, or even sheets of metal, of approximately the same size. Different localities seem to have enjoyed specialists in this kind of portrait making, and now there is quite a vogue in running down the facts about *who* made the portraits. We doubt the propriety even of attempting to cover any phase of this research in this book. It is a very specialized thing. And what could be said about the Connecticut Valley painters, or the Housatonic, Hudson, or Delaware Valley painters of this kind would be of little interest to those whose collecting goes on in the Ohio, Wabash, Tennessee, Missouri, or Mississippi valleys.

Wherever you live, if it was an inhabited place by 1850, it is likely there was some portrait painting done. Even after the big cities enjoyed Daguerrean galleries, where portraits were painted with light and fixed by chemical action on silver salts, this portrait or likeness painting went on in smaller communities. Some of the portraits are in profile because profiles were not only easier to do but admitted of a better likeness. Even when they depict complete figures, with furnishings and familial scenes as do the paintings of Joseph H. Davis made in lower Maine and New Hampshire in the 1830s, the faces are in profile. The Davis pictures were known, but not the painter, until my friend, Frank Spinney of New Haven, located a signed example. That was all that was required to establish the Davis authorship of a great collection of paintings, for, if the man signed but few (only two or three signed examples are known) with his name, he signed them all with his style. And what has proved to be true of Davis will, perhaps, also be found true of many other up to now unknown paintings. There is a Pennsylvania type of full-length painting of women that invariably shows the subject posed with

Top: "Southern Mule Team." A genre woodcut that has been copied in oils by many amateurs.
Bottom: Wooding-up, Currier & Ives.

a rose in hand. Over twenty such were of record before a signed one turned up.

No field of study is still so wide open as this field of American amateur and semi-professional art. Call the semi-professional work artisan paintings, pioneer art, or by any other name you please. They are representative of the painting that, on rare occasions, developed a masterpiece by a nobody.

Collecting Currier & Ives prints, whether just because they are Currier & Ives or whether you collect certain types of scene or subject, is an avocation that needs no spur from this *Reader*. If you cannot own or get to see the great books on Currier & Ives by Harry T. Peters, you can certainly get, or see, a copy of the digested Currier & Ives story with its many plates, published by Doubleday, Doran in 1942.

There is a little warning not out of order here about Currier & Ives reprints. Many small folio reproductions made within the past ten years—some as advertisements and others for cheap framing prints—are now being foisted on new collectors as "old" and original works. Not always does the dealer selling these pictures know they are quite new. He often buys without specialized knowledge and, as the fakers often frame the new prints in old frames, buys also believing he is getting the real thing.

Many antiques shops have a few Currier & Ives and lithographs by other American print makers on hand. But shopping for lithographs in general antiques shops sometimes leaves much to be desired in terms of results. Go to the print shops dealing in old pictures and you'll be in a sort of print collector's paradise. Also, you'll be buying where expert knowledge of supply and demand stabilizes prices. At the specialized print shop you can usually find what you want, no matter whether you seek good pictures for your walls, or whether you want dental, medical, bicycle, railroad, tobacco, steamboat, horse, dog, or cat pictures. There are already some hundred or more special subjects collected in lithographs alone. Pick your subject and go to it.

Early American historic engravings made between 1720 and 1820 constitute a portfolio of hundreds of titles and subjects, with many unbelievably rare. The "Bombardment of Fort McHenry," September 13, 1814, is not merely rare but highly

Top: Bound Down River, Currier & Ives, 1870.
Bottom: American Express Train, Currier & Ives, 1864.

prized because it depicts, in a print, the scene that inspired the writing of our national anthem. There are, however, some several thousands of delightful small engravings of scenes, events, places, and people that can still be had at fair to low prices. Collectors usually like to have a print or two dealing with the locale in which they live, or were born, or which an ancestor inhabited. If you feel that way, enter the lists with high hopes. You have better than a fifty-fifty chance of finding what you seek, no matter where you live.

In 1933 the New York Public Library published I. N. Phelps Stokes's *Early Views of American Cities, Etc.* In this volume, still available, there are listed two hundred cities and towns of which one or more views were published as prints. Tucson, Arizona; Montgomery, Alabama; Fort Smith, Arkansas; Monterey, California; Denver, Colorado, are all included in the two hundred. The dates range from 1497 to 1891. Mr. Stokes could have made his list one thousand cities and towns by extending his date to 1901. In fact, in the opinion of one print seller, it could include some fifteen hundred! Your favorite college; your military, industrial, or philosophical hero; your whim or your choice of man, woman, or scene probably exists in the form of a picture, if only a woodcut from one of the early magazines, or as an early book illustration. Old print shops have these, as well as the formal prints, in stock.

Temperance Prints of 1848.

SKETCH FROM LIFE OF A WESTERN PRAIRIE BEE.—BY F. A. BURR, OF WORTHINGTON, OHIO.

WORKS OF ART.

The undersigned have associated themselves under the firm of
CHANDLER & CLAPP,
DEALERS IN WORKS OF ART,
to which business they will give their exclusive attention. They have
taken House
NO. 34 WINTER STREET,
and fitted up spacious and well-lighted Rooms for the favorable exhibition
of Paintings, Drawings, Fine Engravings, etc. of which they now have
on hand a large and valuable stock, selected with great care, and including many rare works in the most celebrated masters both ancient
and modern. Persons interested in Works of Art are invited to visit the
Esabli-hment, where they will find the finest collection of Engravings in
the country, and every inducement for examining them at leisure. The
stock will be constantly renewed by importations from the best Publishing
Houses in Europe.

G. L. CHANDLER.   GEO. G. CLAPP.

SLEEPING ACCOMMODATIONS IN A PRAIRIE HOME.

Top: F. A. Burr of Worthington, Ohio, Painted This Scene about 1850. After the Woodcut Was Made, Many Amateurs Repainted the Picture.
Bottom Left: Selling Art to Boston in 1855.
Bottom Right: "Libelous," They Said in the 1860s When This Picture Appeared. But It Was Painted from Experience, if Not from Life.

THE PIC NIC PARTY.

Top: Itinerant Painter at Work, 1864. **Bottom:** A Sweet Picture That Was Copied by at Least One Hundred Amateur Artists of the 1850s.

BOSTON

View of The ATTACK on BUNKER's HILL, with the Burning of CHARLES TOWN, June 17. 1775.

GLEASON'S PICTORIAL DRAWING-ROOM COMPANION.

A QUILTING PARTY IN WESTERN VIRGINIA.

Top: Attack on Bunker's Hill. One Hundred Per Cent American Even Though Done in England. An Important Painting from This Print Is Now in a New York Gallery. **Bottom:** Original Woodcut of Quilting Party, October 21, 1854.

CURRIER & IVES' Series of Splendid Colored Pictures

—OF—

THE LIFE OF A FIREMAN.

PLATE 1.—THE NIGHT ALARM.

"START HER LIVELY, BOYS."

Represents the rolling of the engine. The clock seen inside the house denotes that the hour is past midnight, but some of the boys are wide awake, and taking her out handsomely. The lights of the signal lantern, gas lamp in front of, and that seen inside the house, are beautifully managed, and make up a natural and exciting picture.

Size sheet, 26x36 inches. Price, $3.

CURRIER & IVES' Series of Splendid Colored Pictures
—OF—
THE LIFE OF A FIREMAN.

PLATE 3.—THE FIRE.

"NOW, THEN, WITH A WILL." "SHAKE HER UP, BOYS."

A thrilling representation of an extensive conflagration. On the left of of the picture stands a truck from which the members are taking the ladders. Some are already raised, and from an upper window of the burning building emerges a fireman rescuing a little child from the flames, which seem to pursue their prey. Conspicuous in the foreground the Chief Engineer appears, giving his orders. Men are seen upon the ladders with axe in hand, hose upon the roofs of neighboring houses, and all the details in cident to the occurrence of a fire in the city.

Size sheet, 26x36 inches. Price, $3.

CURRIER & IVES' Series of Splendid Colored Pictures
—OF—
THE LIFE OF A FIREMAN.

PLATE 4.—THE RUINS.

"TAKE UP." "MAN YOUR ROPE."

On the right are the ruins, in which the flames still appear, and a heavy smoke rises up; but the enemy is conquered, and the firemen are "limbering up," and starting for home. The position and details of the engines are beautifully represented, and the scene is very pleasing and impressive.

Size sheet, 26x36 inches. Price, $3.

CHAPTER XVIII

Children's Toys

Two men sat in a New York shop chatting with each other, dropping cigarette ashes on hooked rugs, entirely oblivious of the presence of the proprietress. "I saw it only yesterday in an old toy catalogue—a tin boat with a tin man and a pair of wooden oars. You wound it up and put it in a pool and the man would row the boat. I'd like to find one of those!" "Not a chance," replied the second man. "Make up your mind to do without it. Such toys were broken within a year or two. Kids were always hard on toys."

The owner of the shop went to a corner cupboard, removed an object, and stopped before the great big men who were talking about little old toys. "Is this what you mean?" she said. It was. The very toy. The spring was gone. But all the rest was there. It had survived seventy-five years of time, and perhaps as much playing with by grownups as by the youngster for whom it was bought.

Grown-up men and women do play with early toys. There is an editor of a woman's magazine looking right now for a certain kind of hobbyhorse dating from around 1760. There are some thousand or more adults, some bank presidents, some motor tycoons, some insurance executives, who buy mechanical toy banks at what some people think are absurd and ridiculous prices. But it is their fun. The price of a round of golf seems ridiculous, too, when you count up the cost of balls, caddy fees, new clubs, side bets, *and* the annual dues of an exclusive club. There is a woman of parts who, after hours, is a mechanical toy bank hunter; especially shooting banks, the kind that not only portray some kind of shooting action but which also explode a little cap—if you have the cap to put in the proper slot.

Mechanical toys—steam engines, magic lanterns, steam-powered and spring-powered locomotives that run on tracks and

A   **B**

TRICK DOG

SPEAKING DOG   **BANK STUMP·SPEAKER**

D

Mechanical Banks of 1880s and Later.

pull trains! Dolls that are just manikins and others that cry and do other things that babies do; jack-in-boxes, jumping jacks, rocking horses, hobbyhorses, building blocks—the toy parade is endless. Not without charm (and in some cases with fantastic price tags) are such things as early miniature furniture, children's furniture, and magic toys for grownups.

Imagine a box of drawers on the top of which is a hand-painted dial with a pointer. The dial is composed of tiny miniatures of scenes, portraits, et cetera. The pointer points to one of them. Open the top drawer. There is a larger miniature of the scene pointed to on the dial. Take out that picture, open any other drawer and slip another picture in the top one. The pointer slews around, and sure enough it stops at the wee picture of the new one in the top drawer. Date?—1750 or earlier! Where is it? In the Metropolitan Museum? No. It is in an antiques shop—an early, sophisticated, and scientific toy using the magnetic principle: radar in its primitive form.

Hobbyhorses, especially those made between 1840 and 1890, are to be found in some shops—perhaps one in twenty. Horses, ostriches, camelopards or giraffes, deer and swans, from early (1870–90) carousels are now also considered as big toys and sold at big prices. These hand-carved effigies are used by some imaginative or jocund collectors in rumpus rooms and similar household dives. On the other hand, we have heard that bachelor girls consider the camelopards very nice hatracks for apartment foyers.

If you collect toys you'll be interested to know that Louis Hertz's definitive book on mechanical toy banks is in the hands of the printer, and, barring accidents, will soon be published. This book will picture almost every toy bank known to have been made and, in almost every case, the pictures will be the ones used by the original manufacturer to publicize the bank. Meanwhile, go about collecting your toy mechanical banks with an ever enlarging purse or bankroll. These banks are now enjoying, in spite of their late date of production, a price scale that is (here we go again) fantastic. Five hundred dollars was paid for a Harlequin and Columbine bank early in 1945. That's an increase, by multiplication of value, greater than almost anything in the history of antiques generally collected. That Reif-

A, B, C, D, E, G, and **H:** Mechanical Banks of 1880s and Later. The Harlequin and Columbine Bank Is Reported to Have Sold for $500 in 1945. **F, I,** and **J:** Tricycle, Cantering Hobby Horse on Wheels, and Rolling Horse, 1860–90.

snyder sale highboy that brought $44,000 in 1929 probably cost at least $440 when it was made. So antiquity multiplied the original price by one hundred. The Harlequin bank at two dollars retail in 1901 multiplies by two hundred and fifty in forty-four years. It took the highboy at least one hundred and seventy years to get to the one hundred times record. Draw your own conclusions or swear your own swear words. If you do any swearing at all, it will probably be: "Why in the blankety-blank didn't my mother and father lay away a half-dozen Harlequin banks?" I've thought the same thing.

Here are pictures representing the toys—of wood, iron, plaster, paper, tin, papier-mâché, and other materials you can buy today. The miniature furniture, games, blocks, hobbyhorses, dolls, and stuff; the trains and cars and circus parades—all these were made to amuse children and grownups in the last one hundred and fifty years or more. Many of them were made between 1880 and 1920. Yes, some of the toys today sold in antiques shops, and bought without much hesitancy on the part of toy collectors, were made less than twenty-five years ago. Some of the pictures have captions. Others have no captions. Perhaps none of the pictures need a caption. To collectors who understand, they speak for themselves.

Wood Toys and a Stone Block Set, 1870–80.

BROWN & EGGLESTON,

73 FULTON STREET, NEW YORK.

Hobbyhorses and Carriages, 1856.

BOSTON BAZAAR,

DEPOT FOR ALL KINDS OF ROCKING HORSES & CARRIAGES,

302 Washington Street, 302

Corner of Suffolk Place,

BOSTON.

A

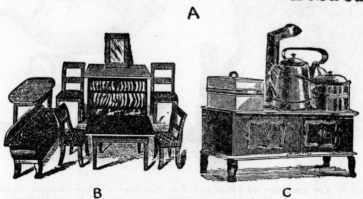

B   C

A: Toy Advertising, 1856. **B** and **C:** Toy Furniture of 1850s—Empire Style;
Toy Stove and Utensils, 1880.

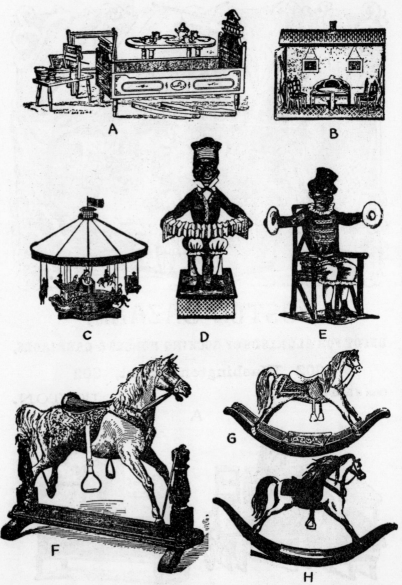

A and **B:** Toy Furniture of 1880s and Toy Furniture of 1850s—Empire Style.
C, D, and **E:** American-Made Mechanical Tin Toys of 1880s. **F, G,** and **H:** Hobby-horses, 1850–80.

A, B, and C: Mechanical Toys, 1885. D: Homemade Toy, 1840. E, F, and G: Hobbyhorses, 1850–80. H, I, J, L, M, and O: Cast-Iron Toys, 1880–1905. K, N, and P: American-Made Mechanical Tin Toys of 1880s.

Glossary and Index

The following glossary of terms, of some importance to the collector of antiques, includes a number of names of craftsmen working in the eighteenth and nineteenth centuries. These are inserted merely as examples of what the diligent researcher can find in some profusion if he will but explore the pages of early newspapers, magazines, and town and city directories. The exemplary listings include names of cabinetmakers working as far west as Chicago. If space permitted we could have included cabinetmakers and other craftsmen of record from Boston of 1660 through to San Francisco of 1860.

Many of the entries deal with terms, habits, customs, textiles, and allied subjects of antiquity that could not, for want of space, be included in the Glossary of the *Primer of American Antiques*. Other entries have to do with objects and subjects covered in the various chapters of this book. Wherever these occur the page reference only is given. Again lack of space prevents the inclusion of many terms and names. These will, eventually, be included in *A Dictionary for Antiques Collectors* now in process of compilation.

THE AUTHOR

AAKIN: Oaken; made of oak.
ABACUS: Flat member at the top of a capital.
ABATTANT: Drop-front or fall-front section of a secretary, desk, or bureau.
 SECRÉTAIRE ABATTANT: A slope-fall or vertical-fall-front secretary.
ABB: The warp yarn on a weaver's loom.
ABBETS, JAMES: Clockmaker of Albany, New York, 1760.
ABDICE: A small ax.
ABELE: The white poplar.
ABEL-WHACKETS: A game at cards—the loser being beaten with knotted kerchiefs.
ABRAHAM'S BALM: The red-willow tree. Bark used medicinally; also as an aromatic.
ACAJOU: French term for mahogany.
ACAJOU NUT: A flavoring used in puddings and combined with cocoa beans in making chocolate.
ACANTHUS: A leaf form, as stylized by ancient Greeks.

ACKERMAN, RUDOLPH: Publisher of colored-plate books, the *Repository*, and furniture style books, England, late eighteenth and early nineteenth century. Also published many prints, fancies, and elegancies.

ACROTERIUM: Pedestal or pediment with urn or other object upon it.

ACYSE: Custom; law.

ADAMANTINE CANDLES: Hardened wax and tallow candles made by Seccomb & Dennis, Salem, Massachusetts, 1845–55.

ADAM CHAIRS: See page 38.

ADAMS CALICO: Adams, Massachusetts, calico prints. Two factories, by 1838, made as much as 5,000,000 yards a year.

ADAMS' RAILROAD ATLAS: Asher & Adams and George H. Adams & Sons, 1870–80, published, in 1876, a monumental elephant folio atlas for use of steamboats and hotels. Many illustrated advertisements of American manufacturers appear in this atlas, including innumerable pictures of the products, some now called antique. About 1880 they published a similar, smaller book, *Illustrated Industries and Geography of America.*

ADAMS WIRE WORK: Samuel Adams, Boston, c. 1828, made bird cages, fender guards, baby play pens, baskets, et cetera, of wire.

ADZE: A planing or smoothing ax, with blade set at right angles to handle, as a mattock or hoe; used in rough-shaping timbers, boards, paneling, wainscoting, et cetera.

AETNA GLASS: Made at Johnson Glass Works, Frederick, Maryland, 1791–1825. Bottles and window glass.

AFFLECK, THOMAS: Philadelphia cabinetmaker, 1760–76.

AGATE: A play marble, turned from real agate.

AGATE, ALFRED: American miniature painter, 1818–46.

AGATE, FREDERICK: American painter, 1807–44.

AGINATOUR: Hawker of small wares; seventeenth-century term.

AGLET, AIGULET: (1) Tags or points on lace. (2) Jewel in a cap. (3) Catkins of the hazel bush.

AIKMAN LANTERNS: Glass bulb lanterns and small hand lamps made by S. M. and E. H. Aikman, New York, 1850–60.

AIR-CYLINDER GRAINER: Hollow cylinder covered with gutta-percha on which a "grain" was impressed to simulate rosewood, chestnut, oak, and other woods. When rolled over wet stain or paint, this grain was impressed on the surface of any soft wood. Advertised in 1860s.

AIR-FURNACE WARES: The Air Furnace Company of New York, 1768, advertised skillets, perpetual ovens, bath stoves, mortars, chimney backs (firebacks), jamb plates, and other ironware.

AIR JACK: A smoke jack; a flywheel placed in the chimney to turn a spit. Also a similar wheel placed on chimney top to improve draft. Eighteenth century. Advertised by Robert Andrews of New York in 1753.

AISIL, AYSEL: Any souring; any vinegar; sour ale, wine, milk, et cetera.

AITKEN, JAMES: American engraver, 1773–1846.

AITKEN, ROBERT: American engraver of Scottish birth, 1734–1802.

ALARUM: A watch clock. A watch with alarm—alarm clock.

ALBARELLO: A drug jar.

ALBIFICATION: Making white. Bleaching.

ALBUMS: See page 122.

ALCOCK, SAMUEL: A Burslem potter who made much ware sold in America, 1830–60, Parian, jasper, and basalt.

ALDEN COFFEE: Cooked coffee, dehydrated to a thick paste after cream and sugar had been added. Sold in pots or jars. "A spoonful makes a cupful." American, 1854.

ALDERNE: Elderberry bush.

ALE BEAM, OYLE BEAM: The olive tree.

ALEC: Fish sauces such as the following, advertised in 1800: walnut ketchup, mushroom ketchup, anchovy essence, Quin sauce.

ALEGER: Sour ale; malt vinegar.

ALE-HOOFE: The ground ivy; -IN-CORNES: New ale; -STAKE: Alehouse sign; -COST: Aromatic bitter "costemary"; -KING: Winter cherry; -WOOD: Olive wood.

ALEXANDER: The great parsley plant.

ALEXANDRIN: Hand-worked or embroidered cloth of the Near East.

ALLELUYA: The wood sorrel.

ALLEY-TOR: A game ball or marble, turned from real marble.

ALLISON: The wood rose.

AMANA: A sect of Dutch origin, settling in Switzerland and emigrating from there to America in the eighteenth century. Related to the Amish, or Omish, and operating weaving mills in Iowa, making exceptionally fine blankets.

AMMEOS: Seeds of the amomum, a grapelike fruit, which yield an aromatic odor similar to camphor.

ANCONY: A "Bloom" or pig of iron, treated for forging.

ANDERSON CLOCKS: Made in Marietta, Ohio, c. 1821-24.

ANIMAL-HEADED PRESSED GLASS: See page 200.

ANNE, CONRAD: Cabinetmaker of Lancaster, Pennsylvania, who made much Empire style furniture, 1835-60. Also made fancy chairs on mass-production basis.

ANNELY POTTERY: Made in Whitestone, New York, c. 1750. "Eight different sorts of earthenware sold at ye fly market."

ANTHRACITE LAMPS: Hard coal worked and turned into vaselike forms to serve as reservoirs in astral and camphene lamps.

ANTI-ATTRITION: Four parts lard, one part plumbago (graphite), used as a lubricant in wood turning.

AQUAMANILE: Covered ewer with a spout. Very early.

AQUATIC BOUQUET: A "mystery" bouquet of the 1850-80 period. "Arrange the bouquet, tying it to stones or lead weights in a deep dish. Submerge the dish with bouquet in a deep tub of water. Submerge a glass shade, bringing it over the bouquet and its dish. Then remove the entire ensemble from the tub. The shade holds all its water and thus the bouquet is in suspension in the water of the shade. Atmospheric pressure holds the water in the shade." (Note to reader: You can try this in miniature first, using a water glass as your "shade." You'll discover it can be done. However, changes in atmospheric pressure cause this aquatic bouquet to act as a barometer. Often it "spills" some of its water when pressure drops.)

AQUAVIVARIUM: An aquarium.

ARCHIMEDEAL PHAETON: A balloon; also called "vertical aireal coach."

ARGAL: Cream of tartar as deposited in wine bottles from wine in which grape seed was crushed in pressing. Best cream of tartar was extracted from grape seeds.

ARGAND LAMPS: See page 158.

ARGENTINE: Silvered white brassware; soy frames, cruets, salts, of Argentine, advertised about 1810.

ARGENT-VIVE: Quicksilver.

ARGILLO: A composition used in making doorknobs, cabinet and drawer pulls, et cetera, 1840s. A large factory for its production was established at Albany, New York, around 1840. Fitted with bronzed collars, rosettes, silvered seats, and other decorations.

ARM LANTERN: A standard lantern of the 1850-70 period, to the bottom of which was soldered a band of tinware through which the arm could be inserted, thus enabling user to have both arms free. Used on railroads.

ASH, GILBERT: A cabinetmaker of New York who advertised in 1759.

ASH, THOMAS: Windsor chairmaker of New York, 1770s.

ASPARAGUS TROUGHS: Troughs of chinaware holding four to six pieces of asparagus for individual service at table.

ASTBURY WARE: John Astbury, eighteenth-century English potter, put raised decoration on colored body wares. This was a phase of Staffordshire figurine making and was indulged in by many potters. Hence most "Astbury" is really a type of ware made since the eighteenth century and still made.

ASTRONOMICAL CLOCKS: Clocks showing moon phases, sunrise and sunset, heavenly aspects, tidal rise and fall, et cetera. Rare and costly.

ATHOL FURNITURE: Made by various manufacturers at Athol, Massachusetts, where, by 1835, an extensive cabinet works was in operation.

ATTLEBOROUGH BUTTONS: At Attleborough, Massachusetts, in 1837, button manufacture ran to over 5,000,000 units, worth over $90,000. Mass-production machinery was in operation. These were metal buttons.

AUTOPERIPETIKOS: Jaw-breaking name for any doll having a clockwork mechanism which caused it to walk or amble. Nineteenth century.

BACHMAN FURNITURE: The monograph on this family of cabinetmakers appearing in *American Collector* for October 1945 reveals makers to have been Jacob Bachman, Swiss-trained, working in Lancaster County, Pennsylvania, 1766-90, and his sons, grandsons, great-grandsons, and thus onward to 1910! See page 82 for further information.

BACHMAN, JACOB, 1766: See page 82.

BACK PORTRAITS: (Hindsights) Daguerreotypes taken of the backs of people who were superstitious of having faces taken, or "stolen."

BADER TABLE: A. Bader of New York, c. 1850, made a table which extended by a refinement of the drawing-table principle. The drawing table (1600 and earlier) had two leaves nested under the main top which could be drawn out at the ends and lifted to a level with the main top.

BADMAN CLOCKS: Made by Joseph Badman of Colebrookdale, Pennsylvania, c. 1780. Tall cased clocks.

BAILEY SILVER: Roswell and B. M. Bailey of Woodstock, Ludlow, and Rutland, Vermont, 1837-72, with partners Parmenter & Parker, made this silver. It is true, or "right," silver, not plated ware.

BAKER SHEFFIELD: William Baker, "late of Sheffield," attempted to make and sell the fine plated ware known as Sheffield, in New York, 1840.

BALDACHIN: A canopy fastened to the wall for suspending over a bed or a chair. Very early usage involved a stonework frame, next a wrought-metal frame, and finally, by the nineteenth century, a wire framework, nailed to any wall, to hold a bed canopy or half canopy.

BALDACHINO: An umbrella covered with leather or parchment, seventeenth century.

BALDWIN LAMPS: Made by C. A. Baldwin, New York, 1845-55.

BALL-AND-CLAW FOOT (CHIPPENDALE): To call the ball-and-claw foot of Chippendale, by Chippendale, or the mark of Chippendale is an error. His published designs do not show this foot. The ball and claw is Georgian, from Queen Anne, and of Dutch origin out of the Chinese taste. It is not Chippendale. Chippendale used the French roll-up or upturned scroll foot on his more ornate pieces. On *his* Chinese styles he used no special footing, many of the legs being carried to floor line without special treatment.

BANISTER-BACK CHAIRS: See page 28.

BANJO CLOCKS: See page 101.

BANKS, MECHANICAL: See page 234.

BANKSON, JOHN: Cabinetmaker of Baltimore, c. 1775, later Gordon & Bankson, c. 1780, and Bankson & Lawson, c. 1785. Made much fine furniture for town houses and plantation mansions. An intensive study of the work of the Banksons is indicated as highly desirable.

BARBER, RALPH: The man who made the Millville Rose paperweights, as late as the 1900s.

BARILLA: Soda deriving from burning the seaweed of the same name.

BAROQUE: Rococo.

BARREL-VAULTED (TUNNELED, WAGON-HEADED): Any ceiling vaulted in the round, as the inside of a barrel. Very early medieval ceilings were actually made of huge oak staves laid over hooplike girts.

BASE FIREDOGS: An iron frame of three straight sides, the front side being the longer, with steps of angle iron mounted on the two shorter sides, the latter serving as "dogs" upon which to lay the fire. A nineteenth-century invention that, by 1860, replaced finer andirons in many American homes.

BASSEL BOWLE: A bowling ball.

BASS MELODEON: A complete bass octave with foot pedals and reeds encased in a separate box, connected to the bellows of a standard melodeon with a flexible hose. Placed upon the floor under the standard instrument, this bass was played with the left foot. Date is in the 1850s.

BATEMAN, HESTER: A female silversmith of London to whom much posthumous honor has been paid—for being a lady silversmith. Her date, 1774–1800. Her children, Peter, Anne, and William, were silversmiths after 1793. In thus making much of Hester Bateman, the antiquarians have ignored Alice Hepplewhite, who published the designs of George Hepplewhite. Also, they have lost sight of, or perhaps did not know of, several lady silversmiths who graced the American scene in the early nineteenth century, and that we had a lady printer at Philadelphia who published some very important books.

BATLINGS: Trimmed lopings and clippings of twigs, bundled for fire kindling. Little faggots. Something like the firelight logs of today.

BATTENS: Cheap, narrow flooring boards in the days when wide boards were used even in cottage construction. Finally, meaning the narrow boards used to cover joints in other boards.

BATTERING: Sloping inward from base.

BAY SOAP: An American soap achieved by boiling animal fats in bayberries and bay leaves, with leaching of wood ashes (lye). The Swedes on the Delaware made soap this way in 1660. If there is a manufacturer really desirous of making a truly early American soap, dig into this and re-create the bay soap of 1660. We have made it in small batches, and it is grand.

BEDROOM AND BOUDOIR FURNITURE: See page 93.

BEDROOM SCALE: An early platform scale invented by Merlin Lord of London, 1786. Ancestor of the bathroom scale.

BED SPRAYS: Sprigged or "spray-of-posies" decoration on fabric for bedspreads and valances.

BED STEPS: Short flights of stairs, sometimes on rollers and with brass bail handles, often made of fine cabinet wood and on occasion having a little railing on one side, used for getting into high beds.

BEECH BUTTER: Churned and thickened oil expressed from beechnuts.

BELEEK: Irish pottery of fine glaze. Now a generic term for any fine pottery with iridescent glaze.

BELGIAN SCHOOL ART: M. deBraekeleer, Jr., came to America in 1853, and opened the Belgian Gallery in New York. He represented Verboeckhoven, Robbe, Wappers, Galland, Rosa Bonheur, Ruyten, and others. He sold to many American patrons, including the Astors, Corcorans, Appletons, Lennoxes, Robbs, and Schoenbruns (Belmonts).

BELKNAP CANDLES: Refined tallow candles made by Belknap & McCann of Newburgh, New York, from 1804.

BELLARMINE JUG: See page 168.

BELL-CAN: Bell-shaped metallic vessel often fitted with tubular spout. Originating in Zurich, Switzerland, and called Gloken-kannen.

BELL POTTERY: Made by Solomon Bell of Waynesboro, Pennsylvania, first half of nineteenth century. Stoneware and redware—crudely decorated. Peter Bell of Hagerstown, Maryland, 1825, and Winchester, Virginia, 1833; John Bell, Waynesboro, Pennsylvania, 1833; Samuel Bell, Strasburg, Virginia, 1834.

BELLOWS FLASK: Eighteenth-century quart flask of glass in the shape of a standing bellows; most likely the shape from which the so-called "violin" or "Jenny Lind" flasks were developed.

BELT, BENJAMIN: Cabinetmaker of Washington, D.C., 1822.

BELTER, JOHN: Cabinetmaker of New York, 1844–64, who worked in the Chippendale revival style that is called Victorian. Once believed to be taken too seriously by his first advocate, Thomas H. Ormsbee, Belter is now considered the Phyfe of his era by the experts who smiled at the Ormsbee enthusiasm. Belter was one of the first cabinetmakers to create Victorian furniture with meticulous care and imagination.

BENNINGTON POTTERY: See page 168.

BERRIAN WARES: Copper, tin, japanned, willow, and wooden wares sold, 1850–60, by one Berrian of New York, at wholesale, to many dealers throughout the states. He was primarily an importer.

BERRY CASES: Cigar cases made by G. G. Berry of North Stafford, New Hampshire, c. 1850.

BETTY LAMP: See page 157.

BIRD BOXES: (1) Battersea enamel boxes composed of a setting bird which, when lifted off its perch, reveals a small patch box or pin receptacle. (2) Porcelain boxes of Chinese make in bird shape (setting hens and ducks), resting on a pedestal. Lid line is usually edge of the bird's wing.

BIRD CANDELABRA: Any candle fixture having figures of birds as a part of its design and structure.

BIRGE CLOCKS: Made at Bristol, Connecticut, 1830–37, and peddled extensively in the South and West.

BISSELL ORNAMENTS: Stucco ornaments for ceiling centers, cornices, and mantels, made by Bissell of Hartford, Connecticut, 1850–70.

BIXLER CLOCKS: Made by Christian Bixler in Lancaster, Pennsylvania, 1753–1800; in Reading, Pennsylvania, by his son Christian, 1785–1820; and in Easton, Pennsylvania, by Christian III, 1790–1830. Tall case clocks.

BLAKE FURNITURE: Empire and Victorian style furniture produced by Kittredge & Blake and by James A. Blake, both of Boston.

BLAKESLEE MIRRORS: Made in Cincinnati, c. 1850, by E. Blakeslee. He produced twenty-five hundred a week!

BLANCHARD PAPERS: Wallpapers by Blanchard & Haley, Philadelphia, 1820–30. Later taken over by W. F. Slaughter.

BLANKET CHEST: See page 90.

BLISS & CREIGHTON CHRONOMETERS: Fine ships' timepieces made by this firm, who advertised 1843.

BLISS, EDWARD: Cabinetmaker of Springfield, Massachusetts, 1815–25 and later.

BLOWN GLASS: See page 182.

BLOWN-GLASS BOTTLES: See page 182.

BLOWN-GLASS FLASKS: See page 182.

BLUE-DASH CHARGER: Early English dishes, tin-glazed. A form of delft.

BLUE DECORATED STONEWARE: See page 167.

BLUNT INSTRUMENTS: Made by sons, Edward and George, of Edward Blunt, the Newburyport hydrographer. Nautical barometers made by E. & G. Blunt are considered fine. Made early nineteenth century.

BOGUE, JOHN: Cabinetmaker of Alexandria, Virginia, c. 1790.

BOSSI WORK: Marble inlay. Of early origin but named for Bossi, a worker in this art, Dublin, late eighteenth century.

BOSWELL: Part of a fire grate.

BOTTLE COLLECTORS: When glass factories used old bottles to make new glass, came the trade, or calling, of "bottle collector." These junkmen in glass did not always sell their wares to glass companies but at times sold them, after sorting as to size and capacity, to nostrum vendors who again used them as new. So common was this practice that a Federal law was passed prohibiting the re-use of wine and spirit bottles. This law may have grown out of the possibility also of re-issue, with the original revenue stamps considered as serving both fillings! At any rate, bottle collectors flourished up to at least 1880.

BOUNCERS: Iron play marbles.

BOUVIER FURNITURE: M. Bouvier was a cabinetmaker of Philadelphia in the first quarter of the nineteenth century. His stock was sold by T. B. Freeman, October 31, 1833, and included thirty hair-seated sofas, two wardrobes, thirteen pairs of tables, ten worktables, twenty-four music stools, fifty easy chairs, eight pairs card tables, nine pairs dining tables, three sideboards, et cetera. Three hundred thousand feet of veneer were also sold. Freeman issued a catalogue of the sale. This stock may be considered exemplary of the finished goods carried by many cabinetmakers of the period.

BOW KNIFE: Sickle-shaped knife affixed to bow of canalboats to sever the ropes of rival craft which did not "pass" their towrope under the hull in passing.

BOXES: FANCY AND PAINTED: See page 135.

BOYD BEDS: Henry Boyd of Cincinnati made bedsteads in some numbers in a factory which, by 1850, employed twenty people.

BOYD CHAIRS: Made in Harrisburg, Pennsylvania, by J. B. Boyd, 1840–65. Cane- and wood-seated chairs, stenciled and painted.

BRADFORD, CORNELIUS—PEWTER: This pewterer of Philadelphia advertised his wares in 1765 as follows: "dishes, plates and basons of all sizes, tankards, quart & pint mugs, porringers, tea pots, sugar pots, cullenders, bed pans, stool pans, half pint & gill tumblers, wine measures, salt sellers, spoons, milk pots, dram bottles, slop bowles, block tin and pewter worms for distilling, candle moulds, and bottle cranes . . ." at the sign of the "Dish" in Second Street!

BRADLEY, HARRISON: Chairmaker of Alexandria, Virginia, 1835.

BRAINTREE GLASS: Made in Braintree, Massachusetts, 1750–56. Mostly bottles.

BRANDED: Done in red and black.

BRANK: An iron frame placed over the heads of convicted common scolds. Seventeenth century.

BRIGADE OF CARS: Original name for a train of railway cars.

BRINNER, JOHN: Colonial cabinetmaker of New York, 1762.

BRITANNIA: See page 151.

BRITANNIA MEDALS: Rewards of merit in medal form, cast in this cheap metal for use of schools, 1835–50.

BRONZE ARGENT: White bronze.

BROOKS-GROVER GRIDIRON: Oblong, round-ended grid with side handle, fitting into the space on top of a range taken up by two lids and the interstice piece; 1850–70.

BRYANT, NATHANIEL: Cabinetmaker of Boston, 1820–35, who made Greek revival-style cabinet furniture, sofas, chairs, and tables.

BURCH, JOSEPH: Washington, D.C., cabinetmaker, c. 1822.

BURCH TINWARE: Solid block-tin ware and japanned tin-plated wares, made by John Burch of New York, c. 1770.

BUREAU, OR SLOPE-FALL DESK: See page 88.

BURLEY & LYFORD: Manufacturers of cottage furniture and ornamental cabinetmakers, Cincinnati, 1840–50. Enameled, scrolled, and landscaped furniture in Italian and Grecian styles—beds, bureaus, toilet stands, some grained to imitate every variety of fine wood. Also makers of steamboat furniture.

BURLING, THOMAS & SON, AND WILLIAM: Makers of looking glasses and cabinet furniture, New York, 1785–1815. JOHN: Cabinetmaker, 1770.

BURNAP CLOCKS: Made by Daniel Burnap of Andover, Massachusetts, and Hartford, Connecticut. Calendar and moon-phase tall-case clocks. Colonial period, to 1838.

BUTLER POTTERY: Stone and earthenwares made by Butler, New Brunswick, New Jersey, 1810–60. Then by Mullen & Connoly, to 1880.

BUTLER & WISWELL FURNITURE: Made at Chicago, c. 1850, by this partnership of cabinetmakers.

BUTTERFLY TABLES: See page 64.

BUTTON-TURNED BEDS: See page 93.

CABINET AND CHAIR MAKERS' PRICE BOOKS: See page 2.

CABINETMAKERS' MODELS: Furniture in miniature, made to scale, anywhere from one-eighth to one-half regular size. Some by apprentices on becoming journeymen, some as "samples" for display.

CALDRONS: Globular cook pots with bail handles and one or two spouts—copper, tin, iron, brass.

CALLING SPOON: Wood, brass, pewter, or silver spoon with a whistle in handle, blown to call servants, sedan-chair men, et cetera.

CAMPBELL POTTERY: Pantiles (roof tiles) and "Philadelphia Earthenwares," made by John Campbell of New York, 1774.

CAMPHENE LAMPS: See page 160.

CANDLESTICKS: See page 157.

CAPTAIN'S DRESSER CHEST: Small chest of drawers with lidded top, side bails, fitted and compartmented trays, folding mirror, withdrawing shelf, and other conveniences. Eighteenth-century ones are often very finely made.

CAPUT FLASK: A "face" flask; a flask in the general form of a head, or bearing a masklike face representing a classic divinity, Christian saint, or holy person. Very ancient, dating from Roman Era through Middle Ages. Made of glass.

CARD WRITER: A local and itinerant trade, practitioners of which often worked on the streets, writing "cards" at a little folding desk. These men (and some women) were experts in the art of calligraphy and were lineal trade descendants of the old "letter writers" of the sixteenth century. As card writers, they specialized in writing visiting cards. Their work generally had the appearance of copperplate printing.

CARMER, HENRY: Cabinetmaker of New York, 1774.

CARMER, NICHOLAS: Cabinetmaker of Maiden Lane, New York, 1767. He advertised chairs, desks, bookcases, tables, and planks of mahogany.

CARTESIAN BOTTLES: Philosophers' toys, named for René Descartes, seventeenth-century philosopher. A hollow glass imp or other figure, airtight, was inserted in a glass tube filled with water or some other liquid and covered with a flexible top, such as parchment. When this cover was depressed it increased the atmospheric pressure in the tube, causing the figure to sink. Release of pressure caused imp to rise. Tubes and "imps" made as late as 1871 by William Demuth, special glass blower of New York.

CARVED WORK: See page 126.

CASE OF DRAWERS: See pages 88, 90.

CASSOLETTE: An ovoid or spherical vessel on a stand. French.

CASSONE: A coffer or casket, usually on feet and richly carved. Fifteenth and sixteenth centuries.

CAST-IRON ORNAMENTS: See page 122.

CATALOGUES OF MERCHANDISE NOW ANTIQUES: See page 112.

CAUGHLEY: Thomas Turner operated the Caughley pottery of England, last quarter eighteenth century. Made willow-pattern plates. Also Salopian wares.

CENTENNIAL LAMPS: Cuplike shades of glass to hold a candle, made in a wide variety of colors and used for the demonstrative art of "illumination" at times of celebration, for political parades, et cetera. The centennial variety is a blown mold, or pressed relation of the earlier blown Christmas-tree light. They were very inexpensive and quite common articles in the carnival trade; 1870–85.

CERMENATI & BERNARDA MIRRORS: Mirrors made by a firm so named, at 2 State Street, Boston, c. 1810. Made tabernacle mirrors of the style miscalled Sheraton. Italian and Swiss-Italian and French mirror makers were not uncommon in America, 1790–1830. It is altogether likely these men introduced the tabernacle mirror—from the French *trumeau* of the period.

CHAMBERINGS: The furniture of a bedroom, or sometimes just a bed.

CHARTA BOMBAZINE: Paper made from cotton.

CHENETS: Firedogs; andirons. French.

CHENEY CLOCKS: Made in East Hartford, Connecticut, 1745–80. Tall-case, wooden-works clocks. Made also in Berlin, Connecticut, 1800–35. Tall-case and mantel clocks. Several makers named Cheney were involved, of course.

CHINA: See page 167.

CHINESE BACKS: Latticework after the Chinese, as used by Chippendale in his chair backs.

CHINESE BLINDS: Advertised name of landscaped and figured window blinds offered by John S. Jones, Philadelphia, in 1833.

CHINESE LANTERNS: "A new and beautiful transparent article suitable for large rooms and gardens, Chinese lanthorns," was offered by John S. Jones of 2 Church Alley, Philadelphia, 1833.

CHIPPENDALE BALL AND CLAW: A common error; see Ball and Claw.

CHIPPENDALE CHAIRS: See page 36.

CHIPPENDALE SOFAS: See page 54.

CHIPPENDALE TABLES: See page 66.

CHIROMANCY: Fancy name for palmistry, based upon the methods of Madame de Normand, palmist to the Empress Josephine. Quite a fad in America, 1840–55, and even later.

CHRISTIAN FURNITURE: A cabinetmaker of New York City, with a shop at 73 Broad Street, "with experience in Europe," made Hepplewhite and Sheraton style furniture in the finest manner, c. 1800–10. He labeled certain of his pieces.

CHRISTMAS BALLS: See page 112.

CHRYSANTHEMUM PLATE: Chinese porcelain plates made in stylized form of an open chrysanthemum.

CINCINNATI FURNITURE: In 1841 the furniture industry of Cincinnati was employing 335 people and making goods valued at $664,000. Ten years later it employed 1,158 and produced $1,660,000 worth of furniture. Most of this production and that of the years before and the years between is now of antique or near-antique status. Cincinnati furniture was sold as far South as New Orleans, as far West as a steamboat could run on the Missouri, as far North as the Mississippi was navigable. It is conservatively estimated that between 1830 and 1850 close to $10,000,000 worth of furniture was produced in Cincinnati. A cabinetmakers' *price book* was published for the cabinetmakers of the city in 1830 and again in 1836. Styles were first a mixture of Sheraton and Directoire, then Directoire-inspired Empire, and finally heavy Empire. Much spool-turned, ball, button, and bulb-turned cottage furniture was also made. Cabinetmaking in Cincinnati deserves a monograph of some scope. If anyone wants to undertake the task this is an invitation to write to the author. We shall gladly contribute what data we have on this important furniture-making center. Among other records, we have one of the Cincinnati Steam Bureau Manufacturing Company which, in 1850, produced 7,000 bureaus annually, and other furniture in proportion. Big business—and all of it that has survived is now nearly, or on the verge of being, American Antique!

CLAIR DE LUNE: A color poetically described as "blue as the sky after rain."

CLAWSON & MUDGE of Cincinnati, 1850, employed 130 people, who produced 130 bedsteads per day. They made 95 styles (!), selling at wholesale from $1.37½ to $75.00. They used poplar, sycamore, cherry, and black-walnut woods, solid and veneered.

CLICHY: French glass, imported in some quantities, 1840–70. They made paper-weights of fine quality.

CLIPPER SHIP: Research thus far conducted seems to indicate that the name "clipper" was applied to ships at least fifty years before the special type of swift-sailing freight and passenger carrier of American make was given that name. Any swift vessel was called a "clipper" in early dockside parlance. There were ships called "clippers" by 1800. Yet the "clipper ship" itself is classified as of 1845–60.

CLOCKS: See page 101.

CLOSE STOOL: Night chair; toilet chair.

CLOSTERMAN CHAIRS: Plain and fancy chairs made by Henry Closterman of Cincinnati, 1845–55. He made mahogany and walnut chairs.

COAD, JOHN: Cabinetmaker of Washington, D.C., c. 1822.

COCONUT DIPPER: Not a dipper made from a coconut shell, but a dipper with a bowl of coconut-shell shape made of brass, iron, copper, Britannia, or silver, with turned wood handle. Made as late as 1875 by G. A. Mix of Yalesville, Connecticut.

CODDINGTON CHAIRS: Chairs made by a Cincinnati furniture manufactory which, in 1850, produced 180,000 chairs, fancy and plain, painted and gilded, at from $4.25 to $22 per dozen. Sold principally in South and Southwest. These chairs are today found in Texas, Louisiana, Arkansas, Mississippi, Georgia, and Tennessee. Made with caned and rush seats.

COFFEE BUSTS: Thomas Coffee, sculptor, of New York, c. 1840–50, made plaster-of-Paris ornaments, busts, et cetera, and sold them in some quantities.

COFFEE DISH: Shallow bowls of Chinese make, without handles, but with under dishes (now called saucers), were the first teacups and coffee cups—but called tea dishes and coffee dishes. Hence, "have a dish of tea or a dish of coffee." Chocolate was also served in such bowls.

COFFIN CUPBOARD: A corner cupboard with one door, having what is known as a fielded panel (a panel with beveled edges and a raised, shaped section inside the beveling) with the general appearance of a wide coffin standing in the corner. Name is not contemporaneous, as the cupboard was made as early as 1710, while the coffin of somewhat similar type was made one hundred years later.

COMFIT BOX: A bonbon box.

COMMERAW POTTERY: Made at Corlears Hook, New York, after 1785; hard earthenware and salt-glaze stoneware.

COMMONEY: Cheap white game marbles of fired white clay, often decorated with multiple hair striping in colors.

COMMUNAL CUP: Any capacious drinking vessel handed around the table for drinking; a tyg; a posset.

COMPOSITE OIL: A patented lamp fluid of the camphene variety, made of resins, turpentine, alcohol, et cetera. It made a lovely light but was highly volatile, and the lamps sometimes exploded.

CONNELLY, HENRY: Philadelphia furniture designer, 1770–1825. Said to have worked in the styles of Hepplewhite, Sheraton, and the Directoire.

CONNER, R., DESIGNER OF FURNITURE, 1842: See page 4.

CONOVER SKATES: Wood-soled, iron-bladed ice skates, 1855–60.

CONSTANTINOPLE CASES: Turkish leather cases for cutlery and razors; eight-eenth-century name.

COOK, LEONARD: Furniture maker of Alexandria, Virginia, c. 1834.

COOLIDGE FURNITURE: Made by John Coolidge, Cincinnati, 1845-55. He made cribs, lounges, tables, stands, desks, and bookcases. Employed forty workmen in 1850.

CORNELIUS & BAKER LAMPS: America's first mass-production maker of lamps of all sorts, sizes, and designs. Philadelphia, from 1828 or earlier. Made lamps by the hundreds of thousands.

CORNICHON: A pair of horseshoes, welded together as an elongated loop, for use in a game similar to quoits.

CORSELIUS POTTERY: The first stoneware pottery of New York, 1730-45, when Clarkson Crolius and John Remmey, who married daughters of Corselius, took over the works, divided it, and continued as two potteries. This pottery made incised and cobalt-blue-decorated stoneware.

COSINOMANCY: Divination with the aid of a sieve.

CÔTE PALEY: A painted dress fabric introduced about 1829.

COULTER BARGAINS: Probably a derisive term for what one bought at the public furniture auctions of Henry Coulter, New York, 1838-45. He sold anything, as the saying goes, and had regularly scheduled auctions twice weekly.

COURT OF DEATH: A painting by Rembrandt Peale, engraved and issued as a print in an edition of 100,000 copies, size 23 by 31 inches, hand-colored, priced at $1.00 each. Offered as a "superb parlor ornament" by G. Q. Colton, 1859. Endorsed by Millard Fillmore and other bigwigs.

COVERLET PATTERNS: Many names were current for the patterns used on the woven two- and three-color coverlets of the nineteenth century: E Pluribus Unum, Washington, Rich Man's Fancy, Bonny's Retreat, Queen, Muscadine, Tennessee Double, Missouri Trouble, et cetera. See *Heirlooms from Old Looms* by the Coverlet Guild for more data.

COVERLETS: See page 130.

COWDEN & WILCOX POTTERY: Stoneware made in Harrisburg, Pennsylvania, c. 1840-70. It is believed they made many snuff jars for Demuth of Lancaster.

COWPERTHWAITE FURNITURE: Fancy chairs and other furniture made by John K. Cowperthwaite of 4 Chatham Square, New York, from 1815. This firm is known to have made Windsor and fancy chairs of many kinds; was in business until the twentieth century; issued catalogues and enjoyed a high reputation.

COX WOODENWARE: Gideon Cox of 335 Market Street, Philadelphia, 1825-40, made bathtubs, bowls, churns, tubs, sieves, butter prints, curly (burl) bowls, hobbyhorses, stepladders, baskets, buckets, beckets, and cedar wares. He had a very extensive manufactory. Many advertisements of this factory appear in Philadelphia newspapers of the period.

COXE, JOSEPH: Cabinetmaker of New York City, 1773, advertised "elboe" and corner chairs, bookcases, cabinets, et cetera.

COZZENS STOPPERS: A screw stopper for bottles; 1855-60.

CRAB CIDER: Crab-apple cider.

CRATER: A metal doughnut-shaped device to place over the glass chimney of a kerosene lamp and make it serve as a small stove; 1855-60.

CREAM EWER: The creamer of any tea set was so called.

CREEM: To shrink, to pulp. Thus, pulped potatoes, apples, et cetera, were not "creamed" but "creemed." People shivering were said to be "creemed with ye colde."

CRESCENT: A neck ornament in the form of crescent, or gorget, worn with low gowns over the V of the breasts. "Impudent lasses will turn up their crescents by moonlight."

CRIBBLE: A colander; a strainer.

CRIMOSIN: Crimson.

CRIMP SOCKET: A socket of crimped metal with a flat, short handle, used in burning candle ends or in making a thin candle fit a large socket; 1835-45.

CRISPELS: Fritters.

CROCUS POT: Half-round or commode-shaped pots of porcelain, fitted with little cups for sprouting crocuses indoors and bringing them to bloom. An elegancy of the eighteenth century.

CROLIUS POTTERY: Stoneware made by the Crolius family, 1745–1850, New York. See also Corselius and Remmey.

CROSS-WICK LAMP: A kerosene oil burner having four narrow wicks fed through a cross-shaped orifice of metal. Lamp required a globe but no chimney. Made in New Orleans around 1858–60. Apparently rather rare, but good.

CROWLET TINWARE: Wine coolers, cellarets, bathtubs, portable kitchens, "conjurers" (quick cookers), japanned wares, et cetera, New York, 1790–1810.

CRYGIER HANGINGS: Wallpaper made by C. & J. Crygier, New York, 1790–1820, "allowed to be superior to any made in the United States." In 1802 this firm advertised these colors: green, blue, pink, and gray, on rich satin or muslin ground.

CUDGEL WORK: Heavy, thick embroidery.

CURRIER & IVES: See pages 216, 219–31.

CURRY SILVER: John Curry and Curry & Preston, silversmiths and silver-plate makers, Philadelphia, 1820–30, produced this ware.

CURTAIN PAPERS: Advertised by Richardson of Albany, 1845, as papers for curtaining walls, covering fireboards, et cetera.

CURTIS CLOCKS: Banjo, shelf, and mantel clocks made by several firms named Curtis, in Concord, Massachusetts, 1814–18, and in Burlington, Vermont, 1818–57.

CURTISVILLE SILVER: Plated silver, the American equivalent of late electroplated Sheffield, and offered in a line that ran from communion chalices to snuffboxes, and from soup tureens and vegetable dishes to cake baskets. Made in Curtisville and Hartford, Connecticut, 1850–75.

CUTLER, ABNER: Cabinetmaker of Buffalo, New York, 1830. He advertised sofas, Grecian couches, sideboards, claw, pier, and card tables, dining tables, et cetera, in one of the earliest-known labor papers in America, the *Workingmen's Bulletin*, 1830. Thus he identified himself as making furniture for the people at large and not only for the well to do.

CUT TISSUES: Die-cut tissue paper for fancywork, 1800–60.

DAVIDSON & STRACHAN: Cabinetmaking firm of New York City, c. 1750.

DAVIS BRASSWARE: Fireplace furniture made by Davis of Boston, late eighteenth and early nineteenth centuries.

DAYTON PICTURES: Dayton & Co., 1855–60, wholesaled prints "engraved and colored in oils." Numbers included Titian's Venus; Molly Pitcher, Heroine of Monmouth; Spirit of the Union, et cetera. Certain of these are considered good, especially the historic prints.

DEAL: Generic term for any timber of the pine family when cut into planks. Name originally applied only to the form of a piece of timber, cut and dressed as a useful board. Finally applied to furniture made from such boards, as a "deal table," a "deal settle," et cetera.

DE COUDRES WARE: Copper-, brass-, and tinware made in Newark, New Jersey, 1825–40, by Thomas de Coudres. Andirons, iron pots, sheet-iron wares also were made by this man. Some of his stuff is marked.

DEDHAM FURNITURE: Much furniture was made in this Massachusetts town in the early nineteenth century. In 1837 production was considered worth $21,000.

DEERFIELD STUFFS: Cutlery and leatherwork from Deerfield, Massachusetts, made in the first and second quarters of nineteenth century.

DE LA PLAINS, JOSHUA: New York City cabinetmaker, 1738–56.

DEL VECCHIO MIRRORS: Made by James del Vecchio of New York City in first half of nineteenth century. He carried on a rather extensive trade.

DENBY & CODNOR PARK POTTERY: See page 172.

DENNIS, THOMAS: Late seventeenth-century joiner of Ipswich, Massachusetts. He worked in oak. The late Irving P. Lyon of Buffalo, son of Dr. Irving W. Lyon, the first historian of Early American furniture, planned a monograph on the oak furniture of Ipswich. Some of his notes were published in *Antiques Magazine*, February 1938.

DESK BOX: See page 86.

DESK BOX-ON-FRAME: See page 86.

DESK-ON-FRAME: See page 88.

DESKS IN GENERAL: See page 86.

DEWEY PITCHERS AND PLATES: Pressed-glass mementos and memorials of Rear Admiral George Dewey, the hero of Manila. Made 1899–1901. Thousands of pieces were made.

DIAPHANIE: Transparent "art" paper upon which various designs were printed in transparent colors. First sold as a specialty to enable homecrafters to imitate stained glass (c. 1848), the stuff became a staple and is still made. It is now considered cheap and in poor taste. Once it was *tres chic!*

DIE MEN: Dice in the form of squatting male figures, with the ace on the posterior, six on his back, et cetera. These date from as early as sixteenth century. **DIE WOMEN:** Similar figures in form of a nude woman squatting. Vulgarly known as "die-doxies."

DIE VASES: Vase-formed dice boxes.

DIETZ LAMPS: Dietz & Company began making lamps early in 1840. This firm is still in business. Between 1840 and 1860 they made a wide variety of candle lamps, oil lamps, and finally kerosene lamps. Catalogues of early issue reveal a comprehensive line.

DIOGRAPH: Drawing instrument for use in making landscapes, enabling the artist to achieve accurate perspective. Invented in 1810 by Simeon DeWitt of Albany, made by Abraham Randel, cabinetmaker of Albany.

DIORASCOPE: A folding, sighting instrument with a scanning screen having twenty apertures formed by crossing cords. Invented by DeWitt of Albany, c. 1810.

DIRECTOIRE CHAIRS: See page 38.

DIRECTOIRE SOFAS AND SETTEES: See page 54.

DIRECTOIRE TABLES: See page 68.

DISSECTED MAPS: Jigsaw puzzles of the 1820–50 period, in which maps were sawed out on state lines for assembly by students.

DOBELL FURNITURE: Cincinnati chairmakers and cabinetmakers of the 1840s include Dobell & Hughes and E. B. Dobell.

DODGE LAMPS: Made by J. F. Dodge of Boston, 1830–60. All manner and styles of lamps, lamp fluids, and lighting fixtures.

DOLL TOYS: Wooden toys of all kinds made by John Doll of Philadelphia, as late as 1874.

DONARKIEL: Scandinavian legend carried to America by Swedes, Finns, and Norwegians, having to do with superstition that all round stones were sacred to Donar. Round stones were "saved" as found, hoarded in piles, placed atop fence posts and on tree stumps. Not a German legend, as some pro-Germanic advocates aver.

DOOLITTLE CLOCKS: Made by Enos Doolittle of Hartford, Connecticut, after 1750. Isaac Doolittle, clockmaker of New Haven, 1769.

DOOR PANELS, NEEDLEWORK: A relic of the old "long" sampler, or "bread cloth," worked in cross-stitch, and often in Swedish, Norwegian, or Swiss patterns, by various sects of Pennsylvania and not infrequently called Pennsylvania-German—which they are not. They were made also in New England, New

York, and, later, in Ohio. New England examples are decorated with English designs not unlike the Norwegian. One of the great enigmas of this day lies in the close resemblance of many Swedish and Norse forms to the early forms of decoration expressed in the Irish *Book of Kells*. It is now believed by some scholars that *Book of Kells* designs are Scandinavian, from early settlers of Scandinavian blood in the north of Ireland and Scotland. On the other hand, certain of the very ancient Swedish décor can be traced to Phoenician influence. The puzzle is very real, but it poses a most interesting problem in solution. One thing is quite sure: it is not German decoration, and any of it that is in Germany was impressed upon Germany by the conquering Swedes of the fifteenth and sixteenth centuries.

DORCHESTER FURNITURE: Dorchester, Massachusetts, had ten furniture and chair factories between 1830 and 1840. One hundred and twenty people were employed as turners, cabinetmakers, and chairmakers.

DORIC FIREPLACE: An anthracite-burning open stove for use in a fireplace. Offered about 1825. Grecian in design. Said to have been invented by Oliver Evans, the American Watt, who, in 1803, had a steam-driven vehicle running on the streets of Philadelphia.

DOUBLE CHEST OF DRAWERS: Another name for chest-on-chest.

DOUBLE GEERED BED: A patented "windlass" bedstead advertised in 1829 by N. Perry of Boston.

DOULTON & WATTS POTTERY: See page 172.

DOWNS CLOCKS: Made in Bristol, Connecticut, and other towns, 1811–43. Downs made many clocks sold by peddlers in New York, Pennsylvania, Ohio, Indiana, and Kentucky. Looking-glass clocks were made by this firm.

DUPUY, DANIEL: Silversmith associated with John Dupuy, clockmaker of Philadelphia, 1770.

DURELL POTTERY: Jonathan Durell of New York, 1773, advertised "Philadelphia" earthenwares: "butter, pickle, oyster, and chamber pots, mugs, bowles, basons, sauce pans, and dishes"!

DUTCH STYLE: The styles the Dutch impressed upon New York and what is now Pennsylvania, from 1650–80, and upon England with some force after 1680; now called William and Mary and Queen Anne. The Dutch appropriated these styles from the Chinese. They were in America before they were popular in England.

DYOTT, THOMAS: Bootblack in boyhood, then vendor of boot polish, then mixer of nostrums and maker of "bitters," finally assuming the title of M.D. and Doctor, and becoming a very successful druggist, patent-medicine, and bitters manufacturer. Needing thousands of bottles, he gained control of a glasshouse at Kensington, near Philadelphia (the scene of his rise to riches), and thus the Dyottville Glass Works. He used child labor, preferably orphans, and worked them hard "for the good of their souls." He next started a workingman's bank. Finally blew up in a mad financial mix-up, losing everything, thus duplicating the life of Henry William Stiegel, the German immigrant who, a stooge for the Stedmans of Philadelphia, also went up like a rocket and came down like the stick. Neither Stiegel nor Dyott were glassmakers. They were speculators. Their workmen, good or bad, made the glass. Many Dyott flasks of the historic variety are now collected. See McKearin's *American Glass*.

EAGLE GLASS: Made at Eagle Works, Port Elizabeth, New Jersey, from 1799. Named "Eagle" in 1817. In operation until 1885.

EARTH FLAX, SALAMANDER HAIR: Asbestos. Also rock alum and stone alum. One early use was weaving into everlasting candlewicks. This proved a failure because the burning candle required a wick that was consumed as the wax burned. Used with more success as a lamp wick.

EARTHENWARE: See pages 167, 170.

EASTLAKE CHAIRS: See page 49.

EASTLAKE SINK: A kitchen sink in Eastlake style (!) offered by Mott Ironworks in 1875.

EASTLAKE TABLES: See page 74.

ECUELLA: A broth cup, oval or round, with loop or flat handles.

EDWARDS LAMPS: H. Edwards of New York, c. 1845-55, made hall lanterns, street lanterns, and lamps.

EGERTON FURNITURE: In New Brunswick, New Jersey, three generations of cabinetmakers named Egerton worked, 1770-1837. They made Hepplewhite and Sheraton style furniture, or so it is reported.

EIDOGRAPH: An enlarging and reducing machine for use in drawing.

ELECTRIC LAMP: Not really electric, but a kerosene burner of great brilliance, using the Argand burner principle and developing a light actually more powerful than an early Edison incandescent bulb.

ELEGANCIES, ADVERTISING OF: See pages 112-37.

ELLIOT, JOHN: Philadelphia mirror maker from 1753. He worked in what has been called the Chippendale style. Most of his mirrors were Georgian style out of Queen Anne. Elliot's mirrors were good to fine. His sons carried on the business until after 1800. John Elliot advertised his mirrors in 1753.

ELLIS DOLLS: All-maple dolls made by J. A. H. Ellis of Springfield, Vermont, c. 1870. The doll heads were die-stamped or "squeezed" from green wood, and the bodies lathe-turned. The first of the so-called indestructible dolls made in America. It is said this doll was also made by Mason, Taylor, Sanders, and others in Vermont.

EMBROIDERED PICTURES: See page 134.

EMERSON PRINTS: Sold by subscription by J. M. Emerson through local agents. One of his biggest hits (1860) was Rosa Bonheur's Horse Fair, which was lithographed by Sarony, Major & Knapp.

EMPIRE SOFAS, SETTEES, AND SEATS: See page 59.

EMPIRE TABLES: See page 72.

ENGRAVINGS: See page 216.

ENTERDEALE: Cohabitation. Term derives from Old Mother Hubbard, when that tale was not for children.

ESCRIN: A cabinet.

ÉTAGÈRES: See page 78.

ETAIN: Tin.

EVANS GIFT BOOKS: George Evans of Philadelphia entered the annual-gift-book business and by 1860 claimed to have sold 6,000,000 copies. Such annuals are now selling at $1.00 a copy as Victorian relics and considered a good buy. They sold for considerably more than $1.00 when new.

EXETER CARPETS: Made by Claude Passavant in Exeter, England, after 1755, and exported to America for sale here.

EXETER WARE: Made at Exeter, New Hampshire, by the Lamson Pottery, 1830-1900. The equipment of this pottery is now in the Edison Institute at Dearborn, Michigan. Output in early days was utilitarian ware. Later product seems to have been chiefly flowerpots.

FAIRY LAMP: A late (1875) lamp made by Gansler, Hoffman & Co. of Philadelphia. It was a night lamp, small and with imitation cut-glass oil fount.

FAMILY BEER: Made from Smith's essence; sold in apothecary shops in the 1840s.

FAN MIRROR: In shape resembling a folding fan, opened, the entire blade being of mirror glass in a lacquered wood frame. Used upright on dressing tables and pendent on walls. Date as early as 1700-25.

FANCY CANED CHAIRS: See page 26.

FANCY CHAIRS: See pages 22, 42.

FANCY SETTEES: See page 58.

FASHION DOLLS: Dolls dressed in the fashion were often the sign of milliners, who also sold such conceits, 1750–1825.

FEDERAL MIRRORS: See pages 108, 110.

FELLOE SAW: A chairmaker's saw.

FIBBLE-DE-DI-DOES: Housekeeping gadgets were so called, 1850–70.

FIGURINES: See page 126.

FIRE HOLDER: A hearthside utensil of iron or brass consisting of a small table with handle, upon which is mounted a pair of spring tension pincers atop a rod, the pincers holding a burning splinter of resinous wood. Eighteenth century.

FIREPLACE EQUIPMENT: See page 128.

FIRE POLISHED GLASS: See page 198.

FITZ-SQUAB: Pseudonym of the illustrator who did the first comic sections for the New York *Mercury*, 1843.

FLOOR SKATES: Roller skates with four rollers of hard rubber, all set in line, giving the effect of one rolling blade. Offered by Frederick Stevens of Boston, 1856.

FOGG CHECKS: Checkered linens and cottons woven by Thomas Fogg of New York, c. 1763.

FOLIATING: Quicksilvering.

FOSTER WRITING SETS: Pocket writing sets of brass, marked "Foster," were sold throughout New England, latter half of nineteenth century.

FOUNTAINS: See page 122.

FRIZZELL MIRRORS: Made by J. W. Frizzell of Baltimore, mid-nineteenth century.

FROBISHER, BENJAMIN: Silversmith and jeweler of Boston, advertised Britannia wares in 1829. (Just in case an expert tells you the date should be after 1835!)

FRONK, LEWIS: Glass blower of Washington, D.C., 1822.

FROTHINGHAM, BENJAMIN: Boston and Charlestown cabinetmaker who was a major in the Revolution.

FUDDLING CUP, BEFUDDLER: A series of six pottery cups bound together with bands of clay and arranged in a triangle so that any cup could be brought to the lips. When fired, the six cups were, of course, one rigid ensemble. There were handles on the three corner cups. Fill 'em up and try to drink from any one. The fuddling cup surely befuddled you. The trick, of course, is to fill any *one* cup. You can drink from it with great ease. But to fill them all and try to drink from any one is to spill the drink all over you. A mid-eighteenth-century tavern and alehouse trick cup. Usually of Staffordshire pottery.

GAITHER, GREENBURY: Silversmith of Washington, D.C., 1822.

GALE STERLING: William Gale & Sons, established 1821 in New York City, were among the first of American silversmiths to stamp their solid silver "sterling."

GALER, ADAM: Windsor chairmaker of Philadelphia before 1773. In New York after 1774.

GALPIN CLOCKS: Clocks marked "Galpin" are clocks made by others but with dials marked with the name of this super-peddler who sold so many clocks he could demand his name be on the dials. Chauncey Jerome made clocks for, and designated, "Galpin." Early nineteenth century.

GARDINER, WILLIAM: Furniture maker of New York, 1835–55.

GARDNER, MASSACHUSETTS, FURNITURE: This town, in 1837, had twenty-five cabinet and chair factories, employing 350 people and producing goods valued at over $100,000.

GATE-LEG TABLES: See page 64.

GAUTIER, ANDREW: Windsor chairmaker of New York, advertising high-backed, low-backed, and double-seated chairs, sack-backed low chairs, children's chairs, and dining chairs, in 1765.

GAYETTY PAPER: Medicated paper for application to cuts, wounds, and sores. It was watermarked "J. C. Gayetty." Sold from 1850.

GEDDES, CHARLES: Clockmaker of Boston and New York, 1770–76.

GEMEL: Oil-vinegar or other "pairs" of flasks, joined, with necks facing in opposite directions. Also GIMMAL.

GEORGE REX JUGS: See page 170.

GERMAN COFFEE: Derisive term for chicory, the roots of which were dried and roasted by Germanic immigrants and used as coffee.

GEYER, JOHN: Cincinnati furniture manufacturer who succeeded to the McAlpin Cabinet Works (established 1835) and by 1850 had a five-story factory, 56 by 100 feet, turning out cottage, Italian, and fancy parlor chairs; sofas, marble-top tables, dressers, *étagères*, papier-mâché tables and stands, desks, and basket-base sewing stands.

GIMMEL RING: Laminated rounds of gold or silver, riveted together and ending in clasped hands. Only when off the finger can the rounds be manipulated and the hands unclasped to reveal a heart or other emblem. Also GEMEL RING.

GINGAWTRE: Cod and haddock, diced small, with bread, broth, wine, and spicing, boiled together. In other words, chowder. Variants of the term point to what may be the origin of the word "chowder"; gingawdry, ginchawdry, ginchawder, chawdery.

GINNA TINWARE: Painted, decorated, and japanned tinware made by Ginna & Co. of New York, late nineteenth century. Much of the ware was for grocery stores and consisted of tea and coffee canisters, spice cans, and such boxes as were appropriate for storing coffee in the bean, sugar, bay leaves, et cetera.

GINORI WARE: Imitation Capo di Monte made after 1860 by the Marquis Ginori, near Florence, Italy.

GITTERN: A zither; a stringed musical instrument.

GLADDING, T. A.: Albany, New York, portrait painter, 1845, who was one of the endorsers of Townsend's sarsaparilla.

GLASS AGATE: A play marble of agate glass.

GLAZE CAP: Glazed-kid (patent-leather) or oilcloth headpiece in military style, 1830–50.

GLOBE IRON FURNITURE: Fancy chairs in Sheraton and Directoire style, made of cast iron, as late as 1868, by the Globe Iron Works of New York. The Chase Iron Works made the same sort of furniture.

GLOBE LAMPS: Advertised but not described by William Mercier in New York *Gazette,* 1755. It is believed these lamps were oil-burning devices fitted with glass globes.

GODDARD BLOCK FRONT: See page 84.

GODEFROY PRINTS: Scenes of the Revolution, engraved by F. Godefroy and N. Ponce, France, 1783–84, and published, with text in French, in a portfolio. Original issues are quite scarce. A re-issue, Paris, 1918, contains the same plates. Expert advice is needed in determining the original and the re-issue, if the re-issue has been "antiqued."

GOELET SNUFF: Francis Goelet (pronounced Ja-lette or Jo-lette), a Huguenot of New Rochelle, New York, was a producer of snuff in 1750. Pierre L'ourilliard [Lorillard] who founded the great tobacco company of that name is reputed to have been apprenticed to Goelet.

GOLDEN-AGE STOVE: An elegant cast-iron parlor stove, 1845–55, having concealed oven and cooking facilities.

GOLDSMITH, DEBORAH: A female itinerant portrait painter, 1826–32. She worked in Hamilton, New York, and nearby Connecticut. Her work is on the crude side and amateurish.

"GONE-WITH-THE-WIND" LAMPS: See page 160.

GORDON & BANKSON: Cabinetmakers of Baltimore, c. 1780–85.

GORGAS CLOCKS: Made by the Gorgases, father and son, of Lancaster County, Pennsylvania, last half of eighteenth century. General Gorgas, of Panama Canal fame, was descended from these clockmakers.

GOUROUD COSMETIQUES: Poudre Subtil, Lily-white (*lys-blanc*), Liquid Rouge, Morphew Soap, and other elegant beauty aids for the ladies of 1840, advertised by "Dr." Felix Gouroud, New York.

GRACE FIRES: Robert Grace of Philadelphia made a Pennsylvania fireplace of iron, 1746, that was the subject of a pamphlet issued by the New York *Weekly Post*, 1744. A form of the Franklin stove.

GRAVES, GEORGE & PHILIP: Cabinetmakers of Boston, 1829. They were factory producers, not retailers, but sold to other stores.

GRAVURES DÉCOUPÉ: Literally, dressed-up engravings. An engraved portrait embellished with bits of fabric, lace, gilt paper, et cetera, to give more reality to the picture. Eighteenth century through to the 1850s.

GREEK REVIVAL: The brothers Adam, about the sixth decade of the eighteenth century, began using Greek forms in furniture and residence design. They worked only for the nobility and the wealthy. Thomas Hope, a Dutchman retiring to England in the late eighteenth century, was the popular champion of Greek Revival, although his designs were also beyond the purse of the common man. Marco Bozzaris, Greek patriot fighting for the freedom of Greece in nineteenth century, gave Greek Revival styles a new lease on life. By 1830 all America could buy Grecian-styled stuffs. Greek Revival architecture seems to have been part and parcel of our early Federal days. It appears to have influenced the designers and planners of all sorts of structures in the new state of Ohio. Greek styles were incorporated in buildings of brick, stone, and wood. Some so-called museum experts still do not believe this was the case. They have failed, perhaps, to study the *Historical Collections of Ohio*, by Henry Howe, issued in 1850. This book, illustrated with hundreds of woodcuts, depicts Greek Revival architecture existing in public and private buildings in every Ohio village and town. New structures in New England, Pennsylvania, Maryland, and Virginia also had elements indicative of the Greek Revival. American architects included it in their books of designs. It was grafted on Empire styles and is reflected in the wallpapers and textiles of the period.

GREEK TEMPLE BATHROOMS: See page 114.

GREEN, JAMES: Cabinetmaker of Alexandria, Virginia, c. 1823, and Washington, D.C., 1831–40. His sons, c. 1850, established a furniture factory in Alexandria which was in operation to about 1880.

GREINER DOLLS: Fabric-covered, molded-head dolls made by Greiner of Philadelphia, c. 1858. Some doll heads were marked by maker, Louis Greiner.

GREY & HEMINGWAY GLASS, CINCINNATI GLASS: Made about 1845, in a variety that included decanters, lamps, bottles, and perfume vials, the latter "in greater variety than made at Pittsburgh." Flint glass.

GRIGGS, THOMAS: Cabinetmaker of New York, 1760–70.

GRIGGS, THOMAS, SR.: 1754.

GRIMACE: A caricature of the human face.

GRINNELL, PETER & SON: Mirror makers of Providence, Rhode Island, first quarter of nineteenth century.

GROTTO: One meaning of this term is a cool cellar, vaulted over, and supplied with a running spring, where butter, milk, and meat were kept cool. Another is an artificial den, fashioned of stone, to which one repaired to keep cool in the heat of the day. The latter was often quite ornately contrived and elaborately laid out.

GUILD MINIATURES AND SILHOUETTES: If you find one signed, know that it was done by an itinerant who began as a peddler from Tunbridge, Vermont, who

Glossary and Index

261

made and cut likenesses in New York, Philadelphia, Lancaster, and York, Pennsylvania, Buffalo, Baltimore, Richmond, Norfolk, and intermediate villages and towns, 1819–24. May be signed "Guild" or "James Guild."

GULLAH: A dialect of the Littoral, spoken also by natives of islands off the Carolina-Georgia coast. Some Negroes of Charleston and Savannah speak, or once spoke, it.

GUTTUS: A boot-shaped jug. Dates from very early to late times.

GYPSY ROSE: The corn rose.

HALL SANDERS: Sandboxes of turned wood, used for blotting ink and often bearing the label "Hall's Sanding Box."

HAMMITT FURNITURE: Countinghouse desks and office furniture of good quality, made by J. T. Hammitt of Philadelphia, 1840–60.

HAMPTON GRATES: Anthracite grates for fireplaces, made 1850–60.

HANAP: "Standing cup with a cover," says H. L. Bond, the antiquarian.

HANCOCK FURNITURE: Made by Henry Hancock of Boston, who closed out his business in 1831. He made fine furniture, advertising "Canterburys, night cabinets, pier tables, sideboards, secretaries, wardrobes, lolling chairs, rocking chairs, and bed chairs." WILLIAM HANCOCK: Also of Boston, 1829, advertised substantially the same line of goods. He also advertised painted transparent window shades in 1828.

HARLAND CLOCKS: Tall-case and wag-on-wall clocks, made by Thomas Harland, Revolutionary patriot who taught clockmaking to Eli Terry.

HASHEESH CANDY: The Gunjah-Wallah Company, c. 1860 (this is all true, no matter how weird it may sound), located in New York, offered the drug, hasheesh, in candy form as "an anti-spasmodic and cure for melancholia, confusion of thoughts, and giver of new energy to all." This was dope peddling à la mode!

HATCH BED: A sack-bottomed bed in which the sacking, instead of being fastened to pegs, was fastened all around to coil springs.

HAT-TIP WORK: Painting in gold leaf on leather bands, or "hat tips."

HAWKES WARE: Tin and sheet-iron wares made by Ezra Hawkes of Boston, 1825–35.

HAY FURNITURE: Good Empire and Victorian furniture produced in York, Pennsylvania, by Hay & Sons, 1840–65 and later.

HAZARD ANTIQUE AND MODERN FURNITURE: Advertised 1856 by Simeon Hazard of Newport, Rhode Island. He offered modern furniture after the latest Parisian models, also mansion and cottage furniture and antique by which he meant what we call Victorian.

HEALY-BUXTON SECRETARIES: A firm by this name, in Worcester, Massachusetts, c. 1845, specialized in making secretaries, washstands, and other bedroom pieces.

HEPPLEWHITE CHAIRS: See page 38.

HEPPLEWHITE SOFAS: See page 54.

HEPPLEWHITE TABLES: See page 68.

HEYNE, I. C.: See page 151.

HEYWOOD CHAIRS: From 1826–1946 Heywood chairs have been made. In 1826, in Gardner, Massachusetts, L. Heywood began making fancy chairs.

HIGHBOYS: See page 79.

HILL, HENRY: Cabinetmaker of Washington, D.C., 1822.

HITCHCOCK CHAIRS AND PARTS: See page 22.

HITCHING POSTS: See page 122.

HOBART BELLS: Aaron Hobart began bell founding about 1769 in Abington, Massachusetts. Church, farm, and fire bells were cast.

HOBBYHORSES: See page 234.

HOFFMAN PRESS BED: A nineteenth-century folding bed of rather nice design. The bedstead folded into a cabinet in the shape of a low case of drawers; the foot of the bed was the front of this cabinet, with its false front of four drawers. The top of the cabinet formed a "hood" over the head of the bed. Made about 1855. A desirable near antique to find and use today.

HONETSIE FLOWERS: This is another weird one. The term is purely a colloquialism for the name "M. Honna et Cie" of Brussels, seedsmen who, in 1842, offered rare plant seeds such as camellias, azaleas, citrus, d'aphne. They had a plant and seed store at 175 Broadway, New York, in 1843.

HONFLEURE: A style of painting invented, or appropriated, by M. and Mme. Honfleure of Boston, 1820. It was a quick method, taught to amateurs in six weeks. The method embraced imitation japanning and flower painting.

HOOKED RUGS: See page 132.

HORN BREAKER: A trade that flourished until about the end of the eighteenth century. The horn breaker was really a horn shaver or horn-peeler, for his job was peeling or shaving thin slices from cattle horn, flattening same, and otherwise preparing for use in lanthorns, watch crystals, binnacle panes, and windowpanes. Such horn was used generally in most cases where mica is used today. It was not used for stove doors, but did have wide use in lantern making. The very term "lantern" means "light-in-horn case."

HORN PAPER: Transparent tracing paper, used also for theorems or stencils, 1750–1850.

HOWE TINWARE: Made by William Howe, Boston, 1820–32.

HOWE WOODENWARES: Made by N. & J. Howe in Fitzwilliam, New Hampshire, 1840s.

HUBBEL & PATTERSON: Cabinetmakers of New York City, 1770.

HUDSON FURNITURE: Late Empire and Victorian sofas, chairs, card tables, chests of drawers, and beds made by B. & W. Hudson of Hartford, Connecticut, 1850s.

HUMMUMS: Turkish baths; sweat baths. Places of resort for such baths. Very popular 1630–1750.

HUMPHREY CHIMNEYS: Lamp chimneys of unbreakable mica. Seem to have been made shortly after 1858. Tubular in shape.

HUNTBOARD: See page 76.

HURDLE BROTHERS: Levi and Thomas Hurdle, cabinetmakers of Alexandria, Virginia, makers of "Grecian, Windsor, and fancy chairs," c. 1830.

HURDY-GURDY: (Hurdi-Gurdi) Early form of mechanical player, first applied to the violin or violoncello. A crank actuated a continuous bow movement while a keyboard "fingered" the strings. Played by streetwalkers called Savoyards. Also played by broom vendors and other peddlers. May be of Swiss or French-Italian (Savoy) origin. Seventeenth and eighteenth century. Said to have been played on streets of Boston, New York, and Philadelphia.

HURTIN & BURGI: Clockmakers of Bound Brook, New Jersey. Late eighteenth or early nineteenth century.

HUTCH TABLES: See page 66.

HUTCHINS CLOCKS: Made at Concord, New Hampshire, 1786–1819. Brass-movement, tall-case clocks.

HUTTON ALBANY SILVER: Isaac Hutton, apparently a prolific silversmith of Albany, said to have worked from 1790–1850—a span of sixty years.

HYGROPHANT: J. S. F. Huddleston of Boston, nineteenth century (probably 1860–75), marketed a combined thermometer and humidity indicator under this trade name.

ICE PITCHER: Water pitcher with compartment for ice, 1850–1900.

IKATS: A method of dyeing yarns in "patterns" before weaving, so that woven cloth shows a pattern even though the weaving is of the simplest kind. Said to be of Malayan origin. Diderot's Encyclopedia describes a similar method used in silk weaving at Lyons. American Indians used the same method in pre-Columbian days. Said also to have been practiced in home weaving in seventeenth- and eighteenth-century Colonial days and known as "yarn-dyed figuring."

INDIA HOUSES: Curiosity shops where Chinese and Indian goods were traded— China for old clothes, India shawls for old lace.

INFUSION POTS: Pewter pots for still-brewing (that is, not over a fire) herbs in boiling water for teas, and to provide inhalant vapors for treating colds. Advertised in 1754.

IPSWICH LACE: Made 1785–1835 at Ipswich, Massachusetts, a lace-making center. First practiced by individual craftsmen, it finally became a manufacturing process, sparked by the Boston & Ipswich Lace Company and the New England Lace Company. Silk and cotton laces were made here.

JACKEMAN CLOCKS: London-made William and Mary period clocks that were imported as new in 1680–90 and have been imported more recently as highly desirable antiques. They are rare timepieces and excellent timekeepers.

JACKSON-BAGGOTT GLASS: Fine-cut glass produced by this firm and sold at their retail store, 76 Chatham Street, New York City, 1815–25.

JACKSON BRASS: Made by Jonathan Jackson of New England prior to 1736. He made door knockers, basins, skillets, stirrups, spurs, firedogs, warming pans, and candlesticks.

JACKSON DELICACIES: In 1765 Benjamin Jackson of Philadelphia offered these delectables: "mustard equal to any from England, in proper glass bottles; chocolate made in the best manner; pickled lobsters in kegs; raw, roasted, and ground-up coffee; rye imitation coffee; spices; salad oyle; pickles; preserves."

JAMS: Buttons made of wire.

JEWELRY: See page 128.

JOHNNYCAKE: "The real name is Journey cake," said a writer in the Philadelphia *Ledger*, May 22, 1836. "Bunk," says an anthropologist. "It derives from 'Shawnee-cake,' a sort of hard bun, baked from pounded corn, leavened with bear's grease, by the Shawnee Indians of the Conestoga and Susquehanna valleys." Take your choice. We vote for number one. It's the bear's grease that turns us from number two.

JOHNSON-BROOKS LAMPS: Made in London, c. 1800–40. Many sold in America. Some are marked with makers' names.

JOHNSON & GODLEY SILVER: Factory-made silverware, Albany, New York, 1845.

JOHNSTON FANCY CHAIRS: Made by C. D. Johnston of Cincinnati, Ohio, 1842–65. This maker had an enormous production. In 1850 he was favored with a standing order from Scarrett & Mason of St. Louis for thirty-five thousand chairs a year. All these chairs would probably be classed as antiques today. Johnston is said to have produced half a million chairs between 1843 and 1853.

JUMBAL: A rich biscuit of early Colonial days. How rich? Herewith the recipe: 1 pound fine flour, 1 pound sugar; mix to paste with egg whites, add ½ pound sweet butter, ½ pint cream, 1 pound almonds, blanched and pounded in rosewater. Shape and bake in gentle oven. Now, weren't Jumbals better than the present-day descendant, the jumble? Early Americans weren't so dumb!

KANGAROO SOFA: The Psyche sofa. Incidentally, we have run across a spelling of kangaroo that is interesting: k'ang-Garu. It sounds Chinese-Indian.

KELSO, JOHN: Windsor chairmaker of Philadelphia, 1770, and New York, 1774.

KERMES OAK: Oak infested with the valued kermes insect from which a scarlet dye was obtained.

KERSE: To cover a wall with flags or slate.

KETTLE STAND: A stand specifically for a teakettle. Known in Queen Anne, Georgian, Chippendale, and Hepplewhite styles. Some have galleried tops, others tray tops. All are fine and scarce.

KEYWORTH, ROBERT: Clockmaker of Washington, D.C., 1822.

KING RUSTICS: Rustic furniture fashioned from laurelwood by one James King of New Haven in 1860s. Advertised for sale to other shops and by mail order.

KISS-COMFIT: Small perfumed and spiced sugar bits to sweeten the breath. N.B.: Halitosis was known in Colonial days but not by that name.

KITTY FISHERS: You tell us the definition of this one. The name appears as something obtainable from Elizabeth Evans, upholsterer and maker of festoon bed and window curtains, wrought quilts, and *slip covers* (which she called "chair, sofa, and settle cases"). All this from her advertising in 1776. But what was a Kitty Fisher? It was the only thing she didn't define. Any reader giving the answer will find the author grateful.

KNIFE BOXES: See page 76.

KOONZ COVERLETS: Made at coverlet factory of Abram Koonz, Albany, in 1840s; sold wholesale and retail and advertised. Marked with his full name and date, or "AK" and date.

LABHART POTTERY: Chicago, 1850–60, are the place and date, and Martin Labhart is the potter.

LACTURE: Mixed greens for salad.

LADDER-BACK CHAIRS: See page 24.

LAMB'S WOOL: "Roast crab or tart apples in sugar. When done, pulp them, with spice, and add to the evening's bedding glass of ale. 'Tis as lambs wool to the innerds." Try it sometime. (The bedding glass was the nightcap or last drink before bed.)

LAMPS: See page 157.

LANCASTER LINENS: Woven in Lancaster, Pennsylvania, 1730–1800. Flemish and French Huguenot weavers established quite an industry. In 1769 they wove 27,739 yards of linen.

LAWRENCE PICTURES: Paper photographic prints ranging from miniature to life size, and tinted. M. M. Lawrence of New York City made a specialty of tinting between 1850 and 1860.

LAWSON, RICHARD: Cabinetmaker of Baltimore, c. 1780–85. In 1785 he became a partner of John Bankson. Lawson worked thirteen years in the London cabinet warehouse of Mr. Seddon before coming to America.

LEAF'S COMPOSITION: A stain eradicator and polish sold around 1800–10.

LEAVITT WARE: Woodenware made by B. Leavitt of Chicopee, Massachusetts, 1830–50, and perhaps later.

LEFFINGWELL & WILLIAMS: Potters of Norwich, Connecticut, from 1771.

LE PRINCE & MARCOTTE: Mid-nineteenth-century cabinetmakers of New York City. Producers of Victorian style furniture.

LEROY CLOCKS: Early Lancaster, Pennsylvania, clockmaker, Abraham LeRoy, of French-Swiss extraction, made these clocks, 1740–70. Tall-case clocks.

LIGHTFOOT PINS: Pins made by the self-acclaimed "first pin maker in America," Richard Lightfoot, New York, 1775.

LIND, OR LUND, MICHAEL: Swedish cabinetmaker of Lancaster, Pennsylvania, who worked between the years 1755 and 1790. It is known that he made walnut chairs in the Queen Anne style.

LINE SPINNER, LINE WHEELS, CORD WHEELS, CORD SPINNER: A rope spinner in miniature, consisting of three small rotating wheels geared to a larger center wheel around which the three rotating wheels moved. Lines tied to the spinners of each wheel thus were formed into cords. We have seen but few of these in antiques shops, but they were apparently factory-made between 1840 and 1870.

LIONESS: Any sportswoman of the 1840s was so called, especially girls of some social position who went in for shooting, swimming, and riding.

LITHOGRAPHS: See page 216.

"LITTLE SCISSORS PICTORIAL": See page 113.

LOWBOYS: See page 79.

LOWESTOFT: See page 172.

LUCKY OIL: Winter-bleached sperm oil, produced by J. N. Lucky and selling at a shilling a gallon, 1840s. Lamp oil.

LYON, DR. IRVING W.: Author of *Colonial Furniture in America,* the first book on American antiques, published 1891. His grandsons conduct the C. W. Lyon, Inc., antiques shops in New York City.

LYON FURNITURE: W. C. Lyon of New York City, as late as 1850, advertised as a custom cabinetmaker, making family furniture to order. An old-school cabinetmaker in the age of machinery.

LYRE SHELF CLOCK: An exceedingly rare item; a variant of the banjo design but constructed as a shelf clock. It is essentially the regulation lyre clock with the regular boxlike element made as a pedestal. A gong bell forms the top of a four-column belfry on top of the dial section. A fine specimen, examined 1945, was marked "Sawin & Dyer, Boston."

MALLARD, P.: New Orleans cabinetmaker, 1838–60. Said to have made furniture in the style of Louis XV.

MANROSS CLOCKS: Made by Elisha Manross, Bristol, Connecticut, 1827–50.

MANWARING CHAIRS: See page 38.

MANWARING, ROBERT (1765): See pages 3, 15.

MARCHPANE (English), MARZIPAN (German), MESSEPAIN (French), MAZAPAN (Spanish), MARCI-PANIS (Latin—Bread of St. Mark; Bread of mercy): All names for the confection of almond paste that was used for celebrations of all kinds, from a firemen's banquet to a Christmas party. Almost always in fancy, historic, and commemorative forms, made in wooden molds which are now objects of collecting interest.

MASSI, S.: Silversmith of Washington, D.C., c. 1822.

McAIDIN FURNITURE: Made by A. McAidin of Cincinnati, 1838–50.

McKEARIN, GEORGE AND HELEN: See page 182.

MEEKS, JOSEPH, FURNITURE FACTORY, 1833: See page 2.

MERCHANDISE BOATS: River-steamboat or -barge stores which sold furniture, groceries, hardware, piece goods, clothing, shoes, et cetera. General stores and fancy bazaars afloat. Plied the Ohio, Mississippi, Missouri and other rivers.

MERRIAM MIRRORS: Pier, wall, and mantel mirrors made by B. W. Merriam, 1818–60. Styles were Regency, Empire, and Victorian.

MERRY-MAN PLATES: Plates of Dutch or Lambeth delft, usually in sets of six or eight, decorated with crowns, flowers, et cetera, but also with inscriptions of a jovial nature, to be read as a series. The "master plate" often bore the portrait of Charles I, Charles II, or William of Orange.

METAL COLLARS: Thin steel or brass collars for men (!), enameled white, offered in "turn-over" and "choker" styles, 1860. They were readily cleaned with a damp cloth.

METZ TINWARE: Made in Chicago in the 1850s by Christopher Metz.

MILLEFLEURS: Thousands of flowers; a style or pattern.

MILLS & DEMING: New York cabinetmakers, 1790, who specialized in sideboards in the Hepplewhite manner.

MIRROR-BACK: A late term given to Victorian chairs having oval backs, somewhat like oval mirror frames.

MIRROR KNOBS: A pair of decorative-headed nails or screws driven in wall to support and keep a wall mirror on an even keel. A mirror could not go awry when supported by two of these at the bottom.

MIRRORS: See page 107.

MOCHA WARE, BANDED AND MOTTLED CREAMWARE: Mugs, tankards, bowls, pitchers, pepper shakers, and other utility wares of lead-glaze pottery, having mocha, buff, mustard, orange, and other tinted banding, also decorated with daubs and blotches, wavy lines, mottles, and general haphazard work; 1800–50.

MOLYNEAUX BRASS: M. Molyneaux of Boston, eighteenth century, a maker of record who produced fireplace equipment of brass.

MOSCOW GLASS: Made at Moscow, Ohio, 1814–32. Made LaFayette, Clay, and other historic flasks.

MOTESPOON: A spoon with a pierced bowl.

MOVING SLIDES: Magic-lantern slides with motion, achieved by sliding sections of glass and also by wooden gears and other devices. The effect of motion was given by moving the glass slides and by turning a small crank. Very realistic. Most date from 1835 to 1875.

MULTUM-IN-PARVO BATH: This device was quite an affair in its day; a sheet-iron, chair-shaped device, japanned and decorated, having deep flanges at sides and serving as a foot, hip, sitz, and sponge bath. Date is in the 1850s.

MUSICAL INSTRUMENTS: See page 136.

MUSIC BOXES: See page 116.

MUTTON HAMS: Salted and smoked legs of mutton, "reeked in smoke of corn cobbs and dry, sweet hay."

NAME SCISSORS: The so-called "modern" idea of having ready-to-wear handkerchiefs, belts, and other accessories with some twenty-five or more "stock" names isn't so modern after all. Name scissors, with the names cut in the metal, were offered in 1825, stock names being Julia, Emily, Maria, Anne, Amelia, Eliza, Harriet, Martha, Lois, Clarissa, Abby, and so on. Thousands were sold in the decade 1825–34. Made by Rogers & Son, Sheffield, England.

NEEDLES, JOHN: Cabinetmaker of Baltimore, 1840.

NEGRO CLOTH: Linsey-woolsey or any half-and-half cloth.

NEW ENGLAND GLASS IMPORTS: Contrary to general belief, the New England Glass Company imported much glassware for sale in its warerooms in Boston. On July 4, 1829, they advertised "10 tierces English white phials in assorted sizes and crates of English crown glass, to be had at the warehouse, 140 Washington Street."

NIGHT STANDS: See page 77.

NIXON, JOHN: Clockmaker and watchmaker, New York City, c. 1773.

NOGGIN: Large-bellied pot; a cup or mug.

NONCHALANTES: Slippers without heels, trimmed with braid, 1840–60.

NORTON POTTERY: See pages 112, 168.

ODDFELLOW KNIFE AND FORK: A Y-shaped instrument with a thick handle, presented a two-tined fork on one branch of the *Y* and a sharp knife on the other. It would require an odd fellow, indeed, to cut with the knife while holding with the fork!

OLD DOMINION COFFEEPOT: A percolator-type coffee maker of the mid-nineteenth century. Some thirty-five patents were granted on coffee makers during the 1850s.

OVAL MIRRORS: These were probably of Chippendale design. Minshull of New York, 1775, offered oval mirrors in white, green and white, purple, or "any color that suits the furniture or the room," or gilt in oil, or burnished gold.

OYSTER CRACKER: (Don't let the term fool you.) A pair of pincers with a sort of pocket in the lower jaw to hold an oyster. Squeeze the handle and presto, the oyster opens. Date is 1830–50. It was patented, and mentioned in the *Scientific American!*

PADELFORD, JOHN: A cabinetmaker of Taunton, Massachusetts, 1800–10. His name appears branded on a secretary-bookcase of Hepplewhite style.

PAILLARD MUSIC BOXES: Swiss prick-drum and comb type, playing from one to twenty-four tunes. Offered by Paillard of New York in 1850s.

PAINTED WINDOW SHADES: See page 120.

PAINTINGS: See page 216.

PAKTONG, TUTENAG: Chinese white brass, somewhat akin to "right," or true, pewter, which was a mixture of copper and tin.

PALMER CHAIRS: Black-and-gold fancy chairs with cane and rush seats, made by William Palmer, New York, 1795–1805. He advertised in New York *Evening Post,* 1802.

PAPERWEIGHTS: See pages 115, 116.

PARIAN WARE: See pages 126, 168.

PARKER, WILLIAM: Cabinetmaker of Washington, D.C., 1822.

PARSONS, JOHN: Cabinetmaker of New York, 1754, formerly an apprentice to Delaplain.

PARTINGTON SOAP: A female Horatio Alger story! Ruth Partington unable to write her name, could boil up a pretty kettle of sweet-smelling and quick-lathering soap from fats, lyes, and herbs. Became a beauty "expert" through selling her soap. She started about 1815. B. T. Babbitt made her soap as late as 1855.

PAULINE POTTERY: An art pottery made in Chicago by one Pauline Jacobus of Chicago and Edgerton, Wisconsin. Finally moved the pottery to Edgerton, 1886. Marked with a crown between two Ps. An art pottery sold by jewelry stores. Not as yet antique, but verging upon that status.

PEARWOOD BOOKS: Memorandum books with leaves of polished pearwood.

PEAT BUCKET: Any bucket of wood or metal to hold the fuel, peat.

PEBBLES: Eyeglass lenses of cut and polished rock crystal or quartz.

PEDESTALS: Small sideboards, often used in pairs, sometimes with doors at the ends rather than front; 1830–45.

PELLATT, APSLEY: See page 198.

PELTON JAPANNED WARE: Made by H. A. & E. A. Pelton of Albany, 1848.

PENCIL'D CHINA: Painted china.

PENNSYLVANIA WARE: See page 170.

PERFUMES, SEVENTEENTH, EIGHTEENTH, AND NINETEENTH CENTURIES: Essences, or spirits, were the perfume; waters were the equivalent of our toilet waters. Of the essences, there were bergamot, lavender, ambergris, musk, rose, jasamine, mint, benjamin, Venus, millifleur, tuberose, cassia, violet, citron, clove, goujak, jonquil, pink, lys. Of "waters," there were lavender, rose, honey, Hungary, Portugal, myrtle, Cordova, mousseline.

PERKINS BEDS: This may have been a derisive term for the mattresses made by the inmates of the Perkins Institution and Massachusetts Asylum in 1840s.

PERUVIAN SILVER: See page 150.

PETERS MEDICINE CHESTS: Here is an item of superlative interest to any collector of medical items. James Peters, druggist and chemist of Lancaster, Pennsylvania, 1765, had one of the largest drugstores in the colonies. He specialized in fitted medicine chests of from three to fifty pounds capacity, neatly made for private families, ships' cabins, and plantations. Peters also dealt in conserves, preserved Lucca and Spanish olives, capers, caviar, ketchup, anchovies, pickled walnuts, mangoes and cucumbers, and West Indian sweets. He advertised in Lancaster and Philadelphia newspapers.

PETTICOAT LAMPS: Nineteenth-century glass, pottery, and china lamps having an oil reservoir that flared out like a petticoat or dress over a hoop-skirt frame.

PEWTER: See page 151.

PHELAN TABLES: Reference would be to billiard tables made by Phelan, and Phelan & Collander, New York, from about 1846.

PHELPS, TIMOTHY, JR.: Cabinetmaker of Hartford, Connecticut, 1725–84.

PHILLIPPE BUTTONS: Mother-of-pearl buttons made by the "secret" machine of M. Phillippe, late from Paris, at 44 Cornhill, Boston, 1829.

PHYFE STYLE CHAIRS: so called: See page 38.

PICKLES AND CONDIMENTS IN 1783: The list makes a gourmet's mouth water. Indian soy, mushroom ketchup, pickled mushrooms, walnuts, onions, capers, mangoes, gherkins, French green beans, anchovies and olives, peaches, greengages, citron and apricots in syrup. All offered by one dealer in New York. The War of the Revolution was over in that shop.

PINCHBECK: Alloy of twenty parts copper and four parts zinc. Named for one Oliver Pinchbeck, born 1670, who used this formula to make imitation gold. By 1760 the term was used for any imitation in the jewelry or fancy line. Also applied to pseudo gentlemen and ladies.

PIPKIN: Among other designations, our ancestors called a brass coal hod a pipkin.

PITKIN SILVER: Made in Hartford, Connecticut, after 1850, and advertised by W. L. & H. E. Pitkin. Spoons, forks, ladles, butter knives, et cetera, from *Pure Coin Silver.*

PITTMAN SILVER: Benjamin Pittman of New Bedford, Massachusetts, from around 1835, maker of flat and hollow silverware.

PITTSBURGH GLASS OF 1797: This is the date given for the first Pittsburgh glass factory.

PLASTER FIGURES: Figures and figurines cast from plaster of Paris have been advertised and sold since 1758.

PLATE CARRIER: A straight-sided bucket made of fine cabinet wood, with brass or silver bottom hoop, top brace, and bail handle. A stave is left out of the bucket to provide an open slot. Plates were carried in this container and removed with ease because slot permitted ready access for grasping the rims. Made in eighteenth century.

PLATE STAND: Imagine a tri-footed candlestand minus its top, and in place of the top three arms extending upward and outward, notched on inner side to serve as rests. Plates of various sizes were stacked in this contraption which, standing by the fireside, kept the plates warm. Queen Anne and Georgian period to 1750.

PLATE WAGON: Deep tray on legs, with castered or wheeled feet for trundling a load of plates to and from dining tables. Eighteenth century. This and the two other entries immediately above were undoubtedly super-elegancies used in large establishments. It is doubtful whether they were used in small private homes, no matter how well equipped.

PLATED SILVER: See pages 147, 148.

POKE-MELY: Cucumbers laid down to pickle in oak, raspberry, black-currant, and rose-geranium leaves, with seeds and spices, in vinegared brine. Said to have been introduced by Russian immigrants, 1790-1800.

POOL BAROMETERS: Made by Charles Pool, New York City, after 1819.

POPE'S HEAD, POPE'S NOSE, POPE'S MUG: American colloquialisms for bellarmine jugs.

POPE'S HEAD, POPE'S NOSE JUGS: See page 168.

PORTRAITS: See page 218.

POST-VICTORIAN CHAIRS: See page 48.

POSSET: A beverage made of milk, curdled with wine and spice. Served hot.

POT CRADLE: A cradle made entirely of pottery, in one piece. Eighteenth century, probably all of English (Staffordshire) make.

POTTERY: See page 167.

POTTERY PICTURE FRAMES: Imitation carved oval picture frames of Victorian style, cast in clay and fired. Many used in back country.

PRESSED GLASS: See page 194.

PRINTED BOWEN KERCHIEFS: Henry Bowen's chemical printworks is said to have produced printed cotton handkerchiefs, 1830-50.

QUADRILLE TABLES: Tables for playing the game quadrille, or quadrille pool, played with "fish" and counters, 1775-1800.

QUAICH: Drinking cup somewhat of the shape of a porringer or bleeding bowl.

QUASSIA CUP: A cup turned from a block of quassia wood, the source of a "bitter" believed to have stomachic qualities. User would fill cup with water and let it stand between meals or overnight. Result: quassia water, or stomach bitters. Mid-nineteenth century marked advent of commercial quassia-cup production, sold in druggists' and apothecaries' shops.

QUEEN ANNE SOFAS: See page 52.

QUEEN ANNE TABLES: See page 66.

QUILTS: See page 130.

QUINCE CREAM, CONNATES ROYAL: Quinces boiled quickly, peeled, papped (pulped), sugared, mixed with rich cream, and beaten stiff. Probably from seventeenth century. A similar recipe used for filling quince pies.

RAG DOLL, POUPEE EN CHIFFONS: Manikins of cloth; printed calico doll patterns. Any manikin made of, or stuffed with, rags.

RAPE OIL: Oil expressed from rapeseeds. Rapeseeds=coleseeds.

RAVENNA LILY: Paperweights and doorstops of glass with a lily enclosed. Made at Ravenna Glass Works about 1880.

RAWSON, JOSEPH & SON, AND ROBERT: Cabinetmakers of Newport, Rhode Island, 1790–1810. Said to have made furniture in Hepplewhite style.

RED JACKET AX: A special ax for pioneers, made by Lippincott & Bakewell of Pittsburgh, mid-eighteenth century.

REFFUS WARE (REFUSE WARE): In pottery, any underdone or overfired ware, distorted, cracked, partly glazed, misshapen, or discolored, and sold at bargain prices to any who came to the pottery for it.

REMICK, CHRISTIAN: A marine artist of Boston who, in eighteenth century, painted six views of Boston Harbor, one of which sold for $790 in 1889. In 1904 Sidney Smith engraved a plate of this view, 1½ by 5 feet. Prints from this plate are now quite scarce and highly valued.

REMMEY POTTERY: (1) Three generations of potters named Remmey made stoneware in New York, 1744–1831. (2) Henry Remmey, Jr., on the Germantown Road at Second Street, Philadelphia, 1825–45, made water jars, bowls, and other "Philadelphia" wares.

REYNOLDS MIRRORS: Made by J. Reynolds, Philadelphia, 1780–1800.

RICE & BARRY: Clockmakers of Baltimore, advertising in 1785.

RINGWOOD IRONWARE: Made at Ringwood furnace, New Jersey, 1760–75.

RISLEY GLASS: Rich cut glass produced by Richard Risley of Philadelphia, 1825–40. Newbold & Trotter conducted the business after 1833. This was a glass-cutting and not a glass-making concern.

ROBBINS & WINSHIP FURNITURE: Made in Hartford, Connecticut, after 1850.

ROBERTS CLOCKS: Made by Gideon Roberts, a pioneer clockmaker of Bristol, Connecticut, who also peddled his clocks.

ROBERTS SILVER: E. M. Roberts, silversmith of Hartford, Connecticut, 1850, manufactured pure silver wares.

ROBINSON BUTTONS: Made in Attleborough, Massachusetts, 1828–40. Gilt (brass) buttons. A factory operation; buttons made by machinery.

ROBINSON PENS AND PENCILS: Gold- and silver-cased pens and pencils made by B. Robinson of Philadelphia, 1830–40.

ROCKINGHAM WARE: See page 168.

ROGERS GROUPS: See Chapter X.

ROOKWOOD POTTERY: Made in Cincinnati since 1879. Fine-quality art pottery. Early production is quite rare and valuable. Some Rookwood now held by many American museums.

ROPE TURNED BEDS: See page 93.

RORKE LAMPS: Edw. Rorke & Co., proprietors of the National Flint Glass Works, made a wide variety of fancy table lamps for burning kerosene or coal oil.

Ross Rug Patterns: Hooked-rug patterns made by the Ross Company of Dayton, Ohio, 1883–93.

Sad: Heavy. Sad ware—heavy ware. Sad iron—heavy iron.

Saffron: Dried stigmata of the yellow crocus, or autumn crocus. Used as a flavoring and coloring agent in cookery from about the fourteenth century.

Saint Louis Glass: (1) A French glasshouse in the Vosges, founded 1682, and among the first to make paperweights, about 1825. (2) A glass factory in St. Louis, Missouri, established about 1845 by Nelson, Case & Eads. Also glass made by Blow & Farrell and by J. Wallace. Several St. Louis glasshouses failed within a year or so after establishment.

Salisbury, L.: Cabinetmaker of Norfolk, Virginia, c. 1840.

Sally Snow: A midget born 1810. She weighed eighteen pounds when twelve years old. Exhibited at many fairs and museums throughout New England, where anything small was dubbed "Sally Snow."

Salt Pouch: Leather sack for carrying salt; used by hunters and pioneer settlers.

Samp Cloth: A sampler.

Sanborn Silver: "The only place in Lowell, or Middlesex County, Massachusetts, where silver spoons are still made in 1850," was the boast of Amos Sanborn, silversmith of Lowell.

Sandwich Glass: See page 194.

San Francisco Glass: In 1860–67 there was a glassworks in Potrero, California, operated by the Pacific Glass Works. Also, in San Francisco, there was a glassworks operated by Hostetter, Smith & Dean. Bottles, flasks, and window glass are said to have been made.

Sanger, Stephen: Cabinet-furniture manufacturer of Alexandria, Virginia, 1834.

Sarcophagus Top: Top sections of clocks or cabinet pieces in the form of a sarcophagus of classic design.

Sawin Clocks: John Sawin, 33 Cornhill, Boston, advertised church, parlor, gallery, bank, and alarm clocks in 1829. Sawin made banjo clocks and other fine timepieces.

Scheppel: Woodenware; a grain measure.

Scientific Antiques: See page 118.

Scrimshaw: See page 126.

Secretaria Bookcase: A name common in first half of nineteenth century, meaning secretary-bookcase.

Seignouret, F.: A cabinetmaker of New Orleans, 1832–53.

Sellers Riddles: "Archimedean screw riddles" made by John Sellers of Darby, Pennsylvania, c. 1770. These were used in sifting grains and seeds.

Settles: See page 50.

Seymour, John: Cabinetmaker of Boston, 1790–1810. He marked certain or perhaps all of his work with a label. He is also the maker who painted the interiors of small secretaries a blue color. His furniture is considered quite fine and rare.

Sgraffito Ware: See page 170.

Shaw & Rettig: Cincinnati cabinetmakers who made furniture in 1838–42 that is quite readily mistaken for work of the Phyfe period in New York. This firm made furniture in the antique, Gothic, Louis XIV styles, painted cottage furniture, and French, Italian, and Grecian bedsteads. They continued in business until after 1860.

Shearer & Paine: Furniture makers of Chicago, 1850.

Shebang: A groggery; a speak-easy; a blind pig.

Sheffield Plate: See page 138.

Sheraton Chairs: See page 38.

Sheraton Mirrors: He designed none. See page 107.

SHERATON SOFAS: See page 54.

SHERATON TABLES: See page 68.

SHILL-I-SHALL-I: A term used to designate people who couldn't make up their minds and who were continually saying "Shall I, shall I, shall I, shall I?"

SHOW UMBRELLA, SHUMBERSHOOT: Advertising umbrellas, often carried by newsboys, teamsters, porters, cabmen, and boxmen.

SIDEBOARDS: See page 75.

SIDE-HUNG MIRROR: William and Mary type mirrors with "ends" that are finished precisely as were the tops of upright mirrors. These mirrors were hung horizontally and were made up of one large center panel of glass with two end panels. This seems to be the first hanging overmantel mirror. Date may be between 1680 and 1700.

SILLIMAN INKWELLS: Made 1820–80 by Silliman Company in Chester, Connecticut. Turned-wood cases with glass wells inserted through bottoms (just in case you have one of those wooden inkwells and wondered how they got the thin glass bottles inside).

SILVER: See page 138.

SKEWER RACK: A wall rack of metal or wood, often with a cresting of some sort, and fitted with six to twelve knobs upon which to hang sets of steel skewers.

SKIN PAPER: A note paper of unusually thin quality, designed for foreign correspondence when the postage rate was excessive for even a half-ounce letter. One might call it early air-mail paper; 1836–50.

SLAT-BACK CHAIRS: See pages 21, 24.

SMITH & HAWLEY: John Broadfoot Smith's son and Mr. Hawley of Cincinnati, were employing sixty people in 1850, making furniture in a factory and producing twelve hundred sofas, twenty-five hundred parlor chairs, one thousand center tables, and other furniture in proportion per annum!

SMITH, JACOB: Chairmaker of New York, 1780s to 1800s.

SMITH, JOHN BROADFOOT: Cabinetmaker of Cincinnati, 1819. So well considered was this cabinetmaker that he was asked to address the mechanics of Cincinnati, July 5, 1819, in celebrating the forty-third year of American independence!

SMITH, WILLIAM: Chair- and cabinetmaker of Richmond, Virginia, 1840.

SNOW & KINGMAN TOYS: Rocking horses, cabs, children's furniture, wheel toys, and other child-size objects, made by this firm in Boston, about the middle of nineteenth century.

SNUFF BOAT: Snuffbox in shape of a ship's hull. The deck is the lid.

SOFA BRITSKA: Sofa on wheels; an invalid's conveyance.

SOMERSET POTTERY: Seven potteries flourished in this Massachusetts town in 1836.

SOMERVILLE PIGS: Pig toys of glass made in Somerville, Massachusetts, glasshouse. This firm moved to Brooklyn, New York, and finally to Corning, New York, and became the Corning Glass Company, 1875. From toy pigs to reflectors for telescopes and Steuben glass!

SOUTHWARK POTTERY: Bonnin & Morris pottery, the first porcelain works in America. Only a very few pieces are known. Eighteenth century.

SPANISH JUICE: Licorice.

SPARABLES: Small nails of iron or copper.

SPEAR, JOSEPH: Cabinetmaker of Alexandria, Virginia, c. 1815.

SPLAT-BACK CHAIRS: See page 28.

SPOOL-TURNED BEDS: See page 93.

SPOONER, SHERLOCK: Cabinetmaker and furniture dealer of Boston, 1820–40. Made fine furniture and imported the latest London and Paris designs.

STAFFORDSHIRE SANITARY WARE: It is a little-known and perhaps somewhat amazing fact that Staffordshire pottery of very fine quality, beautifully decorated in colors, and some in blue willow pattern with gold banding, was made in the form of washbowls and other plumbing wares, 1850–80. The Mott Iron Works of New York catalogued over forty designs in the 1880s and illustrated them in full colors.

STANDS—WHATNOTS, DUMBWAITERS, et cetera: See page 77.

STERLING FURNITURE: Sterling, Massachusetts, in 1837 had twenty-four manufactories of chairs and cabinetware employing eighty people and producing $50,000 worth of goods annually.

STIMSON BOY: Henry L. Stimson, Secretary of War in F. D. Roosevelt's Cabinet, posed as a youth for John Rogers, 1873, when not yet seven years of age. His statue is part of the Rogers "Hide and Seek" group.

STINKPOT: Smudge pot. Fumigating pot.

STONE BEE: A "party" to clear land of stones.

STONER, RUDI: Swiss clockmaker of Lancaster, Pennsylvania, 1750–70. Tall-case clocks.

STOVES: See page 128.

STRETCHER TABLES: See page 62.

STUDENT LAMPS: See page 161.

SUCRIER: Sugar bowl, or basin, with cover. The sugar bowl for the table.

SWISS WARES: See page 172.

SYCAMORE: This wood originally was the timber of the fig-mulberry tree. It was used in making furniture from William and Mary to late Sheraton. In America it is the plane, or buttonwood, tree that we call a sycamore.

TABERNACLE MIRRORS: See page 107.

TALL CASE, OR GRANDFATHER CLOCKS: See page 101.

TAPPIT-HEN: A tankard-shaped measure much constricted below the top. Used as a measure and a drinking vessel.

TERRY CLOCK VARIANTS IN 200 FORMS: See page 104.

TERRY "PILLAR-AND-SCROLL" CLOCKS: See page 104.

THOMAS, PHILIP: Cabinetmaker and chairmaker of Lancaster, Pennsylvania, 1760–90.

TILYOU, PETER, SR.: Cabinetmaker of New York City before 1770.

TIMBERLAKE CARPETS: Made by Timberlake & Bryant, Louisville, Kentucky, c. 1844–56. In 1845 they were weaving three thousand yards per month.

TOILET STANDS: See page 77.

TOYS: See page 232.

TRANSPARENCIES: See page 128.

TREMAIN, JOHN: A retired actor who turned cabinetmaker in New York, 1751.

TRIFOLIATE TABLE: A triangular-shaped table frame and top, the top having three triangular leaves. The top was so constructed as to rotate and, when thus rotated, would bring its three hinged leaves over the corners of the table frame, which acted as supports, and lo! the table was vastly increased in size. Known in Queen Anne style—and a very neat trick!

TRUMEAU: A French Pier mirror, those of Directoire and Empire design having proportions and elements similar to the American tabernacle mirror. See Chapter IX.

TUCKER WARE: See page 172.

TUMBLERS: Originally metal cups with rounded bottoms; they tumbled over. Hence the name. Finally applied to any and all drinking vessels but especially glass-drinking vessels.

TURNERY PATTERNS: Any style or design of turning.

TURNUP BED: A folding bedstead.

UNITED STATES DIRECTORY OF 1822: See page 70.

UNITED STATES POTTERY: See page 168.

VENETIAN BLINDS: See page 120.

VICTORIAN: "It will never be a style, but it is now the fashion," is the way in which we characterized Victorian in our *Primer of American Antiques* in 1944. In case this characterization needs explaining, the following is offered:

Victorian is a *period*, named for Queen Victoria of England, who reigned 1837–1901. The "period" didn't last so long as the Queen's reign, which, even many Englishmen admit, was too long. During that part of Victoria's reign bracketed by the years 1840–90 a great variety of furniture styles were melded, blended, emulsified, and otherwise mixed. Also, certain of the styles were used in almost unadulterated form. "Antique French," as the style of Louis XV (Louis Quinze) was called, enjoyed a resurgence. In America this style was called just "antique," and in the 1840s and early 1850s some of our furniture makers called it "antique furniture"—a designation that is apt to mislead some researchers into thinking these factories also dealt in, or made, what we now call antiques, but for sale then as antiques. The Victorian period enjoyed the following "styles": seventeenth-century Swiss, Provençal, Directoire, Empire, late Sheraton, Grecian, Louis XV, William Morris, Eastlake, Gothic Cottage, and American antique revival. In case you doubt the latter, we have in our possession a lithographed catalogue of furniture offered by an American manufacturer in the 1880s that includes Windsor, Hepplewhite, and Sheraton chairs, hutch and settle tables, and some eighteenth-century Chippendale! Victorian is now the fashion, but keep in mind that the stuff most people regard as typically Victorian isn't "typically" Victorian at all—it is as French as Versailles in 1765 or, if you prefer, as French as Roquefort cheese.

VICTORIAN BEDS: See page 93.

VICTORIAN CHAIRS: See page 46.

VICTORIAN SOFAS, SETTEES, AND SEATS: See page 59.

VICTORIAN TABLES: See page 74.

WALTER, JOSEPH: Proprietor of a steam furniture factory in Cincinnati, 1840.

WARDIAN CASES: See page 120.

WARWICK BED: Reference is to the technique of achieving resilience by use of double slats, the lower serving as the base and the upper slat serving as a "spring" because it was "sprung" away from the lower slat and affixed to it only at the upper or head end of the bed. Date is 1850s.

WASHSTANDS: See page 100.

WATERMAN TINWARE: Made in Boston, 1820–35; plain and japanned ware.

WAX BEADS: Necklace beads of hard wax, sold as early as 1770.

WEATHER VANES: See page 122.

WEAVER, N.: Eighteenth-century cabinetmaker of Newport, Rhode Island.

WEBB & SCOTT: Cabinetmakers of Providence, Rhode Island, 1780–1800.

WESTERFIELD, DAVID: Cabinetmaker of Washington, D.C., 1822.

WEST STATUARY: Imitation of Rogers groups, made by West of Chicago, in 1890s. See page 124.

WESTWARD HO! GLASS: See page 200.

WHILE, L.: Cabinetmaker of Buffalo, New York, 1831.

WHITE, BLANCHE: Lady upholsterer of Philadelphia and New York, 1750–67 and later.

WHITE BRASS: A Chinese invention, improperly called German silver.

WIG STANDS: See page 77.

WILLET, MARINUS: Revolutionary colonel and cabinetmaker of New York City.

WILLETT & PEARSEE (or PERSEY): Cabinetmakers of New York City, 1773.

WILLIAMS, JOHN & JAMES: Cabinetmakers of Washington, D.C., 1822.

WILLIAMS MIRRORS: Established 1810 in New York, J. H. Williams made fine mirrors for forty-five years.

WILSON GLOBES: James Wilson started the first globe manufactory in the U.S.A. about 1812. He was making globes in 1814 and, in 1818, founded the firm of J. Wilson & Sons in Albany, New York.

WINDSOR CHAIRS: See pages 21, 23, 30.

WINDSOR SETTEES: See page 58.

WINE COOLERS AND CELLARETTES: See page 76.

WINNE FURNITURE: John Winne labeled the furniture he sold in Albany, whether from his factory or others. He advertised his furniture in 1845.

WOODRUFF BAROMETERS: Made in Peterboro, New Hampshire, as late as 1865, in the Sheraton style, by Charles Wilder.

WORTHINGTON, WILLIAM: Cabinetmaker of Washington, D.C., c. 1818.